The First Hundred Years

The US Presidents, the Federal Census,
and current events
that influenced the lives of your ancestors
1790 - 1890

Carolyn B. Leonard

The First Hundred Years

Presidents, Politics, Policies

1790–1890

The First Hundred Years

The US Presidents, the Federal Census, and Current Events that Influenced the Lives of your Ancestors 1790–1890

Copyright © 2020 by Carolyn B. Leonard
Photographs from Library of Congress & Wikimedia Commons

ISBN: 978-1-883852-12-2 (softcover)
ISBN: 978-1-883852-13-9 (e-book)
ISBN: 978-1-883852-14-6 (hardback)
Library of Congress Control Number: 2019901259
Visit the author's web site: https://www.carolynbleonard.com

Manufactured in the United States of America
5 6 7 8 9 10

Buffalo Industries, LLC

Acknowledgments

Many thanks to editors:
Judy Hilovsky, former editor
of award-winning *Persimmon Hill Magazine* of the
National Cowboy and Western Heritage Museum;
Mark E. Jones, Political Science consultant;
Margie Roetker, longtime Washington, DC, student;
Jon Heavener, Senior Quality Control Engineer,
retired, Seagate Technology Worldwide;
and the "map lady" **Judith Mills.**

Books by Carolyn B. Leonard, available at your favorite bookstore, and from Amazon.com.

Who's Your Daddy? *(2ⁿᵈ Edition)*
A Guide to Genealogy from Start to Finish
ISBN 13: 978-1-883852-08-5 (softcover) *10:* 1-883852-08-0
Daddy 13: 978-1-883852-11-5 (e-book) 10: 1-883852-11-0
Hardback ISBN 978-1-883852-19-1
Library of Congress Control Number: 2018906060
Size 6x9, 270 pages, 60 illustrations
Spine width 0.614 inches weight 0.891 lb

To Israel, With Love: *(2ⁿᵈ Edition)*
A Journey of Discovery in History,
Mystery, Travel, and Relationships in full color and large print.
ISBN 13: 978-1883852-09-2 *(softcover)* 10: 1-883852-09-9
Israel 13: 978-883852-10-8 *(e-book)* 10: 1-883852-10-2
Hardback ISBN 13: 978-1883852-18-4
Library of Congress control number 2018902864
Size 8x10, 280 pages, 202 illustrations

The First Hundred Years
The US Presidents, the Federal Census,
and Current Events
that Influenced the Lives of your Ancestors 1790-1890
ISBN 13: 978-1-883852-12-2 (softcover) 10: 1-883852-12-9
Hundred 13: 978-1-883852-13-9 (e-book) 10: 1-883852-13-7
Hardback ISBN: 978-1-883852-14-6
Library of Congress control number: 2019901259
Paperback size 6x9, 340 pages, 76 illustrations
Cream paper, Georgia font size 12 text
https://amzn.to/33n82b2

Coming soon:
The Second Century
The US Presidents, the Federal Census,
and Current Events
that Influenced the Lives of your Ancestors 1900-1970.
ISBN 13: 978-1-883852-15-3 (softcover)
Second Century e-book ISBN 13: 978-1-883852-16-0 (e-book)
Hardback ISBN 13: 978-1-883852- 17-7

The First Hundred Years in America — 1790 to 1890

In this period:

Two presidents died of illness in office:
William Henry Harrison died of pneumonia in 1841.
Zachary Taylor died of acute gastroenteritis in 1850.

Two presidents were assassinated in office:
* Abraham Lincoln, assassinated in 1865.
* James Garfield, assassinated in 1881.

The Democratic-Republican Party sometimes called the Jeffersonian Republican Party, was formed by Thomas Jefferson around 1792. They called themselves "Republicans," but this is not the modern Republican Party which was founded in 1854. The Federalists appealed to the business community, the Republicans to planters and farmers. Whigs supported the supremacy of Congress over the presidency and favored a program of banking and economic controls to stimulate manufacturing.

The term Indian in this book refers to Native American Indians. See endorsements on pages 277–278.

Presidents in The First Hundred Years

1)	George Washington 1789–1797	(none)	two terms
2)	John Adams 1797–1801	Federalist	one term
3)	Thomas Jefferson 1801–1809	Demo-Repub	two terms
4)	James Madison 1809–1817	Demo-Repub	two terms
5)	James Monroe 1817–1825	Demo-Repub	two terms
6)	John Q. Adams 1825–1829	Demo-Repub	one term
7)	Andrew Jackson 1829–1837	Democrat	two terms
5)	Martin Van Buren 1837–1841	Democrat	one term
8)	William Harrison 1841–1841	Whig	31 days
9)	John Tyler 1841–1845	Whig	47 months
10)	James K. Polk 1845–1849	Democrat	one term
11)	Zachary Taylor 1849–1850	Whig	16 mo+5 days
12)	Millard Fillmore 1850–1853	Whig	31mo+23 days
13)	Franklin Pierce 1853–1857	Democrat	one term
14)	James Buchanan 1857–1861	Democrat	one term
15)	Abraham Lincoln 1861–1865	Rep/Nat'lUnion	1 term+1 mo
16)	Andrew Johnson 1865–1869	Nat'l Union	46 mo+17 days
17)	Ulysses S. Grant 1869–1877	Republican	two terms
18)	Rutherford Hayes 1877–1881	Republican	one term
19)	James A. Garfield 1881–1881	Republican	6 mo 15 days
20)	Chester A. Arthur 1881–1885	Republican	41 mo 13 days
21)	Grover Cleveland 1885–1889	Democrat	two terms
22)	Benjamin Harrison 1889–1893	Republican	one term
23)	Grover Cleveland 1893–1897	Democrat	two terms
24)	William McKinley 1897–1901	Repub	1 term 6 mo 10 days

Preface

About Presidents, Politics, and Policies

I wished for this book when I was writing my family history. To make your story come alive, you need to know what life was like in those earlier times; what it was like for children and adults, for rich or poor, for master or servant. The job requires utilizing memory, experience, observation, opinion, and various modes of research. I saved my notes, which turned into THE FIRST HUNDRED YEARS.

I won't burden this book with footnotes. You will find a complete bibliography, reading list, index, and online reference list at the end, and the facts are easily researched and confirmed, if desired.

I hope this book is helpful to you in writing your family history, but more than that I hope you find the social and political transformation of our country fascinating.

I wanted to be able to lead my readers on an emotional journey so intriguing they could not bear to lay the book down because our country's history is spellbinding. American history assures us with evidence our nation's success was never pre-ordained or guaranteed. What will you learn about your ancestors?

I learned my grandfather was orphaned and he made the run for land in Oklahoma as a lad barely out of his teens. I learned his father was a twin. The boys joined the Union Army in Illinois and fought together through the war while worrying about what was happening at home. I learned the twins' father, who was born in Vermont, was a Freewill Baptist preacher who led his flock from rocky land in Ohio to the rich green farmlands of the Midwest, became sick and died while his five sons were away at war.

In the prior generation, the preacher's father was born in Connecticut as the son of a Revolutionary soldier. He married a Mayflower descendant, fought Indians and built a community on the wild frontier of the newly opened Northwest Territory. The Connecticut Yankee father served as a sergeant in the Lexington Alarm, and later in the Eighth Regiment of New York Militia.

After the war, that six-foot-tall Revolutionary veteran became the owner of a domestic sheep herd in Vermont and served as an elder on the committee to build the first Presbyterian church in Tunbridge, Vermont, in 1795.

AND BEFORE THAT ... going on back to the immigrant, John Branch. He landed at Scituate, Massachusetts, in 1638 as a ten-year-old indentured orphan on the ship *Castle* from County Kent, England. John's Puritan father died on the way over; his mother and siblings lay buried in St. Mary's High Halden churchyard back in the old country.

Why did they leave their home country? They left because the Stuart King Charles I, King of all England, Scotland, and Ireland, a tyrant who ruled in a total dictatorship, refused to call Parliament for his entire reign. The Thirty Years War was taking place, and the English Civil War broke out just as Charles started a war with Scotland.

Many Puritans were leaving England primarily for religious persecution. Separatist Puritans felt the church too corrupt and wanted to separate from it; however, the church and state were joined in England and the act of separating from the Church of England was considered treason. But that is another story. This one is about America.

Enjoy!

Carolyn B. Leonard
June 2020

Table of Contents

Illustrations

"Liberty, when it begins to take root, is a plant of rapid growth."
—George Washington

ONE—1790

Giving Birth to a New Nation

Who was the only president who did not serve in Washington, DC? George Washington, because during his administration the nation's capital was located in Philadelphia.

Who was the only president to be unanimously elected? George Washington—and he did it twice.

Who was the only president who did not represent a political party when he was elected? GW himself. He remains the only US president never affiliated with a political party.

DEMOCRACY OR REPUBLIC? Think you live in a democracy? The US is not a democracy, never was, and never was intended to be. It is a republic. The Founding Fathers were very explicit about this. The critical difference between a **democracy** and a republic lies in the limits placed on government by the law. A republic offers protection of certain inalienable rights which cannot be taken away by elected officials, such as the right to bear arms. In a true democracy the elected party and government is not restricted by any inalienable rights.

What was going on with your ancestors during the first formative years of our country?

Thirteen years elapsed between the Declaration of Independence (1776) and the inauguration of George Washington as the first president of the United States (1789). During those years our country was governed by a Continental Congress, a group of delegates from two to seven mem-

1

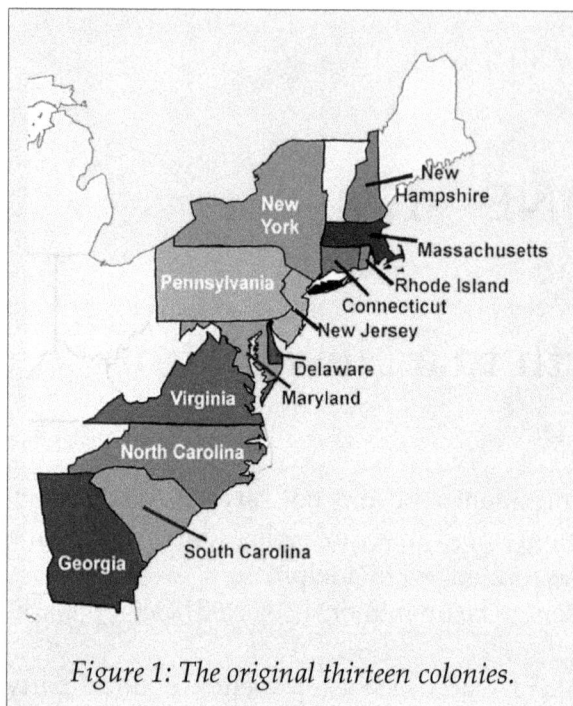

Figure 1: The original thirteen colonies.

bers from each state, and proud you must be if you can claim any of these men as your ancestors. These members assumed the essential functions of government. But they could only accept these powers because the pressure of war united the colonies and made the central body a necessity. Once the burden of war was over, the founders had to establish a new national government.

The First Continental Congress—fifty-six delegates from twelve of the thirteen colonies that would become the United States of America—met briefly in Philadelphia from September 5 to October 26, 1774. Most of the members were not yet ready to break from Great Britain, but they wanted the King and Parliament to act in a manner they considered more equitable.

WHAT WERE WE FIGHTING FOR? The extraordinary conflict of the American Revolution was not a battle of colonists against a foreign power so much as Americans against Americans who allied with the British soldiers.

The war caused chaos in private life in the 1770s with many families divided brother against brother. Some wanted to remain loyal to the crown, while others were "rebels" who cried for independence. About a third of the citizens were Tories loyal to the king. Thousands participated in brutal guerrilla operations; other thousands became caught in the path of contending forces and suffered massive disruptions in their lives.

Military operations conflicted in many ways with living on the home front. The shifting tides of martial fortune caused morale changes that left the final decision in doubt until almost the end of the war. Less than a century later, this internal conflict would be repeated in an internal battle, tearing the country apart again.

WHAT'S NEW ABOUT THAT? We are an old republic, and our two political parties are the oldest and third to the oldest in the world. We've had fewer than fifty presidents, and not all of them were chosen in an election.

The country has seen three uncontested elections (GW in 1789 and 1792, James Monroe in 1820), while six other early presidents were elected under rules significantly different from our current system, and a few moved into office after the death of a sitting president.

LIFE IN THE INFANT COUNTRY: Maine, then a part of Massachusetts, was a center of patriotism during the American Revolution, with less Loyalist activity than other colonies, but travel was awkward all around the provinces. A Connecticut minister on a preaching tour of Vermont during spring 1789 said he found himself in *"mud belly-deep on my horse, and I thought I should have perished."*

There was no Department of Transportation. Each New England town was responsible for building and maintaining all roads within its limits. Colonial laws, with few exceptions, required all adult males to work on roadways a certain number of days each year. It was their civic duty.

The Lancaster Turnpike, chartered by Pennsylvania in 1792, was the first toll road corporation in the United States. There had been a few experiments with toll roads based on the English model of a turnpike trust. Rhode Island established the second such corporation in 1794. Within two years afterward, each of the New England states chartered at least one turnpike.

THE WOMEN BLESS THEM: A monthly magazine, named *The Ladies Magazine*, began publication in France in 1790 with colored plates of the latest fashions and arrived regularly in America. Every woman had to make her pattern because commercial dress patterns had not yet been invented. Instead, they had fashion dolls for sale to demonstrate the latest fashions. The miniatures were not for a child to play with, but for the seamstress to imitate a new style.

Along with the yards of fabric silks and brocades, a seamstress needed some pins. The pins had to be made by hand. Think of that! The workman would cut a piece of wire, fashion the pin, give it a point and add on a large flat head, which was a most difficult operation. Those handmade dress-maker pins were very expensive.

Women of upper class never chewed tobacco, but it was a common habit among the backwoods females, along with pipe smoking. Later, snuff dipping usually replaced the chewing tobacco. Cigarettes were unknown until after the Civil War, and for many years, only boys and young men smoked cigarettes. The habit was frowned upon by preachers, parents, teachers, and employers, so smokers kept it secret.

GUN OWNING DEBATES EVEN THEN: A 1792 act by Congress required all healthy male citizens to purchase a gun and join their local state militia but did not establish a penalty for not complying. Most families still had their long rifles from the Revolutionary War, which replaced the smooth-bore musket. The long rifle was developed on the American frontier in southeastern Pennsylvania in the early 1700s. While they could reload a musket in approximately twenty seconds, the long gun required more time for the average hunter and was much more accurate. Another reason for such popularity of the long rifles is they could be made entirely by hand with hand-operated tooling in a frontier setting.

CREATING A GOVERNMENT: George Washington was both an obvious first choice for president and possibly the only genuinely viable option. He was both a national hero and the favorite son of Virginia, the largest state at the time. Washington also had leadership experience, having served as the commander-in-chief of the Continental Army during the American Revo-lution and president of the 1787 Constitutional Convention in Philadelphia.

With no political parties to nominate and endorse him, George Wash-ington was unanimously elected president of the United States in the first presidential election. He presented the shortest inauguration speech ever, which lasted two minutes and consisted of one hundred thirty-three words. George Washington, who never wanted to be president, served two four-year terms from 1789 to 1797. The new Supreme Court convened for the first time on February 1, 1790.

America's Founding Fathers led the American Revolution against the Kingdom of Great Britain. Most were descendants of colonists who had settled in the Thirteen Colonies in North America. GW was one. Others included John Adams, Thomas Jefferson, James Madison, Alexander Ham-ilton, James Monroe, and Benjamin Franklin.

Franklin is the only founding father to have signed all four of the critical documents establishing the US: The Declaration of Independence (1776), the Treaty of Alliance with France (1778), the Treaty of Paris establishing peace with Great Britain (1783) and the US Constitution (1787). Franklin died on April 17, 1790.

So much work and organization of government had to be done immediately. First, the officials needed to know where to find their constituents and who they were. Uncle Sam prepared to count his children.

WHO LIVES WHERE? President Washington, Vice President John Adams, and Speaker of the House Frederick Muhlenberg signed the first census act. The US Census is a valuable service to better understand our country. It wasn't established to help genealogists. The goal was to count the population of each state primarily for tax purposes, but now because of the census, you can learn where someone lived during a decade, see their household status, and find numerous useful facts.

CENSUS OF 1790: From 1790 to 1820, the censuses were conducted as of the first Monday in August (August 2, 1790; August 4, 1800; August 6, 1810; August 7, 1820) and answers to who lived there on the census date. The first censuses counted the population and provided information on the numbers by county. In 1790, the poll also categorized white males by age: those under age 16 and those age 16 and older.

The count was made within a year from the date of the inauguration of President Washington, and the assembling of the first congress of the United States. The law gave nine months for the completion of the work. Double this time elapsed, however, before all the returns were in. Communication then was slow and uncertain.

The Americans of that day, particularly in the rural districts, regarded the census enumerators with some suspicion. Some thought these agents of the federal government really aimed at getting information on which to base an increase of taxes.

Questions asked on the first census were:

- Name of the head of each household.

- How many free white males age sixteen and older?

- How many free white males under age sixteen?

- How many free white females?

- How many all other free persons in the household?
- How many slaves?

WHAT GOOD IS IT TO YOU? The census can help you distinguish your family from others of the same name. Finding your family in a census verifies the location where they lived at that time, identifies neighbors, and name variations. The census also lists slaveholders.

WHAT CAN YOU LEARN? You might be surprised at how much information you glean from these few questions in the first US Census. Even though only the "Head of Household" is listed by name, look at the surrounding households as you often find other families related to your ancestors living nearby. Ancestry.com has completed the database of all US Census records 1790-1940. Ancestry's database is a most excellent online tool for genealogy research and includes the available collection of 1790 census records enumerated in the United States.

With a paid subscription to Ancestry, you will be able to access the information at home. You can go to any public library and use its subscription for free. You might search online, because some sites offer the census information free, like FamilySearch.org. The LDS (Latter Day Saints) Library in Salt Lake City and its online program (FamilySearch.org) maintains the entire set of US Federal Census microfilms and these also can be found or ordered for a fee at Family History Libraries located throughout the United States. Local libraries often have history and genealogy departments with a collection of microfilm available for research, but these are often incomplete. Sometimes a library will offer its patrons online subscriptions to be accessed at the library.

Under the general direction of Thomas Jefferson who was then secretary of state, US Marshals took the census of 1790, sometimes using berry juice for ink and any scraps of paper they could find. The Marshals traveled on horseback or on foot through the backwoods and buffalo trails to reach settlers. It was a far different country from the United States of today. What is now a land of factories and cities was then a land of forests and farms.

The law required census takers to visit every household and to post the completed census schedules in *"two of the most public places within [each jurisdiction], there to remain for the inspection of all concerned. ..."* They were to transmit to the president *"the aggregate amount of each description of persons"* for every district. However, if they reached a house with no one at home, they could and often did inquire of neighbors for the needed information.

Censuses for 1790 are available in Connecticut, Maine, Maryland, Massachusetts, New Hampshire, New York, North Carolina, Pennsylvania, Rhode Island, South Carolina, and Vermont.

The first census of the new United States of America is missing records for four states which were in existence then: Delaware, Georgia, New Jersey, and Virginia. Kentucky was still a county in Virginia until 1792 when it became the fifteenth state.

Some records burned during the War of 1812. Sometimes only a page or two of the census was lost, or a town or two, or occasionally several counties, or even a poll for a whole state or territory went missing. However, officials reconstructed Virginia's schedules and some others from state information and other alternate information.

Over a hundred years ago the Bureau of the Census published the entire 1790 census, listing the names of all the heads of households. The Bureau published each state in a separate book, and you can see these books in most any research library. While the books are searchable, remember the indexing is not always correct. New Hampshire, Vermont, and Maryland were published in 1907, followed in 1908 by Connecticut, Maine, Massachusetts, New York, North Carolina, Pennsylvania, Rhode Island, and South Carolina.

Because the federal district court clerks did not adequately maintain the records, the 1790 census of Virginia was lost. State enumerations made from 1782 to 1785 were substituted but are deemed incomplete. Some substitutes may be available for the lost state records including Delaware, Georgia, Kentucky, New Jersey, Tennessee, and Virginia. Apparently, the original records were destroyed during the British attack on Washington during the War of 1812.

The Census of 1790 estimated the population of the United States at just less than four million people. For comparison, by the year 2000, the count increased to more than two hundred eighty million people.

Both the US and England claimed Maine until an agreement resolved several border issues between the US and the British North American colonies. Signed under John Tyler's presidency in 1842, the treaty settled the Aroostook War, a nonviolent dispute over the location of the Maine–New Brunswick border.

Now here's an exciting bit of forgotten history: From 1777 until early 1791, Vermont was an independent country, but the people of Vermont wanted to join the United States. They were held back by New York, who claimed land in Vermont and would not allow them to participate unless they paid thirty thousand dollars to New York. Vermonters gave in and paid the ransom in 1791 to become the fourteenth state. So, these new areas came into the union during President Washington's administration: Vermont in 1791, Kentucky in 1792, and Tennessee in 1796.

ABOUT THAT CENSUS COUNT: The United States was the first country to call for a regular census to be undertaken every tenth year. The first census began more than a year after the inauguration of President Washington and shortly before the second session of the first Congress ended. Some other information turned up for most of the missing schedules. Vermont's

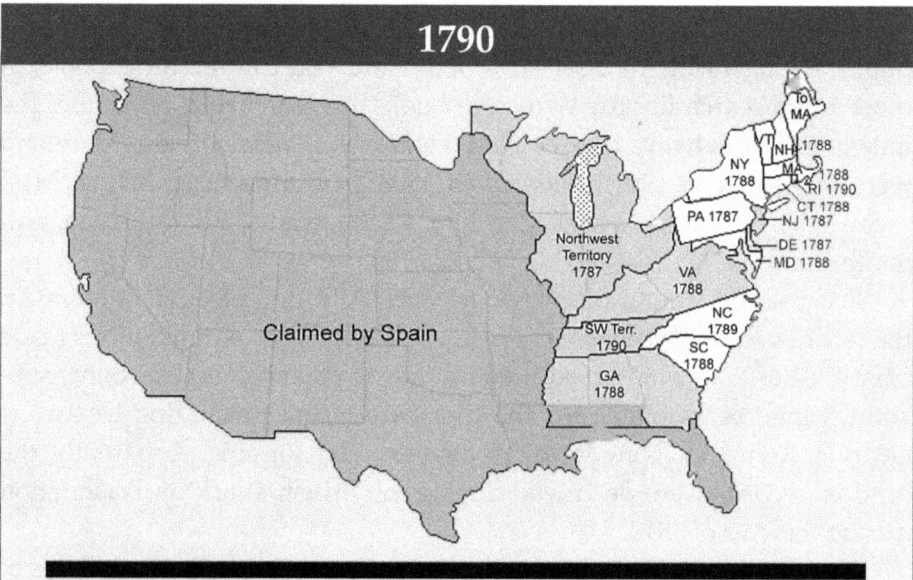

Figure 2: 1790 census under George Washington.

Census schedules are available for the states of Pennsylvania, Connecticut, Massachusetts, Maryland, North Carolina, South Carolina, New Hampshire, New York, Rhode Island, Vermont. The schedules exist for Vermont and Maine, although not admitted as states until later.

census came in 1791. The information exists only for those areas as each achieved statehood. If you cannot find your ancestor where you are searching, perhaps his location was not yet counted in the census.

Over the years, Congress has authorized additional questions, enabling us to better understand the nation's inhabitants and their activities and needs. Initially, one of the nation's founders, James Madison in 1809 suggested the census-takers ask additional questions that would help lawmakers better understand the needs of the country. For example, the 1810 Census also collected economic data (on the quantity and value of manufactured goods). In 1850, the census began collecting "social statistics" (information about taxes, education, crime, and the value of an estate) and mortality data.

Through the decades, the census has collected data on race, ancestry, education, health, housing, and transportation. An examination of the questions asked during each count illustrates changes in our nation's understanding of race, the impact of immigration, growth of the Hispanic population, and computer usage.

As a result of the census's evolution, the constitutionally mandated count has grown to provide valuable information about the population and its housing. Coupled with data from the economic and government polls and demographic and commercial surveys, the US Census Bureau provides governments, scholars, planners, businesses, and individuals the data they need to build schools, plan highways, open markets, and distribute the billions of dollars in federal spending that sustains a growing population.

THE FIRST POTUS: Washington was enormously popular, and his agreement to serve as the first President of the United States ensured he was listed first when the electors cast their votes on the appointed day. The only real question was who the electors would register as their second choice, the person who would be named the vice president. The eligible voting population was limited to white male landowners. Few of those qualified to vote actually knew anything about the candidates, due to lack of mass communication. As the person who received the second-largest number of votes overall, John Adams became vice president. Washington and Adams didn't really care much for each other, but they became more tolerant of each other's styles through the social activities they shared with their wives.

THE PRACTICE OF OWNING PEOPLE: The Constitution, Bill of Rights, and Declaration of Independence were already signed and in place. The founding fathers had done an excellent job for the most part, but they left a big problem for future leaders. Slavery would tear the nation apart. Although the Declaration of Independence states, "all men are created equal," they did not consider slaves as part of the equation. By the time of the Constitutional Convention in 1787, slavery in the United States was a grim reality. Slaves were apparent in nearly every state.

THREE-FIFTHS OF A PERSON: Government representatives were allotted to each state based on population numbers. The word "slavery" was never used. Instead, they used the term "other people." These "other people" counted in the census as three-fifths (3/5) of a person for representation in Congress. The founders left the issue of slavery on the table for too many years.

THE FIRST CABINET: President Washington set a precedent by establishing the cabinet within the executive branch by appointing Thomas Jefferson as secretary of state and Alexander Hamilton, secretary of the treasury, a body not outlined within the Constitution. He also appointed Henry Knox as secretary of war, and although the Department of Justice would not be created until 1870, Washington selected and included Edmund Randolph as attorney general in his first cabinet. He also set the standards for each member's role and how each would interact with the president.

Hamilton put the new country on a stable financial basis even though some of his tariffs and excise taxes caused a great deal of resentment, such as the 1794 Whiskey Rebellion in western Pennsylvania.

TROUBLE IN THE CABINET: Two cabinet officers continually butted heads. Jefferson repeatedly attacked Hamilton as an enemy to American values. Jefferson's opponents, led by Alexander Hamilton, criticized everything Jefferson did as secretary of state. Washington had not imagined the level of hostility the debates of these two would reach. Treasurer Hamilton, never too far from a debtors' prison personally, was a brilliant man but a terrible politician. The two men hated each other, each considering the other a hypocrite with secret plans to bend the president to agree with his plan. It was probably partly Washington's fault. He led each man to assume that his position was the most critical one in the cabinet. Somehow, this great leader had to rein in these two men and enable them to work toward a common good. No easy task.

THE SLAVERY ISSUE AGAIN: George Washington, together with his wife Martha, held more than three hundred slaves. In his will, George wrote he wished to free his servants, but because of intermarriage between his and Martha's slaves, he feared the break-up of families if his workers were set free. His will provided for the continued care of all, paid for from his estate, and his laborers would be set free upon Martha's death.

LADY WASHINGTON: Although the title came into being long after her death, Martha Washington served as the first "first lady" of the

Figure 3: George Washington in 1772.

Our first president presided over the first US census of 1790 and the citizens unanimously elected him to a second term. He served from 1789 to 1793 and 1794 to 1798. The candidate with the second largest number of votes, John Adams, was elected vice president.

United States. During her lifetime, she was often referred to as "Lady Washington." Martha had been born into a world of elite social custom and privilege in the 1730s.

No one could foretell she would marry twice, give birth to four children and lose them all in her lifetime, or bear witness to the Revolution and participate in the creation of a new nation.

At the age of eighteen, Martha married Daniel Parke Custis. He was handsome, wealthy, and twenty years older than Martha. She set up housekeeping on the Custis plantation, where her husband managed their estate of more than seventeen thousand acres. Daniel adored his young, pretty bride and pampered her with the most elegant clothing and gifts imported from England. Daniel and Martha soon added four children to their home, two of whom did not survive infancy.

When Martha was twenty-six, Daniel died after a brief illness leaving her a wealthy young widow with two babies: John Parke "Jacky," Custis, age three, and little Martha Custis called "Patsy," less than a year old.

Washington likely knew both Martha and Daniel Parke Custis for some time before Daniel's death, since his home and property were in the same area.

THE WEDDING OF WASHINGTON: We don't know much about their courtship, but Martha Custis, age twenty-seven, and George Washington, nearly twenty-seven, married on the sixth of January 1759, at the Custis plantation. The wedding was grand.

Washington's suit of blue and silver cloth had red trimming and gold knee buckles. He towered over most of the guests at six feet, three and a half inches tall. The bride, barely five feet tall, wore purple silk shoes with spangled buckles on her tiny feet. The shoes are occasionally still displayed at Mount Vernon.

The couple honeymooned at the Custis plantation house for several weeks before moving to Washington's Mount Vernon estate.

Martha and George Washington had no children together, but they raised Martha's two youngsters. Washington welcomed these children into his home as well as his heart. He was a devout and practicing Christian; as a vestryman, he took regular oaths in the name of Jesus Christ. He regularly prayed in the name of Jesus, asked for a remission of sins, and in a dozen other ways proved himself beyond all doubt to be a Christian.

LITTLE PATSY'S ILLNESS: Little Patsy began to have seizures. The doctor diagnosed her with severe epilepsy at a time when there was no real treatment for it. Dr. Rumney's medical bills in the Custis Papers at the Virginia Historical Society show he came to Mount Vernon to treat Patsy for her seizures at least ten times between 1768 and 1772. He prescribed most of the standard epilepsy medicines of the time: valerian, musk, Peruvian bark, and various "nervous" pills, powders, drops, and he bled her at least once. George and Martha tried taking her to the "healing waters" of Berkeley Springs. The waters provided no benefits, but they met a new doctor there who used herbals.

Although Dr. Johnson visited Mount Vernon only once or twice, packets of his medicines frequently arrived from Annapolis during the early 1770s. They included ether, which like valerian and musk was thought to be a strong antispasmodic. They also tried an assortment of drops, ointments, and concoctions. But all their money and high connections could not save their child. Patsy's "fits," as they called them, grew more severe. The family faced their worst fears during a severe seizure on the nineteenth of June 1773. *"About five o'clock,"* Washington wrote in his diary, *"poor Patsy Custis died suddenly."* She would have been about seventeen. Martha and George were devastated.

GW AND HIS STEPSON JACKY: Jacky was an indifferent student, and Washington despaired of preparing the boy to manage the large inheritance soon coming to him from his father's trust. Jacky quickly became engaged to young Eleanor "Nellie" Calvert of Mount Airy, Maryland, both still teenagers. Although Washington believed his stepson too young to bear the responsibilities of marriage, Martha wanted grandchildren, and the event took place.

Washington attended the boy's wedding on the third of February 1774, although Martha, who was still in mourning for her daughter, did not.

Jacky bought the Abingdon estate, some nine hundred acres on the west bank of the Potomac (now part of the Reagan National Airport in Alexandria, Virginia), about twenty miles from Mount Vernon. GW considered it a bad bargain. The young Custis family had several children in rapid succession and enjoyed many happy hours together, but tragedy struck again in 1781. While acting as a civilian aide to his stepfather, George Washington, at Yorktown, Jacky contracted camp fever and died in November. Martha had lost the last of her four children.

Jacky's widow was twenty-three years old with four youngsters. Eventually, the families decided the two older girls, Betsy and Patty, would remain in the custody of their mother. The two youngest children, Nelly and "Wash" (George Washington Parke Custis), were informally adopted by George and Martha.

While content to live a private life at Mount Vernon along with her homes from the Custis estate, Mrs. Washington joined her husband during the Revolution for all the Continental Army's winter encampments, even at frozen Valley Forge. She helped keep up morale among the officers. Before the revolution, Martha stayed close to home, but during the war, she traveled thousands of miles to be with her husband. Even General Marquis de Lafayette who visited in their home, observed that Martha "loved her husband, madly."

ON THE HOME FRONT: GW needed a secure location for the discussion of major plans and problems, a building that could house what was effectively the "Pentagon" of the Continental Army during the winter. He rented the Isaac Potts house and grounds at Valley Forge for six months with some twelve thousand troops. Isaac Potts, a Quaker, built the house some ten years earlier and he operated a grist mill nearby. The Headquarters camp was about eighteen miles northwest of Philadelphia, which was under control of the British General Sir William Howe.

General Washington moved into Valley Forge with his military family; an estimated two dozen officers, aides-de-camp, and servants. Other generals found housing in various farms around the encampment area, and Washington established his own in the Isaac Potts house, which he rented from its current tenant, Mrs. Deborah Hewes, for a hundred pounds in Pennsylvania currency. The restored building is now part of the Valley Forge National Historical Park and is open to the public.

They ate, worked, and slept in this two-story home. Inhabitants included the personal servants of the aides-de-camp, and Martha Washington, who joined her husband at Headquarters in February of 1778, bringing her own domestic staff, resulting in very crowded quarters.

Meals for the officers were prepared by General Washington's domestics, which included both free and enslaved servants. Housekeeper Elizabeth Thompson, a fine Irish woman in her seventies, managed the household. One of the enslaved servants, Hannah Till, worked alongside her husband Isaac, the cook.

On the second story, the first room on the left was used by General and Mrs. Washington as their bedroom. Martha would have kept personal hygiene and cosmetic items in a dressing table. An upper-class lady's morning routine would have included using some imported items, such as scented oil and skin creams. A pitcher and basin were also important for everyday washing of one's face and hands. In the daytime, the bedroom became a sitting room. Here she entertained the Quaker ladies from Philadelphia who came to plead with the General for the release of their imprisoned husbands.

MARTHA AND THE QUAKER LADIES: Martha took a familiar role as her husband's hostess at camp. On April 6, Elizabeth Drinker and three Quaker friends arrived at Valley Forge to plead with General Washington to release their husbands from jail. The men, all Quakers, had refused to swear a loyalty oath to the United States because of their religious beliefs, even though they reluctantly consented to house a British officer in the Drinker's three-story brick mansion on Front Street overlooking the Delaware River in Philly.

Because the commander was not available at first, the women enjoyed visiting with Mrs. Washington. When he returned, General Washington was unable to release the women's husbands because he could not interfere in decisions by the state of Pennsylvania, but he did invite the ladies to dinner and issued a pass for them to travel to Lancaster to meet with their husbands.

In the daytime, the ground floor provided an office for the military. The aides-de-camp were required to make three handwritten copies of each official document, using the implements available at the time including quill pens, inkwells, and sanders. At two every afternoon the papers and documents were put aside, and the tables pushed together, as the office was transformed into a dining room for the general and his aides. With all the officers together, Washington used this time wisely for group discussion and planning.

Mrs. Drinker described dining with General and Mrs. Washington and fifteen officers as *"elegant but soon over."* This dinner took place in a separate, small log cabin George had added behind the kitchen during the Valley Forge encampment, as headquarters was cramped for space. Their menu was probably marinated roast chicken, savory veal pie, and planked shad surrounded by parsnips. Side dishes on the table could have included pickled cabbage, dressed carrots, and pickled cucumber. When everyone finished dining on the entrée, an attendant cleared away the dishes and carried in the second course, perhaps baked apples in a crust, potato pie, and carrot pudding. It would have been appropriate for plates of nuts and a salad of watercress and winter-cress to be offered, too.

It is apparent the food at General Washington's table was far superior to the continental soldiers' standard fare at Valley Forge—a bit of meat and a chunk of bread. In the evening after dinner, all furniture in the Potts house would have been pushed to the walls to make room for sleeping. No space was wasted when fifteen to twenty-five people shared a house of this size.

WASHINGTON'S TOOTH PROBLEM: Washington suffered severe tooth loss making it difficult for him to eat and even to speak. Legend has it the dental problems were caused by cracking walnuts with his teeth. By the time of his inauguration at age fifty-seven, the new president had lost almost all of his chompers. A single tooth held his dentures. The fake teeth were probably from deceased humans and animals. This style of dentures, although somewhat morbid, was actually very popular well into the nine-teenth century. Probably his sore mouth caused the "pinched" look in his later portraits, which changed the shape of his previously handsome face.

WHAT HAPPENED TO HENRY DRINKER: Elizabeth Drinker worked hard to win the release of her husband, Henry, and eventually, officials allowed the couple to return to Philadelphia together. For the remainder of the war, Elizabeth continued to fend off soldiers from both armies attempting to confiscate her property.

Angered by the Quakers' ongoing lack of support for the Revolution, angry mobs damaged many Quaker homes in October 1781. The Drinkers' house was no exception, with *"seventy panes of glass broken."* Still, the pacifist Drinkers survived.

SMALLPOX: Immunization to smallpox was critical in the Revolutionary War. George Washington in 1790 ordered mandatory vaccination for troops who hadn't survived the disease before. However, inoculation with this live virus was dangerous. It killed about two to three percent of those injected with even small amounts.

Smallpox was the disease every family feared then, and the vaccinations were almost as dangerous as the disease.

MANY FIRSTS FOR THE US: In addition to the first inaugural address, George Washington delivered the first "State of the Union Address" on January 8, 1790, to the Senate and House of Representatives in the Senate chamber of Federal Hall in New York City. Initially built in 1700 as New York City Hall, the Hall later served as the first capitol building. President Washington first took office in New York City, but, when re-elected to a second term in 1792, Congress had moved to Philadelphia where the capitol would remain for a decade.

WHY A CAPITAL IN A SWAMP? Ever wonder why the founders located the nation's capital on the east coast instead of in a more central area and safer inland? Why choose a mosquito-infested patch of swampland between Virginia and Maryland—which is what our future capital city was in the 1790s—instead of an already thriving metropolis like New York City,

Figure 4: Federal Hall, New York City

George Washington statue in New York City stands in front of the reconstructed Federal Hall, which served as the US capital until moving to Philadelphia's Independence Hall by 1792.

Boston or Philadelphia? Looking back to 1783, in recognition of the separate division of the country, Congress first decided to have two capitals, one on the Delaware River near Trenton and another on the Potomac. A year later Congress voted to establish a single federal town near Trenton and to meet in New York City while the buildings remained under construction. That gradually fell into disfavor also.

SHOW ME THE MONEY: In 1790, the question of where to finally locate the nation's capital was one of two very contentious issues Congress faced. The other problem was about money. Who was going to pay the debts incurred during the war for independence?

The winning location was born out of a compromise between those in power.

Alexander Hamilton and the northern states wanted the new federal government to assume Revolutionary War debts. Thomas Jefferson and the southern states wanted the capital placed in a location friendly to slave-holding agricultural interests. The decision was contentious, but Hamilton brokered a deal for the southern states to indirectly pay off the war debts of the northern country in return for Virginia getting all the construction jobs and perks the capital would guarantee.

The "Federal District," or the "District of Columbia" consisted of pieces of land ceded by Maryland and Virginia to become the seat of the new government. Arguments over location of state lines caused problems for census takers.

The new leaders were all quite human. They made big and small mistakes in both their public and their private life, encountering uncertainty, conflicts, struggles, exciting people, failures, triumphs. They became heroes, villains, wise men, knuckleheads, allies, enemies, and were affected by love and hate just as we all are. Our country's success is probably credited more to good luck and God's grace than great leadership.

As it is today.

THE FEDERAL CITY: Today's Washington, DC, is a far cry from the modest place Jefferson entered in 1801. President Washington retained Pierre Charles L'Enfant, a French engineer and former officer in the Continental Army, to design and layout the new capital city in the area we know as the District of Columbia.

L'Enfant, a hot-tempered Frenchman, got fired and went back to Paris, never to return.

According to an undocumented story, a free black American mathematician with an incredible memory named Benjamin Banneker reproduced L'Enfant's drawings, and the work went on as planned.

Washington also approved the design and plans of James Hoban for the "President's House" in July of 1792, but that structure waited in the future. The capital and the presidential mansion would remain in Philadelphia for ten years. During the construction period, Washington City, Georgetown, Washington County and Alexandria became notorious as a center for slavery and the slave trade. African-Americans helped to construct the US Capitol building, the future White House and other public and private projects. The vast majority of those enslaved did not earn money or wages.

BATTLE OF FALLEN TIMBERS: Washington had his hands full of rebellions. The local American Indians, supported and encouraged by British troops, resisted American movement west fiercely. They attacked frontier settlements, killing and scalping most, but taking some prisoners to sell to the British Commander at Detroit. They also inflicted costly defeats on the poorly-trained and scantily equipped defending military forces.

The Washington administration finally called General "Mad Anthony" Wayne out of retirement in the spring of 1792 to command the newly-formed Legion of the United States. Wayne became senior commander in the United States Army charged with building the Legion, while diplomats attempted to negotiate a peaceful settlement with the chieftains.

Failing a peaceful solution, on August 20, 1794, Wayne's well-drilled Legion defeated a combined force of American Indians and a British company of Canadian militiamen in a storm-ravaged section of forest in what is now Ohio. This Battle of Fallen Timbers resulted in the Treaty of Greenville, where the Natives surrendered all claims to Ohio and agreed to return all white captives. There were many captives, mostly children. One of the child captives had been held since she was nine years old. Sara Cozine, a distant cousin of the author, was released about age fourteen. The military record shows only, *"She made her way back to her people in Kentucky territory."*

THE RE-ELECTION OF WASHINGTON 1794–1798: As the election approached, Washington longed to exchange the cares of the presidency for his beloved acres of Mount Vernon and his wife on the banks of the

Potomac, but he yielded and became an unopposed candidate for a second term. He was re-elected president on February 13, 1793. The vote was again unanimous.

Nearly everyone seemed to agree no one but Washington could do the job. In the eighteenth century, people in their sixties were considered elderly, and George was now sixty-two. The first term aged both Martha and George. The second finished the job.

Figure 5: George Washington, re-elected in 1794.

At the time of his first inauguration, GW was described in almost universally glorified terms by the national presses. However, by the end of his second term, hostile newspaper writers were attacking the administration's domestic and foreign policy.

These insults escalated during Washington's second term into personal attacks questioning his integrity, republican principles, and even military reputation. Politicians attacked him also for supporting the national bank, for living in luxury, and for remaining distant and aloof from the ordinary people. They even accused him of wishing to become a monarch. Washington never suggested any action against the papers, though the barrage hurt him deep inside. Martha freely expressed her anger and pain on her husband's behalf.

But the President had more significant problems on the horizon.

THE REIGN OF TERROR IN FRANCE: The French Revolution was underway. Throughout the next year, the Reign of Terror ruled France. People had to be careful of everything they said, what they did, and whom they talked to. The slightest hint of opposition to the French revolutionary government could mean prison or even death. Sometimes they accused people they didn't like or wanted to get rid of. All anyone had to do was accuse someone, and they were considered guilty. The tyrants officially executed almost twenty thousand people and arrested more than two hundred thousand.

The terrorists had control. The French king and queen, Louis XVI and Marie Antoinette went to the guillotine, and the guerrillas ruled France. Marquis de Lafayette who fought so bravely for US independence, barely escaped his country alive only to be thrown into a prison in Austria. Many of the aristocratic French officers who fought alongside Washington and his men were imprisoned and later executed along with their families.

The United States had close ties with France as a result of the Revolutionary War. They were our allies. But now France threatened to drag America into another war.

WAR BETWEEN FRANCE AND BRITAIN: In 1793, France and Britain went to war. By the terms of the treaty of 1784 with King Louis XVI, the United States was obligated to support France. But the king was no more. Again, Washington's cabinet, especially Jefferson and Hamilton, divided on whether the treaty was still in effect. American citizens argued about the issue as well.

Finally, Washington declared the United States would not take sides. Saying we would stay neutral was easy, but with America tangled in the affairs of those European nations, both sides criticized Washington for not taking up arms.

BARBARY PIRATES: At the same time, the Barbary Pirates continued harassing American commercial ships in the Mediterranean in 1793. The Barbary pirates, mostly Muslims, were part of the long-running war between Christians and Muslims in the Mediterranean Sea. They operated from the Barbary Coast in North Africa as far back as the time of the Crusades. Most maritime nations found it easier and cheaper to bribe the pirates rather than fight them.

Before the United States achieved independence from Britain, American merchant ships were protected on the high seas by Britain's Royal Navy. After the Revolution, American ships lost Britain's protection. This problem needed a solution.

BRING OUT YOUR DEAD: If those concerns were not enough, the yellow fever epidemic struck Philadelphia in July 1793, carried in by a mosquito and aggravated by infected immigrants living in crowded conditions. By August, the raging fever, black vomit, bleeding orifices, delirium, and jaundice—all symptoms of the disease—even spread to more privileged neighborhoods. Fatalities doubled, tripled, quadrupled.

Gravediggers driving wagons through the deserted streets would cry, *"Bring out your dead."* Carpenters piled up ready-made coffins around buildings, and the diggers dug trenches in the poor people's "Potters field" to bury the bodies in mass graves.

The death toll continued to mount. Federal authorities finally evacuated the city because of the raging epidemic. Eventually, a cold front eliminated Philadelphia's mosquito population. The death toll fell to twenty a day by the end of October.

The 1793 yellow fever outbreak raised doubts over the safety of this place to be the nation's capital. In September, the president laid the cornerstone to the United States Capitol building, which took several years to complete. The government continued to meet and work in Philadelphia until May 15, 1800, when they moved to Washington, DC.

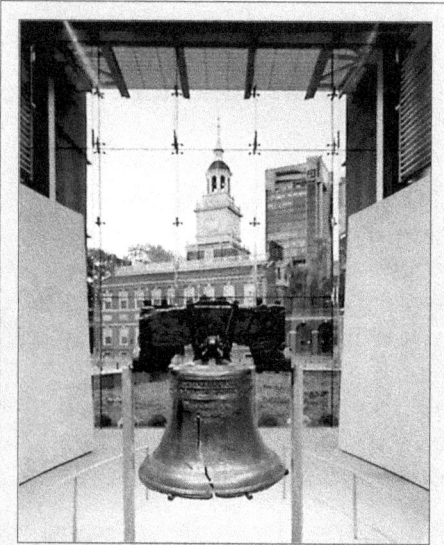

Figure 7: Independence Hall

The old cracked Bell in Philadelphia still proclaims Liberty and Independence Hall echoes the words, "We the People."

The Founding Fathers met in Philadelphia to sign the Declaration of Independence that started the War in 1776. In 1787 they signed the Constitution here. Philadelphia also served as the US capital from 1790 to 1800 while Washington, DC, was under construction.

GERMAN IMMIGRANTS AND THE AMERICAN FARM: The first significant movement west of the Appalachian Mountains began in Pennsylvania, Virginia, and North Carolina as soon as the US won the Revolutionary War.

Pioneers housed themselves in a rough lean-to, a dugout, or at most a one-room cabin. The main food supply came at first from hunting deer, turkeys, and other abundant small game. By the 1820s, the diverse peoples who settled the Valley of Virginia had lived together for several generations. Shaped by the everyday experiences of the American Revolution, the founding of the United States, and the market revolution, ethnic differences began to fade. Cultural persistence remained strongest among the Virginia Germans. Many of this group maintained their language and unique customs throughout the 1800s, but after 1820 they began moving toward the mainstream of American life.

Activities in and around German farmhouses in Virginia were reminiscent of their Central European heritage. Wives and daughters worked as hard as the men and were known to assist the men and boys with fieldwork. In the house, women did the spinning and weaving and made linen and wool cloth to be traded for goods at local stores or made into coverlets or rag carpeting. Meals prepared by German housewives were distinctive and included dishes of sauerkraut, scrapple, and raisin pies.

COTTON WAS KING: Before Eli Whitney invented the cotton gin in 1793, the price of average upland cotton was about forty cents a pound. Ten years after its invention the increased production of cotton brought the amount down to twenty-one cents a pound, but even when sold at the lower price the profit was enormous. The prime field hand slaves sold for five hundred dollars apiece, and a slave working in a cotton field might earn half his own cost the first year. The all-powerful cotton gins of later years handled thousands of bales of cotton work the same way as Whitney's little model of the eighteenth century. Cotton was king of the South and slavery operated the kingdom, especially in the cotton fields.

THE TROUBLE IN PENNSYLVANIA: In 1791 Congress levied a federal tax on corn liquor. In frontier Pennsylvania, farmers distilled whiskey to use up surplus corn, and the product gradually became a bartering product for them. They refused to pay the tax. Throughout Western Pennsylvania, protesters used violence and intimidation to prevent federal officials from collecting the whiskey tax. More than five hundred armed men attacked the fortified home of tax inspector and collector, General John Neville. In return, Neville and his slaves fired at a group surrounding his house, killing a member of the military. The next day, a group of militia members seeking Neville fired on a group of federal soldiers, causing casualties on both sides.

As word of this rebellion spread across the frontier, a whole series of loosely organized resistance measures were taken, including robbing the mail, stopping court proceedings, and the threat of an assault on Pittsburgh.

RIVALRY IN THE CABINET: Secretary of State Jefferson blamed Secretary of Treasury Hamilton for the rebellion, and in turn, Hamilton criticized everything Jefferson did. The two men, each convinced of the rightness of their personal view, glared at each other across the cabinet table and even on occasion trembled with rage, ready to lay hands on each other. Each man begged the president to choose between them and let the other resign, but Washington asked both to remain during his administration. And so they did, but always at each other's throats.

WHISKEY REBELLION: Washington endorsed Secretary of the Treasury Alexander Hamilton's new twenty-five percent (25%) federal tax on whiskey, but that brought on the Whiskey Rebellion in 1794. Thomas Jefferson opposed Hamilton's financial plan of course, but more importantly, farmers in western Pennsylvania protested against paying tax on their homemade moonshine, which the settlers shipped across the mountains to earn extra money.

Whiskey sales brought in much more money than crops, and the firewater also served as a medium of exchange. The farmers refused to give up their private income profit to the government. What was the president to do?

This was the first severe test of the new government. Washington ordered federal marshals to serve court orders requiring the tax protesters to appear in federal district court. By summer 1794, the protests became dangerously close to outright rebellion. Resistance took the form of threats, gunfire, assault, arson, and even tarring and feathering directed at federal tax collectors.

The entire United States Army was in Ohio fighting Indians with General Wayne, so President Washington took charge. He called out the voluntary militia from Maryland, New Jersey, Pennsylvania, and Virginia for federal service. Washington himself rode at the head of an army to suppress the insurgency, with thirteen thousand militiamen from those four states. This incident in Pennsylvania was the first and only time in United States history a sitting president donned a uniform to command troops in battle.

By December most of the militia force had returned home and were mustered out of service. After crushing the Whiskey Rebellion, Washington publicly blamed the Democratic-Republican societies for the trouble, and Jefferson began to view Washington as "the head of a party" rather than "the head of a nation." A few years later, when Thomas Jefferson was president, the whiskey tax was repealed. It had been almost impossible to collect anyway.

THE BIRTH OF POLITICAL PARTIES: Throughout his tenure in office, Washington passionately counseled his countrymen against forming political parties, which he believed would lead to destructive factionalism.

However, as Washington's second term was winding down, America saw the birth of those pesky rival factions. For their part, the Republican press viewed the Washington administration as heading in the direction of an English-style corrupt monarchy.

The peak of press attacks against Washington came with the public announcement of the controversial Jay Treaty with Great Britain in 1794, which attempted to ward off an impending war with Britain at the expense of American-French relations. The Federalist Party, led by Alexander Hamilton, and the rival Democratic-Republican Party, led by Thomas Jefferson and James Madison, joined opposing forces to contest the election, and seize power in the new government. The Federalists appealed to the business community, the Republicans more to the planters and farmers.

By 1796, the two parties monopolized politics in every state. Washington decided to step down when his term was up. His friends urged him not to, but he was determined. The negative press attacks may well have been a primary reason for Washington's decision to retire. The most violent attacks on Washington's reputation came just as the president was preparing to leave the office.

Thomas Paine inspired rebellion with his *Common-Sense* pamphlet. He wrote these famous words, *"These are the times that try men's souls: The summer soldier and the sunshine patriot will, in this crisis, shrink from the service of their country; but he that stands it now, deserves the love and thanks of man and woman. ..."*

Paine moved to Paris to become involved with the French Revolution, but the chaotic political climate turned against him. He was arrested and jailed for crimes against the country. The new American Minister to France,

James Monroe, who would later be elected president, secured Paine's release in November 1794.

Paine was furious Washington had done nothing to get him out of the French prison. He accused Washington of using his presidency to enrich himself and his allies at the expense of veterans and the country at large.

Conflicts over British loyalty began to simmer down. Life became calmer as Washington's presidency closed.

THE NEXT ELECTION: In 1796, Federalist John Adams won the election. Democratic-Republican Thomas Jefferson lost by three electoral votes, which under the law of the time awarded him the second office under his vanquishing opponent.

John Adams, America's first vice president under George Washington, was now the nation's second president, 1797 to 1801. Popular George was a hard act to follow, while Adams seemed to have way too many political enemies.

The short, rotund Adams and tall, thin Jefferson, the two men at different times the best of friends and the worst of enemies, would have to learn to work together.

Figure 6: John Adams

The second president of the US for one term 1797 to 1801.

Vice President: Thomas Jefferson.

DEATH OF THE PRESIDENT: On the evening of December 14, 1799, at Mount Vernon, George Washington passed away of a throat infection at the age of sixty-four. He was buried four days later in the family vault at Mount Vernon.

Robert E. Lee's father, "Lighthorse" Harry Lee, delivered the eulogy at Washington's funeral. By coincidence a few years later Martha's grandson, George Washington Parke "Wash" Custis married Mary Lee Fitzhugh in 1804 and they had one daughter, Mary (later Mrs. Robert E. Lee).

ABIGAIL ADAMS: John's outspoken wife Abigail became almost as well-known as her husband, at a time when women were expected to remain silent and invisible. Abigail Smith, daughter of Congregational minister, the Reverend William Smith and Elizabeth (Quincy) Smith, first met John Adams when she was fifteen years old. John accompanied his friend Richard Cranch to visit Abigail's older sister, Mary, to whom Cranch was engaged. Abigail's younger sister Elizabeth was engaged to John Shaw. The family secret was that Abigail's brother William Smith Jr. had become an alcoholic at a young age.

NO FLIRTING: Marriage, by necessity, was the first objective of a woman. Those unmarried by the time they reached age thirty were considered "old maids." People generally believed something was wrong with a girl if she never married, yet a young woman could do very little to secure a good husband. Behavior considered only mildly flirtatious today would have been labeled indecent then. All a girl could do to catch a man was to look her best, be shy and modest in public, and meek in manner. On the other hand, if she seemed highly intelligent and possessed an education or appeared too independent, she would be labeled a "bluestocking" and would be politely shunned by most males.

John Adams reported he found the Smith sisters neither "fond, nor frank, nor candid." Still, he married Abigail a few years later in 1764, in the Smiths' home in Weymouth, Massachusetts, with Abigail's father performing the ceremony.

Abigail was nineteen and John ten years older.

Over the next twelve years, they became parents of six children. The first twenty years of their marriage, the busy young lawyer was away from home tending to the business of the new country. He was appointed Ambassador to France, and Abigail did not see him for three long years.

While John was running around the world, Abigail tended the farm and raised the children.

WIFE, MOTHER, MANAGER OF FARM BUSINESS: Childbirth was dangerous business. Many women died while giving birth and their babes succumbed with them. Still, they did not call a doctor for something so commonplace as birth, and even if a medic did show up, they often did more harm than good. Luckily, Abigail and four of her six children lived.

As the war raged around them, although pregnant or nursing a babe, she managed to weave the cloth, pay the bills, oversee tending of crops and livestock, feed the family, and maintain constant letter-writing exchanges with her husband, who was away taking care of the country's business.

The curse of Abigail's family seemed to be the disease of alcoholism, the secret everyone knows, affecting her siblings and their spouses, and later her children and their spouses, and even grandchildren. All the children of John and Abigail Adams were prolific, and nearly every one of the grandchildren came to live under the Adams' guardianship at some point.

By November 1798, the president's house workers in DC were white-washing the sand-colored stone walls and declared it "move-in ready." The Adams family would be the first to live there, but it wasn't called the white house yet, just the president's home.

NO SCHOOL FOR GIRLS: Abigail Adams was known for advocating education for girls in public schools equal to boys, although she received no formal training. She was taught to read and write at home. As an intellectually open-minded woman for her day, Abigail Adams' ideas on women's rights would eventually play a significant role. She loved both her husband and her son, yet she could not vote for them.

A woman was not admitted to a school, or allowed to own property in her name, let alone to think of voting or expressing her opinions in public. A wife was in the same relationship to her husband as an indentured servant to his master. She was his property; all children, the woman, and all she possessed belonged to the husband. A wife had little recourse against a brutal, selfish mate. Luckily for Abigail, John Adams was a good husband.

IMMIGRATION, A PROBLEM FROM THE BEGINNING: The Alien and Sedition Acts were four unpopular bills promoted by Alexander Hamilton, passed by Congress and signed into law by President John Adams in 1798. These acts granted Adams broad new powers to arrest virtually anyone who criticized his policies.

The first three acts aimed at the rights of immigrants.

1) One made it harder for an immigrant to become a citizen, extending the residency requirement from five to fourteen years.

2) The second act allowed the president to imprison and deport non-citizens who were deemed dangerous.

3) The third authorized the president to deport any male citizen above age fourteen, who was from a hostile nation during times of war.

4) The fourth controversial Sedition Act, in direct violation of the Constitution's guarantee of freedom of speech, criminalized making statements critical of the federal government. More than twenty Democratic-Republicans, mainly journalists, were prosecuted and some imprisoned under the act. For instance, Congressman Matthew Lyon of Vermont served four months in jail for criticizing the president.

CONTROVERSIAL THEN, CONTROVERSIAL NOW: Abigail Adams supported the sentiment behind her husband's Alien and Sedition Acts as a legal means of imprisoning those who criticized the president in public print. The Virginia and Kentucky legislatures passed resolutions declaring the federal laws invalid within those states. The prosecutions fueled furious debate over the meaning of a free press and the rights afforded to political opposition parties in the United States. Within five years all but one of the unpopular Alien and Sedition Acts had been repealed or expired.

As a result, many Japanese, Germans, and Italians were arrested and confined for the duration of the war, and later deported to their nations of origins. These acts were significant political issues in the elections of 1798 and 1800, controversial then and remaining so today

THE HATED 1798 DIRECT TAX: Under Washington and Adams the Federalists established a stable government, but sometimes they followed policies that alienated the citizenry. For example, in 1798 to pay for the rapidly expanding army and navy buildup in anticipation of a possible war with France, the Federalists enacted a new tax on houses, land, and slaves. This 1798 Federal Direct Tax affected every property owner in the country.

Genealogists will rejoice at the records taken in Pennsylvania under the Direct Tax. Rich with detail about the house in which the families lived, they provide not only dimensions of the dwelling but also the number of panes of glass in each window, and the sizes of barns, sheds, and blacksmith shops. The tax records are also available for ten counties including Baltimore City and the District of Columbia. The listing shows occupant name, land tract name, and the number of acres owned. An added feature includes structure types and dimensions such as "a frame house fourteen feet by twenty-four feet, or stone mill house thirty by fifty."

This 1798 tax assessment resulted in the creation of at least three types of documents. "Particular Lists" included the first description of each dwelling house and outbuilding valued at more than a hundred dollars on lots not exceeding two acres. Vermont was designated to contain five divisions for this tax. Vermont was a frontier state; houses worth over a hundred dollars were rare. The second list detailed land, including dwelling houses valued under a hundred dollars. The third list enumerated slaves. Owners later had to auction many of these properties and slaves to pay the Direct Tax.

These tax sales produced large numbers of land transactions providing valuable information to family historians. The Treasury Department never required the states to send direct tax records to Washington, so papers concerning this tax are tucked away in various archives where researchers must hunt for them. Since the Direct Tax was a federal tax, any state deemed to be part of the United States in 1798 created these records. The question is whether the records survived. Some did not.

Maine was divided into five counties and was a district in the state of Massachusetts. The five counties in Maine were Cumberland, Hancock, Lincoln, Washington, and York. Maine did not become a state until 1820, although we know settlers were living there at least ten years before.

FOREIGNERS BECAME CITIZENS: The government did not require passenger lists until 1820, but naturalization records have always been vital. During the Revolutionary War, many people took oaths renouncing their allegiance to King George III and swearing allegiance to the state in which they were living.

From 1798 to 1828, local courts required a new immigrant to appear before a local court and register his arrival recorded in the court minutes. Sometimes the court created a separate document called a Report and Registry or Aliens' Register. The immigrant could obtain a certificate showing he had registered. The registration would prove his residency later when he applied for citizenship. So, researchers should check the court records at the port of arrival—once you know which port he/she arrived in, as well as the courts surrounding the one where they filed Declaration of Intention. Both a Report of Registry and a Declaration of Intention petitioned the court for naturalization.

The amount of information to be learned makes it worth the time to search. The Report of Registry might include the following on your ancestor, depending on the court recording the information, in addition to age:

- Name of immigrant
- Birthplace
- Nation of allegiance
- County of migration
- Place of intended settlement
- Occupation

THE XYZ AFFAIR: This incident with the strange-sounding name was a diplomatic incident between France and America in the late eighteenth century leading the US to an undeclared war at sea. Here is how it happened.

France went to war with Great Britain in 1793 while America remained neutral. President Adams refused to consider joining France in its fight against Britain, so a bitter quarrel with France filled Adams's administration, and preparations for war began.

Three different diplomats were sent to France to resolve the issue, but France was so angry about their American friends abandoning them that they seized several American merchant ships. Some members of Congress asked to see the diplomats' reports regarding what had transpired in France. Adams handed these over, with the names of the French agents replaced with the letters X, Y, and Z.

This X Y Z affair led President Adams and Congress to create the Navy Department. Ships were built and armed. War appeared inevitable until—just in the nick of time—Napoleon Bonaparte became Master of France. Bonaparte desired peace with America.

So, at the beginning of the new nineteenth century, the United States was at peace with the world, however briefly.

Chapter 1 in Summary from 1790 to 1800

- ✓ George Washington and John Adams elected as first President & VP
- ✓ Only white, male, landowners were allowed to vote
- ✓ First census act signed March 1790, first country to call for census
- ✓ George and Martha Washington held more than 300 slaves
- ✓ George Washington delivered the first "State of the Union Address"
- ✓ Supreme Court convened for the first time
- ✓ Census 1790 records missing for four states
- ✓ Vermont paid $30,000 to join the USA in 1791
- ✓ The census was not planned for genealogy
- ✓ Some of the 1790 census was burned by the British
- ✓ Some original census listings were alphabetized
- ✓ The first census takers were US Marshals
- ✓ Dark berry juice was sometimes used for ink, all copies were handmade
- ✓ The cotton gin was invented in 1793
- ✓ The Whiskey Rebellion erupted 1794 western PA
- ✓ Political parties by 1796 were Federalist and Democratic-Republicans
- ✓ John Adams became the elected second president 1797
- ✓ John Adams signed Alien and Sedition Acts and the unpopular 1798 Direct Tax
- ✓ Department of Navy created, warships ordered
- ✓ New immigrants recorded on Report and Registry
- ✓ Napoleon Bonaparte wanted peace with America
- ✓ 1793 Barbary Pirates attacked US merchant ships

"Old minds are like old horses; you must exercise them if you wish to keep them in working order."

—John Adams

TWO—1800

The New American People

THE FAMOUS ADAMS FAMILY

In late 1800, President John Adams and wife Abigail moved into the unfinished president's home which would in years to come be known as the White House. He began the tradition of receptions on New Year's Day. Any citizen could stand in line, enter the mansion, and shake hands with the president. The tradition endured until well into the twentieth century.

George Washington had a salary of twenty-five thousand dollars but no house, nor carriage, nor servants, nor even a secretary. All expenses had to come out of the president's pocket. That wasn't a big problem for George since he was a wealthy man, but for John Adams it was a significant problem, so Congress allocated a one-time expense budget of fourteen thousand dollars.

Adams was born the thirtieth of October 1735, in Braintree, (now known as Quincy) Massachusetts on the family farm. Named for his father, John was a deacon of the church and a descendant of John and Priscilla (Mullens) Alden, pilgrims who landed at Plymouth in 1620.

John Adams married Abigail Smith on October 25, 1764, in the Smiths' home in Weymouth where Abigail's father presided over the marriage. After the reception, the couple mounted a single horse and rode off to their new home, the small cottage and farm John had inherited from his father in Braintree. Later they moved to Boston, where his law practice expanded.

Figure 8: Abigail Adams.

She is pictured during the Revolution period.

The couple welcomed their first child nine months into their marriage and five more within the first twelve years.

With such a large family to care for and her many responsibilities, Abigail had no time to dilly-dally. Today we use electric lights and gas or electric cooktops every day. In the 1800s electricity had been discovered but was not in practical use. People lit their homes with candles and oil lamps. Homemakers cooked food in a large cast-iron pot over an open wood fire or in a fireplace. Abigail also had a farm to manage while caring for John's aging parents. His mother, Susanna Boylston Adams, had a cranky disposition and a fiery temper.

Abigail did not attend her husband's inauguration as she was busy tending to John's dying mother.

By the time Congress adjourned, Abigail was exhausted and ill with fever, diarrhea, and diabetes. Because of her own ill health, Abigail was unable to join her husband until after the second recess of Congress.

Of the four years of his presidency, Abigail Adams was truly present first in the temporary capital of Philadelphia and later, the permanent "Federal City" of Washington, DC, for a total of only eighteen months. She nonetheless made a strong impression on the press and public in that short time.

She became the first president's wife to reside at the president's palace, as it was then known. Abigail moved in during November 1800, living there for only the last four months of her husband's term. The new city was still a wilderness, the house far from completion. John described it as no city at all, just shabby buildings and tormenting heat. Abigail found the unfinished mansion in Washington "habitable" and the location "beautiful;" but despite thick woods nearby Abigail could find no one willing to chop and haul firewood for them. Abigail did use the unfinished East Room on a rainy week to hang up the laundry.

While John was president, Abigail continued a formal pattern of entertaining. She took an active role in politics and policy, unlike the previous quiet presence of Martha Washington. Both Abigail and John were highly intelligent and well educated.

"There are two types of education," John Adams has been quoted, *"One should teach us how to make a living and the other how to live."*

About this time, male supporters of the Revolution adopted the practice of wearing trousers instead of knee-breeches. The pants became popular in America among the working class, but those higher up did not immediately embrace the fashion. For some unknown reason, perhaps because of muddy roads, the long trousers were cut above the shoe tops. About three inches of sock showed between the pants and the shoes. Rubber raincoats, boots, or overshoes were unknown.

THE SECRET EVERYONE KNOWS: Abigail brought the children of brother William Smith, her sisters Mary Cranch and Elizabeth Shaw, and Abigail's own son Charles, all to live in the president's house in Philadelphia during her husband's presidency because the children's respective fathers all struggled with alcoholism. Just days before Charles' death in 1800 Abigail brought her three-year-old granddaughter, Susanna, to live with them.

Historians are familiar with Abigail and John's relationship through their correspondence and other writings. Letters exchanged throughout John's political obligations indicate he sincerely trusted in Abigail's knowledge. Abigail wrote about the troubles and concerns she had as an eighteenth-century woman. Abigail was an advocate of married women's property rights and more opportunities for women, particularly in the field of education. She was quite a reformer for her time and is quoted often for her shocking March 1776 letter to John and the Continental Congress, requesting them to:

"Remember the ladies and be more generous and favorable to them than your ancestors. Do not put such unlimited power into the hands of the husbands. Remember, all men would be tyrants if they could. If particular care and attention is not paid to the ladies, we are determined to foment a rebellion and will not hold ourselves bound by any laws in which we have no voice, or representation."

TRAVEL IN 1800: Despite traffic jams on the roads and congestion at airports, we don't know how good we have it today compared to our ever-so-great grandparents.

In 1800, the only practical way to travel was skimming along the nation's natural waterways. As a result, settlement clung to the nation's coasts and rivers. A few roads existed, mostly narrow paths following old Indian trails or animal paths. Travel on these footpaths was difficult and time-consuming—presenting impassable mud when it rained or choking dust in dry weather.

For the working class, trips had to be by horseback or stagecoach. Children and more destitute adults walked everywhere. Only a few farmers owned horses and wagons. One Revolutionary War pension applicant in 1830 described how the veteran, at age ninety, had walked more than thirty miles each way to get a signature on his affidavit.

Slow-moving oxen pulled many loads of freight. Even on a good horse, depending on the weather it took from four to six days to travel from Boston to New York on the best roads, which only ran between larger cities along the coast. According to Fisher Ames, the former Federalist Congressman and president of a turnpike company, "Most New England toll roads were built only to facilitate country produce on its way to market."

THE 1800 CENSUS: John Marshall, secretary of state in 1800, was the nominal head of census operations. The completed census shows more than five million people living in the United States; however, almost nine hundred thousand, or nearly one-fifth of the population, were slaves.

Twelve counties made up Massachusetts in 1800: Barnstable, Berkshire, Bristol, Dukes, Essex, Hampshire, Middlesex, Nantucket, Norfolk, Plymouth, Suffolk, and Worcester. In 1800, Maine was still part of the Commonwealth of Massachusetts.

WHAT IS A COMMONWEALTH: The Commonwealth was created in the early 1900s when nations formerly a part of the British Empire began to secede. Its main goal was to ease the process of British decolonization. Four states, former British colonies, still call themselves commonwealths: Kentucky, Massachusetts, Pennsylvania, and Virginia. The distinction in the US is in name only.

WHERE ARE THE DC PEOPLE: The District of Columbia (DC), founded in 1791, is not listed in the confusing 1800 census. The DC inhabitants are counted under Virginia and Maryland. Furthermore, Maryland records are available, but the Virginia records are lost.

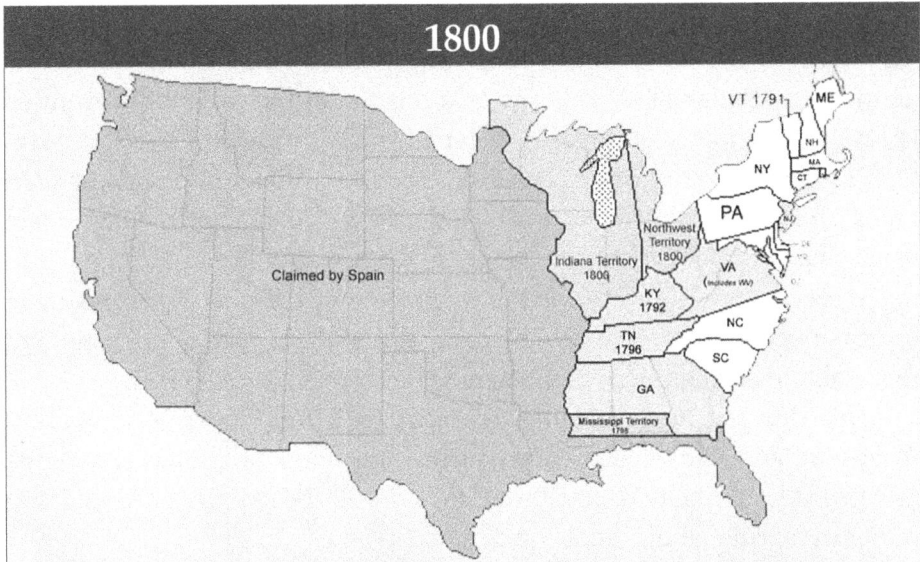

Figure 9: 1800 census under President John Adams.

This was the second population count for the USA. Schedules exist for the new states of Vermont, Kentucky, and Tennessee, but not for New Jersey. Both Maine and District of Columbia have census schedules on record but have not attained statehood.

Most surnames in this census are transcribed in the order of visitation, which is good because you can identify your ancestor's neighbors who might be close relatives. However, some census takers copied and rearranged the names to appear in alphabetical order by surname.

WHO DID THEY COUNT: This second census included the following categories: head of the household, number of free white males and females in age categories: under age ten, ten to sixteen, ages sixteen to twenty-six, twenty-six to forty-five, and over forty-five. Also listed you can find the number of other free persons except "Indians not taxed," the number of slaves, and the town or district and county of residence. These categories allowed Congress to determine persons residing in the United States who should pay taxes and qualify for seats in the nation's House of Representatives.

INDIANS NOT TAXED: This item, included in each census, is finally explained in the 1880 instructions. The phrase "Indians not taxed" is defined as: "Indians living on reservations under the care of government agents, or roaming individually, or in bands, over unsettled tracts of country." Indians who are **not** in tribal relations, whether full-bloods or half-breeds, mingled with the white population or residing in white families are listed as a part of the ordinary people of the country. They could be working as servants or laborers or living in huts or wigwams on the outskirts of towns or settlements. Still, for the constitutional purpose of apportioning representatives, these individuals are to be counted in the census.

This difficult governmental gobbledygook for "Indians not taxed" means Indians who have renounced tribal rule and who exercise the rights of citizens under state or territorial laws should be counted. Those living under tribal rule would **not** be included.

COUNTING THE SLAVES: Slavery in New Jersey began in the early seventeenth century when Dutch colonists imported African slaves for labor to develop their colony of New Netherland. American involvement in the international slave trade was limited when the US Congress passed the Slave Trade Act of 1794. The law prevented international slave trade on US vessels and controlled the business of foreign ships in US ports.

Six years later, the 1800 Slave Trade Act built upon the former Act, limiting American involvement even more in the trade of human cargo. Several similar acts of Congress did not ban slavery but did eventually outlaw the importation of slaves. The 1800 Act increased fines and penalties and prohibited US citizens' and residents' investment in the trade, and restricted employment of US citizens on such foreign vessels.

New Jersey's slave population was said to be about twelve thousand in 1800 and became the last northern state to emancipate its slaves. After the Revolutionary War, many northern states rapidly passed laws to abolish slavery, but Jersey did not follow until 1804, and only then by gradual emancipation similar to New York.

Before the Civil War, owners considered their slaves and indentured servants as personal property. The slave or their descendants could be sold or inherited just like any other property. Laws of individual states primarily governed human chattel.

SLAVE OR SERVANT: In contrast, many early immigrants came as indentured servants. These people sold their labor in exchange for passage to the New World and housing upon arrival.

Pennsylvania was the first to agree to abolition during the Revolution. The Gradual Abolition Act in New Jersey made African Americans free at birth but required children born to slave mothers to serve indentured service until early adulthood. Freedom was only given to those born after the fourth of July 1804, although they were still required to work for the person whose land they lived on until they reached age twenty-five (if male) or twenty-one (if female). The state paid to support the children. Even then, technically, these "free" people could be sent south and sold to the slave-owning southerners. Slaves were most often engaged in agricultural labor, especially in the South, but they also filled skilled artisan jobs in shipyards and industry in coastal cities.

APPLE ORCHARDS PLANTED: John Chapman (a.k.a. Johnny Appleseed) began handing out apple seeds and seedlings to Ohio settlers in 1800. The favored image is of Johnny Appleseed spreading apple seeds randomly everywhere he went. In reality, he planted nurseries rather than orchards, built fences around them to protect from livestock, left the plantings in the care of a neighbor who sold trees on shares, and returned every year or two to tend the nursery. Children enjoyed his stories as he spread his New Church gospel to adults, receiving in return a floor to sleep on for the night and sometimes supper. He preached as he traveled, converting many Native Americans, whom he admired. The NAs regarded him as someone who had been touched by the Great Spirit and even hostile tribes left him strictly alone.

ADAMS END: President Adams faced a daunting re-election campaign in 1800. He had spent much of his first term at his Massachusetts home, *Peacefield*, preferring the quietness of domestic life to political endeavors at the capital. He ignored the political patronage and office-seekers other politicians utilized.

The campaign between Adams and Jefferson was bitter and characterized by malicious insults by partisan presses on both sides. James Callender, a Republican propagandist secretly financed by Jefferson, degraded Adams' character and accused him of attempting to make war with France.

Adams had Callender arrested and jailed under the Sedition Act, which only further inflamed Republican passions, as previously mentioned.

DIRTY POLITICS: Each side believed a victory by the other would ruin the nation. This election ushered in a new type of American politics, a two-party republic, and acrimonious campaigning behind the scenes and through the press, which continues today. On top of this, the election pitted the "larger than life" Adams against Jefferson. The former close allies became political enemies.

Benjamin Franklin said of President Adams, *"He means well for his country, is always an honest man, often a wise man, but sometimes, and in some things, absolutely out of his senses."*

Beat the drum cadence, here come the combative political parties. The Democratic-Republicans nominated a ticket consisting of Jefferson and Aaron Burr while the Federalists nominated a ticket consisting of John Adams and Charles Pinckney. At first, the 1800 election led to a tie between Jefferson and Aaron Burr, members of the same party. Thirty-six contentious ballots were required before the House of Representatives finally broke the deadlock. Jefferson won as president and Burr became vice president. Jefferson entered office with a profound distrust of his vice president (Burr), whom he cut out of all governmental, political, and party matters.

Burr would later kill Alexander Hamilton in a duel and be charged with murder, as well as being prosecuted for treason, but he was acquitted in both cases. Contemporaries often remained suspicious of Burr's motives to the end of his life, continuing to view him as untrustworthy.

PRESIDENT NUMBER THREE: Jefferson, the new president, had been troubled by several incidents in John Adams' presidency. He was convinced that radicals within Adams' Federalist Party were waging war against what he called the "Spirit of 1776"—goals the American people had hoped to attain through the Revolution. The experiences of the 1796 and 1800 elections spurred legislators to pass the Twelfth Amendment changing the presidential election process so that each member of the electoral college cast one electoral vote for president and one electoral vote for vice president. Under the new rules ratified in 1804, this ended the possibility of multiple candidates winning votes from a majority of electors.

Thomas Jefferson was elected for two terms and served from 1801 to 1809. Born into one of the most prominent families of Virginia's planter elite, Jefferson spoke six languages, was a talented violinist, and an excellent singer. He also loved to dance. His mother, Jane Randolph Jefferson, was a member of the proud Randolph clan, a family claiming descent from English and Scottish royalty.

THE DUEL THAT STUNNED THE NATION: Alexander Hamilton was a brilliant man but not a very good politician. He made a dangerous enemy when he helped engineer Burr's defeat in the presidential nomination, advising his fellow Federalists to vote for Thomas Jefferson instead.

The two, Hamilton and Burr, had long been political rivals, but Hamilton made disparaging remarks about Burr at a dinner. That was a bridge too far.

When Burr learned of Hamilton's remarks about his character, he demanded an apology for every slanderous thing said about him. Hamilton refused, and the pair exchanged a series of letters which culminated in arrangements for a duel.

Figure 10:
Thomas Jefferson

Our third US president served two terms, 1801 to 1809.

Vice President: Aaron Burr

Alexander Hamilton was born out of wedlock, orphaned as a child, and taken in by a prosperous merchant before being sent to New York to find his way.

Similarly, Aaron Burr was orphaned when he was two years old, his father, mother, and both maternal grandparents all died within a year. So, the two men had that in common. But unlike the impoverished Hamilton, who worked tirelessly as a clerk, Burr relied on his influential family lineage.

While dueling may seem primitive to us now, it was a ritual that made sense in a society in which male honor was paramount. A man's integrity was the most important aspect of his identity, and his reputation had to be kept untarnished. Duels were a way for men to prove their courage and manliness publicly. The challenged party usually had the choice of weapons, and Hamilton chose guns. Arms makers even created sets of pistols specifically built for dueling, so that the equipment of both challengers would be equal.

Each man would have a "second" who was responsible for seeing the men conducted the duel honorably. Seconds would locate a proper dueling ground, usually a remote area away from witnesses and law enforcement, since dueling remained technically illegal in most states, though rarely prosecuted. The two men traveled to New Jersey because even though dueling was unlawful there, officials were less likely to prosecute duelists than in New York.

Hamilton missed. Burr did not.

On July 11, 1804, Burr's shot mortally wounded Hamilton, who died thirty-six hours later. Facing potential murder charges, Burr returned to his estate in lower Manhattan for a hearty meal and showed no remorse for the action. However, even though he retained his office as vice president to the end of his term, Burr's professional and personal life remained in tatters until his death.

Laws were different then. Political duels in the early republic were part of the political game, even though outlawed in two states. For example, Thomas Jefferson and James Madison were once arrested together in Vermont for taking a carriage ride on a Sunday, which was against state law at the time.

JEFFERSON'S FIRST TERM: During his first term, Jefferson doubled the size of the country through the Louisiana Purchase in 1803. The cattle and timber of Montana, wheat of Minnesota and the Dakotas, corn of Kansas, and the sugar and cotton of Louisiana contributed to America's wealth.

The Territory of Louisiana included all of present-day Arkansas, Missouri, Iowa, Oklahoma, Kansas, Nebraska, plus part of present-day Minnesota, North Dakota, South Dakota, New Mexico, Montana, Wyoming, Colorado, and Louisiana. After months of negotiation with France, Jefferson's representative secured five hundred thirty million acres of land for less than three cents per acre plus cancellation of debts worth eighteen million francs. The total cost ran to about fifteen million dollars, equivalent to about six hundred billion in current money.

The Louisiana Purchase was the most significant land bargain in US history. The purchase doubled the size of the United States, strengthened the country materially and strategically, and provided a powerful drive for westward expansion.

To Jefferson's dismay on moving into the president's house, domestic necessities such as shelters for fowl, goats, and cows had begun to supplant the workers' shanties that had sprung up around the house during construction. Jefferson found other needs wanting. The stables were two blocks distant; guests and servants shared an exterior privy; keeping ice was difficult without an ice-house; the basement offered inadequate storage for wood and coal; and other functions such as a hen house and smokehouse were needed and best placed outside the basement.

Jefferson began remodeling with the easiest projects related to convenience and service: replacing the outdoor privy with two indoor water closets from Philadelphia; establishing a cooled wine cellar; hanging service bells throughout the house; upgrading the kitchen for his French chef by installing stew stoves, boilers, and ranges; and having the unsightly and dangerous south stairs removed in favor of a bridge-like entrance on the north side of the house, which had been intended for public access.

Construction of the White House wings in 1805 according to Jefferson's plan, would include three spaces on each side: ice-house, coal and wood room, and privy on the west; and meat house with vault, stairway, and privy on the east. The east privy would be reserved for the family and guests. At 10-feet wide it might have been divided into two stalls and was probably still "unisex," as per the custom. The west "necessary" would be for the servants.

Jefferson received some unusual pet presents when he asked his representatives to send back samples of what they found. Captain Zebulon Pike sent two grizzly bear cubs that stayed in a cage on the front lawn for at least two months. When they outgrew their cages, they roamed the president's house lawn with the peacocks and partridges.

Jefferson's favorite pet, however, was his mockingbird, Dick. He bought the bird from one of his father-in-law's slaves. Jefferson's good friend Margaret Bayard Smith described how the bird would land on Jefferson's table and *"regale him with its sweetest notes, or perch on his shoulder and take its food from his lips. Often when he retired to his chamber, it would hop up the stairs after him."*

THE CORPS OF DISCOVERY: Less than two months after acquiring Louisiana, Jefferson commissioned his private secretary, Captain Meriwether Lewis to head an expedition to the far Northwest. Meriwether Lewis selected William Clark, age thirty-three, a veteran, as co-leader. The Lewis and Clark expedition began after congressional approval in 1802 and ended on the return of their Corps of Discovery in 1806.

A SHOSHONE GIRL GUIDE: Sacagawea, a young Shoshone woman, traveled with the thirty-some member expedition over the thousands of miles from North Dakota to the Pacific Ocean. She helped establish cultural contacts with other Native American people in addition to her contributions to natural history. A party from the Hidatsa tribe had kidnapped Sacagawea and several other girls when she was about twelve years old.

Sacagawea was sold into a non-consensual "marriage" when she was about thirteen to a French trapper named Charbonneau, who was at least twenty years her senior. Sacagawea was pregnant with her first child when the Corps of Discovery arrived at the Hidatsa village to spend the winter of 1804. Lewis hired Charbonneau as an interpreter because his very young pregnant wife spoke Shoshone. While on their journey, Lewis recorded the birth of Sacagawea's baby, Jean Baptiste Charbonneau, on February 11, 1805, nicknamed Little Pomp.

Figure 11: The Sacagawea gold coin is a US dollar.

An Oklahoma sculptor, Glenna Goodacre, designed the coin, which has been minted every year since 2000.

SACAGAWEA: She helped navigate the Corps through a treacherous mountain pass—today's Bozeman Pass in Montana—to the Yellowstone River. Sacagawea remembered being there when she was kidnapped and taken east to Mandan country. At one stop to purchase horses for the Corps, Sacagawea was surprised and happy to recognize the Shoshone leader, Chief Cameahwait, as her brother, and they had an emotional reunion.

Sacagawea's work as an interpreter certainly helped the party to negotiate with the Shoshone; however, her most significant value to the mission may have been merely her presence during the arduous journey, which demonstrated the peaceful intent of the expedition.

Sacagawea was a highly skilled food gatherer. She used sharp sticks to dig up wild licorice, prairie turnips (the explorers called these tubers "white apples") and wild artichokes that mice had buried for the winter.

When a canoe overturned, this young girl also rescued essential papers, books, navigational instruments, medicines and other provisions which might have otherwise disappeared—all while being sure her baby was safe.

For the two-year trip, Charbonneau was paid five hundred thirty-three dollars and received a land warrant for three hundred twenty acres in Missouri. Sacagawea received nothing.

After the expedition, Charbonneau and Sacagawea spent three years among the Hidatsa before accepting William Clark's invitation to settle in St. Louis in 1809. They entrusted Jean Baptiste's education to Clark, who enrolled the young man in the Saint Louis Academy boarding school. It is believed Sacagawea died of a fever in 1812, and Clark became a guardian of the children, Jean Baptiste and his little sister Lisette. Jean Baptiste became an adult guide, hunter, and trader, but Lisette died soon after her mother.

JEFFERSON'S PRIVATE LIFE: We know our founding fathers were not saints. They were human and inflicted with the usual human frailties. Although Jefferson kept slaves—in a typical year he owned about two hundred—he is famed as a champion of political and religious freedom. This tall, gangly young man with reddish-blond hair, hazel-gray eyes, and a burnished complexion married Martha Wayles Skelton, an attractive and delicate young widow whose dowry more than doubled his holdings in land and slaves. Martha's mother had died when Martha was just a two-week old babe in 1748.

Now, this gets more complicated. Martha's widowed father, John Wayles not only lost his first wife, Martha's mother, but his second and third wives also died young. He did have several children by his second wife. After the death of his third wife, he took his half-white slave Elizabeth "Betty" Hemings as a concubine for the rest of his life. According to this legend, in twelve years they had six children, the youngest child named Sally Hemings, born two months after John Wayles' death in 1773.

After her father's death, Martha inherited the mulatto servant Betty Hemings. She and her ten children came to live with young Martha not long after she married Thomas Jefferson in 1772. Throughout their almost eleven-year marriage, the Jeffersons appeared to be devoted to each other and had a good life. Jefferson arrived as a delegate to the Second Continental Congress in Philadelphia 1775 in an ornate carriage drawn by four handsome horses and accompanied by three footmen. They had six children before Martha died age thirty-three, eighteen years before the country elected Thomas Jefferson president.

She left him with their three surviving children. The young daughters, Lucy, four months old; Mary "Polly," age four, and Martha "Patsy," age ten.

Before she died, Mrs. Jefferson asked her husband to promise he would not remarry. Step-mothers had raised Martha, and she didn't want step-mothers raising her children. Her grief-stricken husband held her hand and promised he would never remarry.

THE WIDOWER AND THE SLAVE GIRL: Continuing the family tradition, which was not at all uncommon at the time, the widower Thomas Jefferson formed a long-time relationship with Martha's much younger half-sister, Sally Hemings, who was only a quarter black.

Virginia widowers frequently had long-term relations with enslaved women; polite white society simply expected these men to be discreet about it. Sometime after his wife's death, Jefferson reportedly had several children with Sally Hemings. Speaking of the concept of historical recurrence, Mark Twain once said, "to wit, no occurrence is sole and solitary, but is merely a repetition of a thing which has happened before, and perhaps often."

According to Sally's son, Madison Hemings, Sally became Jefferson's mistress and mother of five children by him. A small number of historians disagree, but Madison Heming's memoir states that his mother Sally Hemings told him his father was Thomas Jefferson. His brother Eston said the same thing. Their relationship started in Paris, where Jefferson was serving as a diplomat.

The record shows that in May 1787, Sally Hemings, aged fourteen, accompanied Jefferson's daughter Mary "Polly," age five, to London to visit John and Abigail Adams and then on to Paris, where the widowed Jefferson, aged forty-four, was serving as the US Minister to France. His older daughter, eleven-year-old Martha "Patsy" was already in Paris with him. The baby, Lucy, had died of whooping cough while he was overseas. (Monticello.org Report of the Research Committee on Thomas Jefferson and Sally Hemings, January 2000)

Under French law, Sally spent two years there and could have petitioned for her freedom, because the 1789 revolutionary constitution in France abolished slavery. Sally had a legal right to remain in France as a free person. If she returned to Virginia with Jefferson it would be as a slave.

Her son's memoir says Sally agreed to return home based on Jefferson's promise to free her children when they came of age.

Based on DNA evidence, historians agree Jefferson probably did father all four of Sally Hemings' surviving children: Beverly, Harriet, Madison, and Eston. The teenage Sally's first child, a girl born soon after the return from Paris, lived only a few months.

Madison Hemings said although Jefferson did not display fatherly warmth to the Hemings children, he did give them lighter work responsibilities compared to other slaves. According to the 1873 memoir, his older brother Beverly and sister Harriet moved to Washington, DC, in 1822 when they "ran away" from Monticello. No one went after them. Indeed, Jefferson ensured Harriet was given money for her journey. Because of their light skin and appearance, they identified with the white community. Hemings said they married white spouses of satisfactory circumstances and moved into white society.

In his will, Jefferson gave immediate freedom to only three slaves: John Hemings, a brother of Sally, to whom he also bequeathed *"the service of his two apprentices Madison and Eston Hemings."* Jefferson instructed John Hemings that the brothers must each be set free on reaching age twenty-one. Jefferson did not release their wives and children, so all had to be sold along with Monticello's one hundred thirty slaves at auctions in 1827 to settle the massive debts against his estate.

Madison, his brothers, and their friends worked to buy the freedom of their families. The brothers rented a house in nearby Charlottesville, where their mother Sally joined them for the rest of her life. She died in 1835, but the 1830 Albemarle County census classified Madison, Eston, and Sally Hemings all as free whites.

Thomas Jefferson was one of the earliest and most fervent supporters of the cause of American independence from Great Britain. He is the author of the Declaration of Independence and became the first president to be inaugurated in Washington, a city he helped plan.

Jefferson encouraged agriculture and westward expansion, most notably by the Louisiana Purchase and subsequent Lewis and Clark Exploration team. Believing America to be a haven for the oppressed, he reduced the residency requirement for naturalization to five years. Immigrants from Europe poured into the country. By the end of his term, the population of the USA numbered more than seven million.

YO-HO-HO AND THE BARBARY PIRATES RETURN: Jefferson eliminated the whiskey tax, reduced the national deficit, and repealed the hated
Alien and Sedition Acts. He also confronted the Barbary Pirates who were
harassing American commercial ships in the Mediterranean. With dag-
gers in their teeth and cannons firing at close range, pirates could and did
quickly overpower merchant ships, stealing the products in the hold and
capturing the ship crews, forcing them into slavery and holding them for
ransom.

The Pasha (ruler) of Tripoli demanded more tribute and declared war
on the United States. Tripoli was part of the Ottoman Empire, where the
governments in North Africa supported an enormous amount of white
slavery under the Muslims in the Mediterranean. The Pasha's demand for
tribute conflicted with Jefferson's determination to stop all the extortion.

Despite his opposition to the expense of maintaining a navy, Jefferson dispatched an American naval squadron to Tripolitan waters. Jefferson
refused to pay any more tribute to the Barbary pirates. While negotiating
to free Americans held by North African pirates, he knew that paying their
bribes invited more problems. The new US Treasury could not afford to
pay the exorbitant ransoms the pirates demanded. The Pasha declared war
on the US, not through any formal written documents, but in the customary Barbary manner of cutting down the flagstaff in front of the US Consul-
ate in Tripoli on 14 May 1801.

The young US Navy prepared to deal with the problem by building a
few ships destined to fight the pirates off the Barbary coast of Africa near
Tripoli. One of those vessels, named by George Washington after the Constitution of the United States, and nicknamed "Old Ironsides," the *USS
Constitution* still floats in Boston Harbor. It is the world's oldest commissioned naval vessel still afloat.

After a series of inconclusive battles, the Marines captured the Tripolitan city of *Derna* in 1805, the first time the United States flag was raised in
victory on foreign soil. The action is memorialized in a line of the Marines'
Hymn—"*. . . to the shores of Tripoli.*" Capturing the city gave American nego-
tiators leverage in securing the return of hostages and the end of the war.

A peace treaty was signed aboard the *Constitution* and ratified in 1806.
The wooden-hulled, three-mast heavy frigate launched in 1797, was rated
as a forty-four-gun frigate, but often carried more than fifty at a time. Paul
Revere supplied the copper sheets replaced on her hull in 1803.

This part of the 1806 Treaty of Tripoli is especially interesting:

> *As the Government of the United States of America is not, in any sense, founded on the Christian religion, —as it has in itself no character of enmity against the laws, religion, or tranquility, of Mussulmen [Muslims], and as the said States never entered into any war or act of hostility against any Mahometan [Mohammedan] nation, it is declared by the parties that no pretext arising from religious opinions shall ever produce an interruption of the harmony existing between the two countries.*

Twenty-three of the thirty-two sitting Senators were present for the June 7th vote which unanimously approved the Treaty. However, before anyone in the United States saw the Treaty, its required payments, in the form of goods and money, had been made in part. Not until the final goods were delivered did the Pasha of Tripoli recognize the Treaty as official. By 1807, Algiers had gone back to taking US ships and seamen hostage.

JEFFERSON'S SECOND TERM: Jefferson was re-elected in 1804 and spent most of his second term protecting the neutral rights of American merchants from the British and French. He attempted to prevent US involvement in the Napoleonic Wars by restricting American shipping.

The embargo was unpopular and did not work very well. The Embargo Act of 1807 was an attempt by Jefferson and the US Congress to prohibit American ships from trading in foreign ports. It was intended to punish Britain and France for interfering with American trade while the two major European powers were at war with each other.

At the beginning of his second term, Jefferson began construction on the first east and west wings of the White House, a project dragging on until the end of his presidency.

THE BURR CONSPIRACY: Jefferson focused his attention on the trial of then former Vice President Aaron Burr for treason. The President ordered Burr arrested and indicted for treason, despite a lack of firm evidence.

Burr's true intentions remain unclear to historians to this day. Some people claim he expected to take parts of Texas and the Louisiana Purchase for himself. Others said he intended to capture Mexico, and yet others claimed he planned to conquer most of the North American continent.

The prosecution eventually resulted in an acquittal, but the test destroyed Burr's already faltering political career.

The Jefferson vice presidency under Adams and the Burr vice presidency under Jefferson were miserable experiences because of conflict. At every turn they faced potential disaster, so legislators began seeking an alternative to naming the electoral runner-up as vice president. The proposed amendment was adopted and ratified as the Twelfth Amendment in 1804, providing the procedure for the Electoral College to cast separate votes for president and vice president.

Jefferson was also concerned with the issue of slavery, specifically the importation of slaves from abroad. He denounced the international slave trade in 1806 as a "violation of human rights" and called upon Congress to criminalize the action.

HE CAN'T LIVE WITHOUT BOOKS: Communication methods in the 1800s included paper and pencil, newspapers, and narratives. Very few people could read and write, so storytelling became an essential part of history. People would pass the oral history of their family and town to others through stories.

After leaving the presidency, Jefferson needed money. The British burned the first Library of Congress in the War of 1812, so he sold his collection of books to the government to be the first books to form the new Congressional library in spite of his famous quote: *"I cannot live without books."*

He founded the University of Virginia (UVA), even designing its buildings and planning its curriculum. He claimed UVA as his most significant accomplishment and never mentioned his presidency of the US in the epitaph for his tombstone.

Rising tensions between the United States and Britain dominated the final years of Jefferson's second term, as the Royal Navy began capturing sailors from American ships and forcing them to work on British crafts and attacking American shipping. Jefferson rejected war and instead used economic threats and embargoes, ultimately hurting the US more than Britain. The disputes with Britain continued after Jefferson left office in 1809, which would eventually lead to the War of 1812.

During his presidency, Thomas and Martha Jefferson's eldest daughter, also named Martha but called "Patsy" (Mrs. Thomas Mann Randolph), served during 1802 to 1806 as the hostess in the president's house. After

Jefferson's retirement, Martha and her children spent their time primarily at Monticello.

The financial difficulties of both her father and husband were a continual strain on Martha.

Thomas Jefferson left "the splendid misery" of the presidency to his friend and protégé James Madison in March 1809.

Figure 12: The "president's house" 1814 after English burned it.

Figure 13: The White House on the $20 bill.

THREE—1810

The Capitol is Burning!

THE CENSUS OF 1810

Jefferson's secretary of state and close friend, James Madison, succeeded him as US President in 1809 and served to 1817. Like Jefferson, Madison inherited a plantation in Virginia, and he owned hundreds of slaves. Both men collected books throughout their lifetimes for their libraries. While Jefferson founded the University of Virginia (UVA), Madison graduated from Princeton, where he completed a three-year degree in two years.

While the two men had similar backgrounds, they contrasted greatly in appearance. Jefferson was over six-feet tall, but the wiry Madison barely reached his friend's shoulder at not quite five feet four inches. He was the shortest president on record and the first president who habitually wore long trousers. The stylish breeches that stopped just below the knee probably made Madison look even shorter.

Madison was sickly as a child, yet he lived to the age of eighty-five. Washington Irving described him as a small, wizened man, appearing old and worn; "a withered little apple-John."

In contrast, Madison's wife Dolley was the toast of Washington. People spoke of her beauty, warmth, and joyfulness. Born Dolley Payne in North Carolina, she married a young lawyer, John Todd, in Philadelphia. The 1793 yellow fever epidemic hit Dolley particularly hard, as her husband, son William, mother-in-law, and father-in-law all succumbed to the disease.

Figure 14: James Madison

The fourth president served two terms from 1809 to 1817.

Vice President: George Clinton

Aaron Burr, a mutual friend, introduced the young Quaker widow to James Madison, who was not a Quaker, so once Dolley accepted his proposal, she was expelled from the Society of Friends.

Madison is considered the most influential contributor to the United States Constitution, and he worked passionately to see the document ratified. Madison's political views changed little throughout his life. He drafted the first ten amendments to the Constitution and is known as the father of the Bill of Rights. He also contributed to The Federalist Papers explaining why he advocated for a robust federal government. Madison was president for the Census of 1810 on census day, the sixth of August.

The third census (1810) counted people in seventeen states and five territories. Included are Vermont and the original thirteen colonies: Connecticut, Delaware, Georgia, Massachusetts, Maryland, New Hampshire, New Jersey, New York, North and South Carolina, Pennsylvania, Rhode Island, Virginia, as well as Kentucky and Tennessee, and the District of Columbia (DC), plus the new state of Ohio.

This census also counted six territories: Illinois, Indiana, Michigan, Mississippi, Louisiana, and Orleans Territory. Louisiana Territory was later renamed Missouri Territory in 1812. Orleans Territory would become Louisiana, the eighteenth state in 1812 followed by Indiana the nineteenth, Mississippi the twentieth in 1817, Illinois the twenty-first, and in 1819 Alabama became the twenty-second state.

In Ohio Territory, all the census records became lost except for Washington County. There's a partial loss of census records in Illinois Territory, and a complete loss of schedules for the District of Columbia, Georgia, New Jersey, Tennessee, Indiana Territory, Michigan Territory, Mississippi Territory and Louisiana Territory (Missouri). If your ancestors were in any of those areas, you might have to rely on other information to find them.

THE THIRD CENSUS: Marshals in 1810 collected the same information as in 1800. The authorization act for the third census stipulated an assistant marshal must personally visit each household or the head of each family within his designated enumeration district. They were not to rely on hearsay to complete the count.

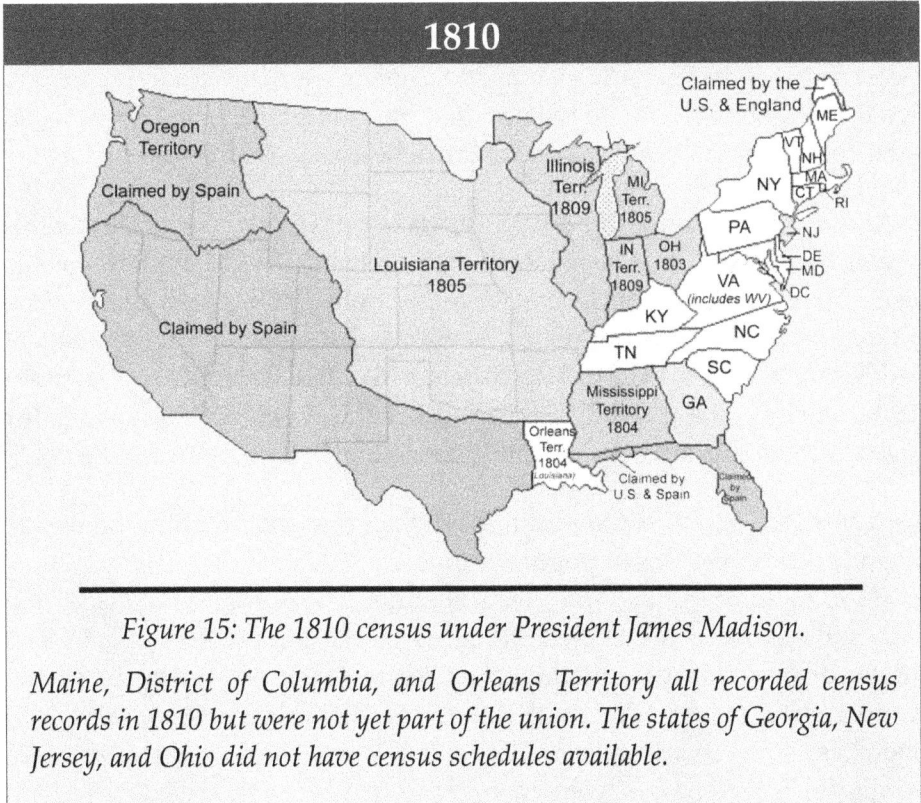

Figure 15: The 1810 census under President James Madison.

Maine, District of Columbia, and Orleans Territory all recorded census records in 1810 but were not yet part of the union. The states of Georgia, New Jersey, and Ohio did not have census schedules available.

IF I FIND THE RIGHT PERSON, THEN WHAT: Use the age categories to determine an approximate birth date range. Use the residence to locate other records such as land, probate, tax, and church records. Continue to search the index and records to identify other relatives

When looking for a person who had a common name, look at all possible spellings for the surname before deciding which is correct. You may need to compare the information of more than one family or person to make this determination

NEW MADRID EARTHQUAKE: One of the worst earthquakes ever to strike the United States started on 16 December 1811 and followed with three more upheavals a few weeks later in February. With an estimated magnitude of 7.4 to 8.3, the last quake shook Missouri so vigorously, it destroyed one-half of the town of New Madrid and was felt strongly for fifty thousand square miles. The earthquake created new lakes, caused numerous aftershocks, and temporarily reversed the course of the Mississippi River.

THE RICH AND HOW THEY GOT THERE: On June 23, 1810, John Jacob Astor founded the Pacific Fur Company. The success of this trading company would make him the United States' first multi-millionaire, and even when adjusted for inflation, he was one of the richest men in American history.

WAR OF 1812: During his presidency, Madison led the US into the controversial War of 1812 that lasted until 1815 against Great Britain. Britain was using its navy to prevent American ships from trading with France. The United States, as a neutral nation, saw this as a violation of international law. Worse than that, even though Britain had ceded the Northwest Territory to the United States by treaties, they shocked the population by sending Brit soldiers to assist Native Americans in harassing settlers on the frontier.

MR. MADISON'S WAR: Madison asked Congress for a declaration of war in spite of a severe lack of popular support.

The nation's coffers were lean because Jefferson and Madison had closed the Bank of the United States, narrowed the tax system, and also reduced the military. Both Britain and France endeavored to block the United States from trading with the other. The British accosted American merchant ships to seize alleged Royal Navy deserters, carrying off thousands of US citizens who were then forced to serve in the British navy.

Madison finally prevailed, and the United States declared war on Britain in 1812 even though the US was far from ready. The vote on the declaration of war in the Congress was very close, reflecting how unpopular the fight seemed to large segments of the American public.

The new Americans had not fought a war or even needed an army for a long time. After the American declaration of war, the president learned the British had already repealed the offending trade restrictions but that was too late. The battle was on.

WE FIRED OUR GUNS, BUT THEY KEPT A'COMIN': The Brits fought battles on land and sea. The conflict kept grinding on for three years, and so did opposition to the war. Newspapers blasted the Madison administration, and some state governments even went so far as to obstruct the war effort. Northeastern newspapers especially denounced Madison as corrupt and greedy. The military situation suffered from unpopularity, especially in New England, where citizens derogatorily called it "Mr. Madison's War."

The Massachusetts governor refused to allow the state's militiamen to join the campaign in Canada. The British concentrated their assault on the southern coastline from Florida to Delaware Bay. Madison had great difficulty financing the war with the US national bank disbanded and private bankers in the New England states opposed to the war. Madison's rebellious House denied him additional taxes, and his Treasury secretary had to lower the defense budget for the country to stay solvent.

"THE STAR-SPANGLED BANNER": On 14 September 1814, Francis Scott Key witnessed the bombarding of US forces at Fort McHenry during the Battle of Baltimore. The experience inspired him to write a poem that later became lyrics to the national anthem, The Star-Spangled Banner. Seeing the large flag with fifteen stars and fifteen stripes flying triumphantly above the fort following the victory inspired Key to write the song.

The first official US flag flown during a battle was on the third of August 1777, at Fort Schuyler (now Fort Stanwix) during a siege. Massachusetts reinforcements brought news Congress adopted the official flag. Soldiers cut up their shirts to make white stripes. Scarlet material for the flag's red stripes came from red flannel petticoats of officers' wives, and they carved the blue union from Capt. Abraham Swartwout's blue cloth coat.

Congress later reimbursed Capt. Swartwout for his blue jacket, but the assembly did not compensate women for their red petticoats.

THE FIRST US MILITARY DRAFT: With only eight thousand soldiers, Congress passed a conscription act. Luckily the war ended before the draft took effect. The young USA knew little about fighting a war. Ragtag American land forces rarely eked out battlefield victories and never secured their principal strategic aim, which in actuality meant control of Canada and the St. Lawrence valley.

TIPPECANOE AND TECUMSEH: William Henry Harrison, governor of Indiana Territory (and later president), formed a large force to try to capture Detroit from the British. Harrison's men did not succeed, but they did chase the British from Detroit as well as from a British fort at Malden, in Canada. Harrison, in 1811, led an army of more than a thousand men north to near the Wabash and Tippecanoe Rivers to intimidate the Shawnee into making peace. A confederation of Native Americans from various tribes gathered there under Shawnee leader Tecumseh and his brother Tenskwatawa, commonly known as "the Prophet."

The tribes launched a surprise attack on Harrison's men in what became known as the Battle of Tippecanoe. Harrison and his troops stood their ground for more than two hours until the natives ran out of ammunition and withdrew.

Harrison's men burned Prophetstown to the ground, even destroying food supplies stored for the winter. The soldiers hailed Harrison as a national hero, and the battle became famous.

Later Harrison's men caught the Brits and defeated them in the Battle of the Thames in Ontario, Canada. The great Indian chief Tecumseh, who had been fighting for the British, was killed in this battle.

THE FORT DEARBORN MASSACRE: More soldiers usually died from disease than from fighting. However, when the British allied with Potawatomi Indians to attack Fort Dearborn (modern-day Chicago), the results became devastating. The incident, known for years as the Fort Dearborn massacre, left more than sixty men, women, and children dead on the shores of Lake Michigan. Captain Nathan Heald commanded the fort as war broke out with Great Britain during the summer of 1812. The settlers at Fort Dearborn were already consumed by fear because Native Americans, incited by the British, had been conducting raids on white settlements for months.

Ordered to abandon the fort and hoping to win over the Potawatomie and secure their help as escorts, Captain Heald promised to give them the contents of the fort including food, calico, and other provisions. However, at the last minute before departing, he decided to destroy the fort's supply of alcohol and ammunition, concluding whiskey would only inflame the Potawatomi. He feared they might use any powder or shot against the soldiers. The Indians considered this another white man's broken promise.

At nine o'clock on a hot and sunny Saturday morning of August 15, a mixed column paraded out of Fort Dearborn including fifty-five soldiers, twelve civilian militiamen, nine women, and eighteen children. Some of the women were on horseback, and most of the children rode in one of the two wagons. Five hundred Potawatomi surrounded the wagons, defended by a twelve-man militia desperate to protect their wives and children. When the attack began, the soldiers discharged their muskets and then brandished them like clubs before they were all slain.

A solitary Potawatomi climbed into the wagon with the children and indiscriminately bludgeoned them to death with his tomahawk.

Four years later, when soldiers arrived at Chicago to build a second Fort Dearborn, the bleached bones of the battle's dead still lay unburied on the Lake Michigan shoreline.

MADISON'S SECOND ELECTION: Despite the problems characterizing his first term, Madison won a second term in 1812. Vice President George Clinton (no relation to Bill Clinton) died in office. Elbridge Gerry was elected to fill the vacancy, but in 1814 he died too. Madison guided the nation through the War of 1812 with Great Britain, which many called the second American Revolution.

WASHINGTON IS BURNING: On the twenty-fourth of August 1814, the British naval force attacked Washington and set fire to the Capitol and other buildings. Royal Navy officer George Cockburn directed the capture and burning of Washington, DC. Before setting fire to the president's home, Cockburn took as souvenirs one of Madison's hats and the seat from one of Dolley Madison's dining chairs. British sailors enjoyed feasting on food using the president's silverware and china before burning the building.

When the British invaded, President Madison and his officials were forced to flee suddenly. Dolley received a letter from her husband, urging her to leave Washington at a moment's notice. She packed a wagon and saved the red silk velvet draperies of the Oval Room, the silver service, and the blue and gold Lowestoft china set she had purchased for the state dining room. Most reports say she saved Gilbert Stuart's life-size portrait of George Washington, though that act is in dispute. The original is now in the National Portrait Gallery, and a copy hangs in the East Room.

One of the most dramatic events in the War of 1812 was when invading British sailors burned the executive mansion to its stone walls in retaliation for the American attack in June on the city of York in Ontario, Canada. They flew the Union Jack on top of Capitol Hill and burned the public buildings in the young nation's capital—including the Capitol Building (missing its uncompleted rotunda), the president's house (i.e., White House), and the Treasury Building.

The British looted the Capitol, which at that time housed Congress, the Library of Congress, and the Supreme Court. The red coats first set fire to the southern wing containing the House of Representatives, then the northern wing with the Senate. They intended to burn the Capitol to the ground, but the flames multiplied so quickly the British could not collect enough wood to burn the stone walls completely. However, the contents of the Library of Congress in the northern wing contributed to the blaze. Fuel was added to the fires to ensure they would continue burning into the next day.

Out of the blue, less than a day after the attack began, a sudden, very heavy thunderstorm put out the flames. The storm also spun off a tornado. The circular winds passed through the center of the city, sat down on Constitution Avenue and lifted two cannons before dropping them several yards away, killing British troops and American civilians alike. British occupation of the capital city lasted only about twenty-six hours.

AFTER THE STORM: The "storm that saved Washington," as it soon came to be called, moved out, and so did the Brits. After the enemy withdrew, the Americans returned. Madison found most public buildings burned beyond repair. Among the destruction was the three-thousand-volume collection in the Library of Congress. The carnage included the Capitol building, the Senate House and the House of Representatives, the arsenal, dockyard, Treasury, war office, president's mansion, the bridge over the Potomac, a frigate, and a sloop.

In the winter of 1814, leaders decided to repair the president's house as it was, but restoring the Capitol took much longer than anticipated. The Old Brick Capitol had taken only five months to complete; the new US Capitol required twelve years. After the devastating fire, President Madison declared that all must be rebuilt as before, without deviation. Phoenix-like the house, and then the burned wings, rose again and returned to use in 1818.

The final battle of the 1812 war between Britain and the United States occurred when the Brits attempted to invade New Orleans. Major General Andrew Jackson defeated the English in that one. The battle took place directly after the signing of the Treaty of Ghent on December 24, 1814, because news of the treaty had not reached the United States. Unfortunately, the 1815 peace treaty between the two countries settled very few of the continuing issues.

NAPOLEON MET HIS WATERLOO: Napoleon, who was friendly to the US, was defeated for the last time at the Battle of Waterloo (in present-day Belgium) near the end of Madison's presidency.

As the Napoleonic Wars ended, so did the US Wars with the British. The War of 1812 conclusively established the United States as a permanent fixture among sovereign nations. The battle definitively ended the series of wars convulsing Europe and many other regions of the world since the early 1790s.

Almost four decades of international peace in Europe followed.

PRESIDENTIAL ELECTION OF 1816: Our young country being so near disaster in the War of 1812 did not prevent Virginia Republicans from choosing another man from Virginia. Revolutionary War veteran James Monroe was comfortably elected to become the fifth president. Monroe was the last Virginian and the last of the Founding Fathers to be president. He was also the last president to wear a ponytail or queue.

SEMINOLE WAR OF 1817: Settlers in southern Georgia and Florida attacked the Seminole who then retaliated by attacking homesteads. In 1818, General Andrew Jackson decided to invade Pensacola. The Spanish territory divided into West, East, and North Florida. It had become a sanctuary for runaway slaves from northern states and several tribes of Indians. The governor of West Florida said most of the Indians at Pensacola were women and children and the men were unarmed, but Jackson did not stop. When he reached Pensacola, the governor and the hundred-seventy-five-man Spanish garrison retreated, leaving the city to Jackson. The two sides exchanged cannon fire for a couple of days, the Spanish surrendered, and Jackson went home. The first Seminole War continued through to 1819, but with no conclusive winners.

FLORIDA TERRITORY: In 1819, Secretary of State John Quincy Adams achieved a diplomatic coup with the signing of the Florida Purchase Treaty, which officially put Florida into US hands without cost except for the assumption of some five million dollars in claims by US citizens against Spain. Florida became a US territory in 1822 and came as a slave state in 1845.

There were international repercussions to Jackson's military action in Florida. Secretary of State John Quincy Adams had just started talks with

Spain for the purchase of Florida. Spain protested the invasion and seizure of West Florida and suspended negotiations. Adams apologized and said it had not been American policy to seize Spanish territory. Spain accepted the apology and eventually resumed talks.

LIFE IN THE YOUNG NATION: Malaria and tuberculosis topped the list of leading causes of death for adults during this period, while children most commonly died from measles, mumps, and whooping cough.

More than four out of every five Americans still lived on farms. Many farmers constructed goods by hand like barrels, furniture, or horseshoes for their use, for barter, or to sell.

The Industrial Revolution arrived. Textile mills and cotton-spinning plants spread across the country. More than a hundred such mills employed women and children at less than a dollar a week and operated throughout New England. Singing and sheet music became available, particularly "broadside songs" or sheet lyrics that sold for a penny. For recreation, horse racing increased in popularity. Washington Irving published *Rip Van Winkle* and *Legend of Sleepy Hollow.* Jane Austen's *Pride and Prejudice* became a best-seller.

Long-distance travel by horseback or uncomfortable stagecoaches moved slowly over rutted roads. Cargo by horse-team was limited to twenty-five or thirty miles a day, but in 1811, Congress signed a contract for the construction of the National Road, the first highway built by the government. The National Road moved across the Appalachian Mountains, fostering westward expansion. The road did not complete until 1834. Americans discovered steamboat travel in 1817 when construction kicked off on the Erie Canal connecting the Great Lakes and the Ohio and Mississippi valleys with the Hudson River and the Atlantic Ocean.

Protestant evangelism swept across the country. Tens of thousands of people would attend a single camp meeting, marked by enthusiastic preaching with audience singing and participation. Spontaneous services, led by itinerant preachers, helped unite settlers on the Western frontier to the cultural life of the rest of the country.

Most Americans ate whatever they hunted or grew, such as corn and beans with pork. In the north, cows provided milk, butter, and beef. In the south where cattle were rare, venison and other game provided meat. Without refrigeration, meat required smoking, drying, or salting. Vegetables were stored in a root cellar or pickled.

The first installment of Washington Irving's *Rip Van Winkle* appeared in the May 1819 edition of The Sketch Book. The famous story follows a Dutch American villager in colonial America named Rip Van Winkle, who falls asleep in the Catskill Mountains and wakes up twenty years later, having missed the American Revolution.

PRESIDENT NUMBER FIVE: James Monroe, age twenty-six, married Elizabeth Kortright, age seventeen, on the sixteenth of February 1786, at her father's home in New York City, but little more is known about Elizabeth except she suffered poor health. Elizabeth gained a reputation for being aloof, and many disapproved of her European tastes.

Monroe formed a close friendship with the Marquis de Lafayette, a French volunteer who encouraged Monroe to view the war as part of a broader struggle against religious and political tyranny. After the war, Monroe was appointed American Minister to France soon after the French Revolution. In private, the Monroe family spoke only French.

Figure 16:
James Monroe

Our fifth president served two terms from 1817 to 1825.

Vice President: Daniel Tompkins

THE MADAME LAFAYETTE: Mr. and Mrs. Monroe were living in Paris during the Reign of Terror when Elizabeth learned Adrienne, the wife of Marquis de Lafayette and the daughter of a Duke and Duchess, could soon face death on the guillotine.

The arranged marriage in 1774 of Lafayette and Adrienne had turned out well. Although she was only fourteen, she was happy in her new position, yet Adrienne and Lafayette could not have been more at odds over social affairs. Adrienne loved them as much as Lafayette hated them. Three years after the marriage, Lafayette became enamored with the American Revolutionary War and wanted to go to America to make a name for himself. He remained in the US, even spending the winter in Valley Forge with Washington, with a few

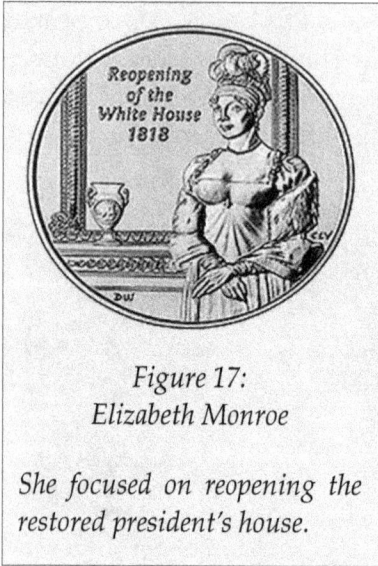

Figure 17:
Elizabeth Monroe

She focused on reopening the restored president's house.

occasional trips home until 1782, where the public hailed him as a hero at Versailles. The Marquis and his wife named their first son George Washington.

Adrienne's grandmother, mother, and her sister had been arrested and guillotined on 22 July 1794. Elizabeth Monroe helped secure Adrienne's release a year later to join her husband, who was still held captive in Austria. James and Elizabeth Monroe's daughter Eliza became friends with Napoleon Bonaparte's step-daughter and they attended Napoleon's 1804 coronation.

Elizabeth began her tenure as the nation's first lady on March 4, 1817, when her husband commenced his first term. However, the president's house was still under reconstruction after having been burned, so Elizabeth hosted the inaugural ball at their private residence on I Street in Washington, and part of the time the first family lived in The Octagon House, now a museum.

Since the British attack destroyed all the presidential mansion furnishings, the Monroe family brought some from their private residences.

On New Year's Day 1818, President Monroe opened the reconstructed house at a gala New Year's reception. The president's house had previously been painted gray. When Monroe began his presidency in 1817, the mansion was painted white, so many people informally called the building the white house long before Theodore Roosevelt officially adopted that name in 1901.

FEELING GOOD: Monroe's presidency ushered in what was known as the "Era of Good Feelings." However, it also ushered in a new Democratic political party organized by Congressman Martin Van Buren, and his plan to save the Union by "bribing" people in the northern states to support the party in office by giving them government jobs.

This new Spoils System meant any government job was going to go to the person most effective at getting out the vote in the election, not the most qualified.

Chapter 3 in Summary from 1810 to 1820:

- ✓ James Madison succeeded Jefferson 1809-1817
- ✓ Dolley Madison was the toast of Washington
- ✓ Madison inherited his plantation in Virginia with hundreds of slaves
- ✓ Census 1810 counted 17 states and 5 territories
- ✓ New Madrid (MO) 1812 quake destroyed half the town
- ✓ Madison asked Congress for a declaration of war, but the treasury was empty
- ✓ Madison declared war anyway, so the people called War of 1812 "Mr. Madison's war"
- ✓ The British captured and burned Washington
- ✓ Major General Andrew Jackson defeated British in New Orleans
- ✓ Battle of Tippecanoe involved Shawnee Tecumseh and Tenskwatawa "the Prophet"
- ✓ Fort Dearborn (Chicago) massacre in 1814
- ✓ Revolutionary War veteran James Monroe of Virginia elected President in 1816
- ✓ Industrial Revolution begins
- ✓ Diseases: malaria, tuberculosis, measles, mumps, and whooping cough
- ✓ Most people lived on farms and traveled by horseback or stagecoach on dirt roads
- ✓ New states: Louisiana #18, Indiana #19, Mississippi #20, Illinois #21, Alabama #22
- ✓ Jane Austen's *Pride and Prejudice* published before 1813
- ✓ Many people called it the White House long before Teddy Roosevelt named it in 1901

"The best form of government is that which is most likely to prevent the greatest sum of evil." —James Monroe

FOUR—1820

A Hillbilly Housewarming

CENSUS OF 1820

The United States now stretched from the Atlantic Ocean to the western edge of the Mississippi basin, even though Florida, Michigan, and Wisconsin had yet to attain statehood.

ELECTION TIME AGAIN: James Monroe of Virginia, a founding father who fought under George Washington at Valley Forge, was nominated for a second term in 1820. A protégé of Thomas Jefferson, Monroe served with the Continental Army before embarking on a long political career. He ran virtually unopposed.

He is best known for the Monroe Doctrine, preventing European interference in the West. This document warned European nations to keep their hands off the independent countries of North and South America.

THE MISSOURI COMPROMISE: Slavery remained a contentious issue during Monroe's presidency. The North had banned slavery, but Southern states supported it. Monroe signed the Compromise Bill of 1820, a temporary solution to the brewing controversy over slavery.

An aging Thomas Jefferson said news of the Compromise shocked him like a *"fire bell in the night."* He feared it was the *"death knell of the Union."* This significant bill attempted to equalize the number of slave-holding states and free states. The Missouri Compromise provided for the admission of Maine as a free state and Missouri as a slave state, keeping them in balance.

The amendment also drew an imaginary line across the former Louisiana Territory, establishing a boundary between free and slave regions.

While the Missouri Compromise eased the under-lying tensions caused by the slavery issue only temporarily, it did create an interim peace and hold the nation together. Critics in the South objected to the federal government imposing any restrictions on a state wishing to have slavery as an institution. As new states came in, officials were to keep equal the number of free and slave states.

The balance would shift in 1850, but for now, Monroe's high approval rating assured his election to a second term in 1821. The Constitution, written when James Monroe was a young man, avoided coming to terms with the slavery issue, and the Missouri Compromise, passed at

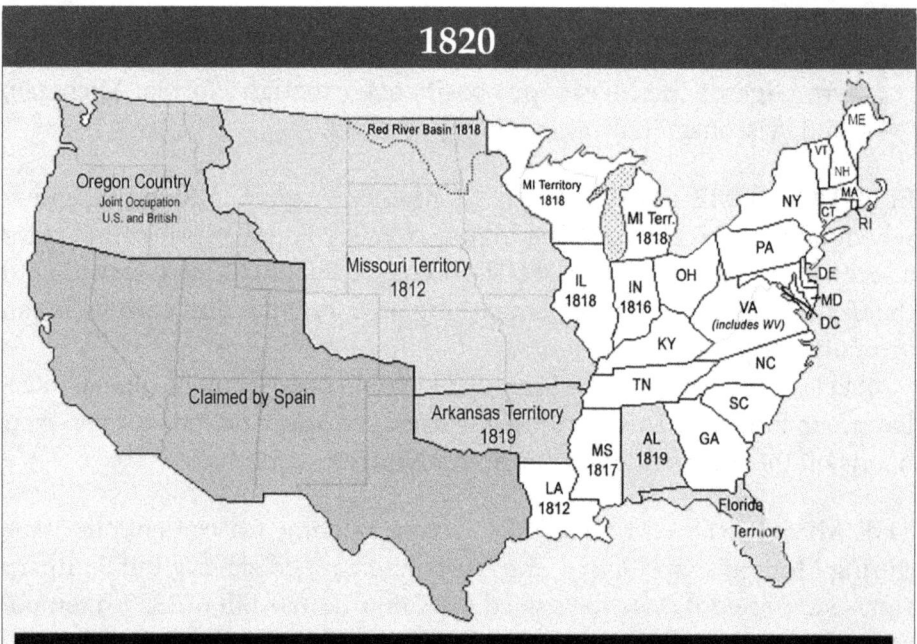

1820

Figure 18: The 1820 census, James Monroe, president

The 1820 Census included six new states: Louisiana, Indiana, Mississippi, Illinois, Alabama, and Maine. However, census taking was not yet an exact science. Census schedules were lost for Arkansas Territory, Missouri Territory, and New Jersey. Census information is available for the white colored states.

the end of Monroe's first term as president, merely patched together a framework for dividing the nation between free and slave states.

THE FOURTH CENSUS: The 1820 census lists the original thirteen colonies: Connecticut, Delaware, Georgia, Maryland, Massachusetts, New Hampshire, New Jersey, New York, North Carolina, Pennsylvania, Rhode Island, South Carolina, and Virginia, plus three more: Vermont, Kentucky, and Tennessee.

Six new states came in for this census: Alabama, Mississippi, Illinois, Indiana, Louisiana, Maine; and three territories: Arkansas Territory, Michigan Territory, and Missouri Territory. Note: Wisconsin Territory was not split off from Michigan Territory until 1836 when the state of Michigan prepared for statehood.

Maine remained a part of Massachusetts until 1820, when as a result of the growing population and a political agreement regarding slavery, Maine became the twenty-third state on the fifteenth of March under the Missouri Compromise, and then Missouri became the twenty-fourth state the next year.

However, a district-wide loss of data occurred for Arkansas Territory, Missouri Territory, and New Jersey. Some of the schedules for these states have been re-created using tax lists and other records. Partial losses included half the counties in Alabama and about twenty eastern Tennessee counties.

Existing records show the head of household name, number of free white males and females by age group, number of foreigners not naturalized, number of free colored males and females by age group, number of male and female slaves by age group, and number of other persons—except for that one pesky item, "Indians not taxed." All questions asked and answers given refer to the official enumeration day of 7 August 1820 in regard to births and deaths.

The census count showed the total population had grown to almost ten million in just thirty years.

WATCH OUT FOR DUPLICATES: The census of 1820 presents a pitfall if you do not know what questions they asked. Under "Free White Males," there is a breakdown by ages: under 10, 10-16, 16-18, 16-26, 26-45, 45-up. Those listed in the 16-18 column are duplicated in the 16-26 column so it could look like there are additional males in the family.

Census takers also counted the number of persons to be naturalized; how many engaged in agriculture, commercial, or manufacture; how many "colored" persons (sometimes in age categories); and the count of other persons, except for Indians. The 1820 Census is the first to obtain data about foreigners not naturalized (by count only, not by name).

The other "special" schedules counted foreigners not naturalized, and persons involved in commerce. Census takers were told to count each individual in only one of the occupational columns. For example, if an individual was engaged in agriculture, commerce, and manufacture, the census taker had to choose which one in which he thought the individual was primarily involved. Census takers were asked to use double lines, red ink, or some other method of distinguishing these columns so double-counting would not occur.

A VISION FOR THE MORMON CHURCH: In 1820 in Palmyra, New York, fourteen-year-old Joseph Smith witnessed a vision. The fifth of eleven children born to a poor farming family, Joseph received only three years of formal schooling and was educated mainly at home from the family Bible. He said he went into the woods to pray where he met two figures. Joseph referred to them as "personages." They introduced themselves as father and son. Smith describes them as "standing in the air." Smith asked the figures which church he should join. They answered, "none." All of the existing churches had corrupted their creeds and misconstrued the true gospel, the figures said. You will learn more about this young man in the next chapter.

BILL OF RIGHTS, FIRST AMENDMENT: *Congress shall make no law respecting an establishment of religion or prohibiting the free exercise thereof; or abridging the freedom of speech, or of the press; or the right of the people peaceably to assemble, and to petition the Government for a redress of grievances.*

FREEDOM OF RELIGION: The freedom of religion has changed over time in the United States and continues to be controversial. For instance, from 1780 to 1824, Massachusetts residents were all required to attend a parish church, the denomination of which was chosen by majority vote of town residents, and in effect this established Congregationalism as the state religion.

They discontinued the remaining state churches in 1820 and abolished teacher-led public-school prayer in 1962. The North Carolina Constitution of 1776 disestablished the Anglican church, and until 1835 the NC Constitution allowed only Protestants to hold public office. From 1835 to 1876 NC allowed Catholics and all Christians to hold public office.

Until 1877 the New Hampshire Constitution required members of the state legislature to be of the Protestant religion. Until 1968 the state funded Protestant classrooms but not Catholic classrooms.

Freedom of religion is also closely associated with separation of church and state. The government is not allowed to hinder the free exercise of religion and is not allowed to sponsor any particular religion through taxation of favors. Notwithstanding the clear separation of government and religion, the predominant cultural and social nature of the nation did become strongly Christian.

MISSOURI'S BACHELOR TAX: Missouri imposed a one-dollar bachelor tax on unmarried men aged between twenty-one and fifty.

BUILDING THE ERIE CANAL: George Washington was the first to present an idea of building a canal from the east coast to mid-America. Washington actually attempted such a thing in the 1790s, and while Washington's canal was a failure, citizens of New York thought they might be able to construct a canal that would reach hundreds of miles westward. That idea was a dream, and many people scoffed. But when one man, DeWitt Clinton, became involved, the crazy dream started to become reality.

When the Erie Canal opened in 1825, it was the marvel of its age, and soon a huge economic success.

Built between 1817 and 1825 to link Lake Erie to the Hudson River and New York City, the Erie Canal brought together goods and people from across New York state and from the far reaches of the Great Lakes. Area farms and industries benefited from the traffic on the canal. New York City was the leading market for commerce on the new channel.

The labor force numbered three thousand men in 1818 and nine thousand in 1821. The men dug the four-foot-deep by forty-foot-wide canal mainly by hand, aided by draft animals, explosives, and tree stump pulling machines. Their wages of fifty cents a day, or about $12 a month, sometimes included food and a bunk. Residents and new immigrants alike were happy to find work on the project.

The Ohio and Erie Canal was constructed during the 1820s and early 1830s in Ohio, connecting Akron with the Cuyahoga River near its outlet on Lake Erie in Cleveland, and a few years later with the Ohio River near Portsmouth. The canal carried freight traffic from 1827 to 1861 when the construction of railroads ended demand. The canal was so successful the government considered extending channels into the new lands that stretched from Kentucky to Alabama and on to Texas.

THE LAND LAW OF 1820: This land act allowed purchasers to buy as little as eighty acres of public land for a minimum price of a dollar and a quarter an acre. The new law became effective on the first of July 1820 and required full payment at the time of purchase and registration.

Previously, seekers could purchase public domain lands on credit or an installment system over four years. Financiers considered the law necessary because many farmers were having trouble paying off loans due to the additional economic hardships brought by the Panic of 1819.

Squatters broke the rules by trying to get land more cheaply; they moved onto the property before it was put up for auction. Congress did not like these encroachments on Indian Treaties and had to do something. The act was instrumental in ushering in a new age of Western influence. The 1820 Land Act was suitable for the average American and it was also favorable for the wealthy investors who had sufficient money to buy the lower-cost property. It was terrible for Native Americans because the Act allowed increased confiscation of land.

BUREAU OF INDIAN AFFAIRS CREATED: The Bureau of Indian Affairs replaced the Office of Indian Trade. When Congress passed a law prohibiting the sale of alcohol to Indians in 1822, a disruption in the fur trade pattern occurred. This industry relied on the Indians to trap and hunt for the furs in exchange for alcohol and other goods, so the change of rules created a new problem.

General Andrew Jackson resigned his commission in the US Army to be appointed military governor of Florida Territory in 1821.

THE FIRST PHOTOGRAPHS: A French inventor, Joseph Niépce, succeeded in recording a light-sensitive image with silver chloride. His ongoing research into using a type of asphalt to fix the picture gave him success.

JOHN QUINCY ADAMS, THE SIXTH PRESIDENT: American railroad mania began with the Baltimore and Ohio Railroad in 1826 and flourished for several decades until the Panic of 1873 bankrupted many railroads and temporarily ended growth.

As for what was happening in Washington in this decade, John Quincy Adams was elected president in a close and controversial four-way contest. He did bring two new things to the presidential palace if you can imagine, a pet alligator and a pool table. The son of second US President John Adams and his wife Abigail, John Q. possessed vast experience, unassailable ethics, and deep intelligence.

He had a grand vision for America but is generally considered a failure as president.

Adams did not believe in patronage at a time when the spoils system was the primary tool political parties used to get out the vote. The post office was one of the crucial patronage arms in government, with thousands of jobs to be given away.

Figure 19: John Quincy Adams

The sixth US president served one term 1825 to 1829.

Vice President: John C. Calhoun

Every sitting president either has been or will be featured on presidential one dollar coins, though these coins are printed only for collectors.

John Q. renominated all political appointees from the Monroe administration, including those appointed by his own political opponents, assuring he would not have a strong base of support for his policies.

While serving abroad as US Ambassador in 1797, he married Louisa Catherine Johnson, who had been born in London. He was the first president with a foreign-born wife. John Q. developed an interest in charming nineteen-year-old Louisa when they met in London in 1794. Three years later they moved to Berlin where he was serving as a diplomat. When John Quincy Adams was a candidate for president in 1824, his wife was his unofficial campaign manager, although John Q. usually ignored her except when he needed her to hostess official receptions. Louisa had experienced multiple pregnancies, miscarriages, a stillbirth, and numerous other health issues, but the Johnsons eventually became parents of three sons and a daughter. Louisa's health was not good. Suffering through menopause during her husband's presidency, the once affable and gregarious first lady withdrew into herself.

Louisa remained a very private woman caught in an intensely public life. *"There is something in this great, unsocial house which depresses my spirits beyond expression,"* Louisa Adams said of her life.

THE PREZ WENT SKINNY-DIPPING: Some historians say John Quincy Adams liked to swim in the Potomac River during his presidency, but no one caught it on video. Every morning at five a.m., he laid his clothing on the bank and went skinny-dipping. One morning someone stole his clothes, and he had to ask a boy passing by to run to the house and get him something to wear.

When John Q. was elected, his father, the former president, wrote to him, *"No man who ever held the office of president would congratulate a friend on obtaining it."*

Shortly after Adams' defeat in the 1828 election, their eldest son, George, either fell overboard or committed suicide by jumping off a ship in April 1829. He was on his way to visit his parents in Washington, DC. He had been called home to consult with his parents about his fathering a child out of wedlock. Only five years later, their second son, John, died of acute alcoholism.

LIFE IN THE USA: Men's fashion by the mid-1820s changed. Coats became knee-length, featuring broad shoulders with inset sleeves, a narrow waist, and flared below the waist. Trousers were worn for smart day wear, while knee-breeches continued in use at court and in the country.

Fashionable women's clothing styles transitioned away from the empire silhouette and demonstrated full skirts and visible corseting of the natural waist. For our ancestors at this time, new modes of communication spread messages of religious revival, social reform, and party politics. The world had changed. Improved transportation moved goods, money, and people more rapidly. However, slavery remained widespread.

By the 1820s, farmers in the valley of Virginia were providing a comfortable lifestyle for themselves and their families. They furnished their homes with tables and chairs, pewter and ceramic tableware, coarse earthenware, chests, books, and bed and table linens, though rarely would you see fashionable goods such as mahogany furniture or porcelain. The Virginia Germans often added cast-iron heating stoves and clocks to their household furnishings.

Roads were greatly improved. Stagecoaches were familiar vehicles along the main byways of the East and the South before the coming of railroads.

As for John Quincy Adams' success as a president? He operated well within the confines of the Constitution, but like his predecessors, he just kicked the can of slavery on down the road.

PRESIDENT ANDREW JACKSON: When Andrew Jackson lost the election of 1824, his supporters got busy preparing for the next one. A faction split off from the older established Democratic-Republican Party to become the Democratic party.

At age thirteen in the Revolutionary War, the future president acted as a courier and was captured by the British.

Jackson was orphaned as a teenager and fathered no biological children, although he became the guardian and father to many children, including a Native American orphan Jackson found in battle. In a few years he went on to become the hero of the War of 1812. Even though a treaty was already signed, communication was slow. Jackson won a decisive victory over the British army at the Battle of New Orleans in 1815, making him a national hero. His soldiers gave him the nickname "Old Hickory," saying he was as "tough as old hickory."

Figure 20:
Andrew Jackson

The seventh president, he served two terms from 1829 to 1837.

Vice Presidents: John C. Calhoun and Martin Van Buren

Representatives of both America and Great Britain had signed the "Treaty of Ghent" on Christmas Eve day 1814, in the city of that name in the United Netherlands. The treaty solved no problems but did restore relations between the two nations and moved the borders of the two countries to the lines before the war started.

REPRESENTED BY A DONKEY: Opponents told all who would listen that Jackson was a stubborn jackass. Jackson was so proud of his reputation for stubbornness he started using the image of a donkey on his campaign posters. Democrats have used the donkey icon to represent their party ever since.

Jackson was the victor of the dirtiest-ever presidential election in 1828. Jackson had a thing for taking it outside, being involved in an estimated one hundred duels, usually because someone said something negative about his wife. In 1806 during one of these duels, he was shot in the chest. Seven years later, he took a bullet to the arm in a bar fight with a senator. Jackson once killed a man in a duel over a matter of honor regarding his wife. In our modern age, solving a problem by asking someone to step outside is generally considered an immature, low-class thing to do. Despite putting on a brave front, no gentleman relished having to fight a duel and risk both killing and being killed—except perhaps Andrew Jackson.

RACHEL ROBARDS JACKSON: Naturally, Jackson's record of dueling made a scandalous print for the opposition, but the worst gossip concerned Jackson's beautiful wife, Rachel Donelson Robards, whom he met and fell in love with. They eloped and married in 1788 in Mississippi.

The couple later learned Rachel's alcoholic first husband, Lewis Robards, had failed to legally terminate their marriage.

Andrew and Rachel re-married six years later after finalizing her divorce, which led to a great deal of gossip.

During the cruel prelude to Jackson's first presidential election, Rachel was the subject of extremely negative attacks from the supporters of her husband's opponent, John Quincy Adams. Jackson believed these attacks hastened her death. She died suddenly, probably of a heart attack, before her husband became president. Jackson always blamed his political enemies for her death because she was so distressed about the slander.

Rachel and Andrew Jackson lived at their home, The Hermitage, where she died just days after his election and before his inauguration. Rachel's niece, Emily Donelson, assumed the role of presidential hostess.

A HILLBILLY HOUSEWARMING: Jackson was the first president to invite the public to attend the White House ball honoring his first inauguration. On the fourth of March 1829, Jackson held an open house after his swearing-in ceremony. Many poor people came to the inaugural ball in their homemade clothes and backwoods manners. Quickly the crowd swelled to more than twenty thousand, turning the usually dignified presidential mansion into a boisterous mob scene. Jackson's guards could not keep control. Eventually, dishes and decorative pieces inside were broken. Some people stood on upholstered chairs in muddy boots to get a look at the

Figure 21: The first Hermitage.

Andrew and Rachel Jackson lived in the home for several years. Once they moved out, the cabin was turned into slave quarters.

Wikimedia Commons by Rennett Stowe

president. Finally, the attendants poured punch in tubs and served it on the lawn to lure people outside.

As Jackson appointed his government heads, he started the process whereby the way to get elected was to promise more jobs than your opponent.

GO WEST, YOUNG MAN: In the 1820s, America's population continued moving ever westward in search of opportunities and advancement. Frontier settlers are often seen as fiercely independent and strongly opposed to any government control or interference; however, they did receive a lot of government help, directly and indirectly. The national roads, such as the Cumberland Pike (1818) and the Erie Canal (1825) created by the government, helped move them move West, and also helped deliver farm produce to market.

Chapter 4 in Summary from 1820 to 1830:

- ✓ James Monroe continued as 5th president through 1825
- ✓ Six new states and three new territories came in
- ✓ Monroe signed Missouri Compromise
- ✓ American Railroad mania began
- ✓ Monroe Doctrine prevented further European colonization
- ✓ Joseph Smith saw a vision in Palmyra, NY
- ✓ 1825 John Quincy Adams became 6th President
- ✓ John Q., was the first president to marry a woman of foreign birth
- ✓ 1828 Andrew Jackson elected as 7th President
- ✓ Jackson was angry about people gossiping about his wife
- ✓ Jackson held a wild housewarming in the executive mansion
- ✓ Citizens continue the westward movement
- ✓ Maine became the 23rd state in 1820
- ✓ Missouri became the 24th state in 1821
- ✓ Democratic party created in 1828, and donkey icon adopted
- ✓ The Erie Canal opened in 1825
- ✓ Missouri compromise allowed slavery in Missouri on May 3, 1820
- ✓ The US took possession of territory of Florida from Spain

FIVE—1830

A Slave Rebellion

WOMEN'S RIGHTS IN THE 1830s

Jane Robinson of Washington County, Virginia, wrote her will on the twenty-first of February 1835 stating she had no children or lineal descendants.

Being elderly, she instructed her executor, William Trigg, to petition the Virginia Legislature for passage of a bill allowing her slaves to remain in the state of Virginia as free people. Should such a bill pass, she asked that her slaves not only be freed but she also left them her real and personal property. If the bill was defeated, Jane stipulated her entire estate, including the slaves, should go to Mr. Trigg. No doubt they made a private agreement on emancipation of the blacks.

She singled out one servant named Mark and instructed him to be freed and provided with money to secure passage to Liberia or to the country of his choice.

The will was introduced in Washington County court on the twenty-fifth of August 1836 by William Trigg.

It was contested by Jane's brother in law, Mitchell Robinson, and her deceased sister's sons, Jane's nephews: John Robinson, James Robinson, Moses Robinson, Alexander Robinson, and Jane's brother, John Edmiston. The first court refused to record the will, but after much legal wrangling, it was finally accepted and recorded. William Trigg obtained clear title to the land and sold it soon after. So, what happened to the slaves that Jane wanted set free? In Virginia, a slave set free after 1836 had to obtain the permission of county court to remain legally in the state for more than a year after his manumission. Until the mid-1850's, the Fairfax county court routinely permitted reputable, newly emancipated slaves to remain in the county. But not always.

The *Journal of the House of Delegates of Virginia*, states that on the third of March 1840 [Bill] 166: A bill granting permission to certain slaves emancipated by Jane Robinson, deceased, to remain in the commonwealth, was read a second time, and was determined in the negative. Resolved, that said bill be rejected. (*books.google.com S3073*)

THE GAG RULE: A gag rule imposed by southerners and their northern Democrat allies in 1836 forbade members even to discuss the subject of slavery upon the floor of Congress, under threat of censure. Not only was the enslaved black person denied freedom, but now the supporting white person was not allowed to talk about it.

BETTER TO STAY SINGLE THAN TO MARRY: The laws of Virginia at the time did not support married women owning property, including slaves, in their own right. This doctrine was known as coverture, which provided that upon marriage a husband and wife became one legal entity with the husband holding legal title to the couple's property. A single woman did have some rights of her own, as did a widow. Even then, if such a female owned property and died without children or a will, the property reverted to her father and/or siblings.

CENSUS OF 1830: The fifth census of the United States is the first in which census takers used uniformly printed schedules. In prior counts, marshals used any paper they could find. They designed and bound the sheets themselves. Sometimes the homemade ink was so faint and watered-down, reading became a difficult task. Answers to the census questions on 1830 to 1880 and in 1900 referred to the situation on June 1 of that year.

Included are the original thirteen states: Connecticut, Delaware, Georgia, Maryland, Massachusetts, New Hampshire, New Jersey, New York, North Carolina, Pennsylvania, Rhode Island, South Carolina, Virginia, plus Vermont and the District of Columbia.

Added in are Alabama, Mississippi, Illinois, Indiana, Kentucky, Louisiana, Maine, Missouri, Tennessee; and the three 1820s territories: Arkansas

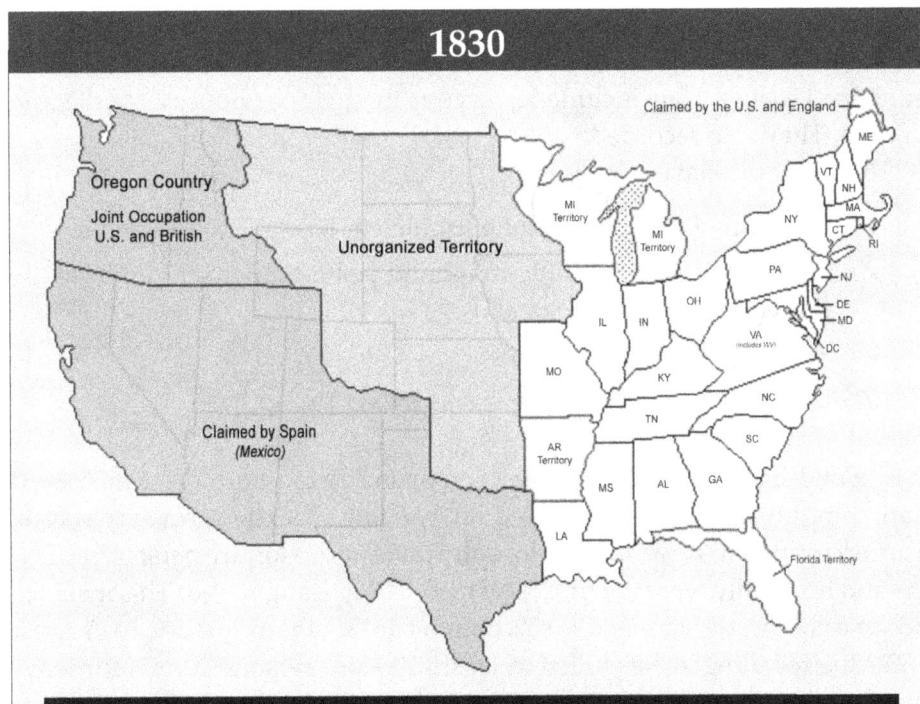

Figure 22: The 1830 census, Andrew Jackson, president.

Twenty-four states and four territories were included in the 1830 census. The only loss of census records for 1830 involved some countywide papers lost in Massachusetts, Maryland, and Mississippi. The newest state included in 1830 was Missouri.

Territories included: Arkansas, Florida, Michigan, including the Wisconsin and Minnesota area, and Oregon Country which was also jointly occupied by Britain. Michigan Territory contained parts of what we know today as Wisconsin, Michigan, and a portion of Minnesota. Census schedules are available for the white colored areas.

Territory, Michigan Territory, and Florida Territory. Massachusetts, Maryland, and Mississippi lost a few county-wide censuses. One new state, Missouri, attained statehood in this census, which now included twenty-four states and three territories. This tabulation included all the 1820 information plus: the number of blind persons—white, colored, or slave; the number of deaf-mutes (same designation), the number of white aliens, and the total number of persons in the household, except Indians not taxed, as explained earlier. They included everyone living in the house as of the first of June. They also recorded:

Name of the slave's owner.

✓   The sum of foreigners (not naturalized) living in a household.

✓   How many deaf, "dumb," and blind persons. (Being "dumb" at the time meant unable to speak.)

✓   Total count of slaves.

✓   Count of male and female slaves by age group.

A SLAVE REBELLION: Nat Turner, son of an African-born slave mother in Southampton County, Virginia, led an uprising of sixty or seventy slaves. Turner testified his own master, Joseph Travis, was a kindly person, yet Travis and his family were the first to be mercilessly slaughtered. This instance became the best-documented slave revolt in Southern history. In August 1831, the rebelling slaves killed at least fifty-five persons. They murdered men, women, and children, most of them helpless in their beds.

Turner often fasted, could be seen praying, or found immersed in reading the stories of the Bible. He often saw visions which he interpreted as messages from God, and he believed these visions were instructing him to lead his fellow slaves in rebellion. He started with several trusted fellow slaves, and ultimately gathered more than seventy enslaved and free blacks, some of whom were on horseback. The rebels traveled from house to house, freeing the slaves. They killed any white people they encountered. Muskets and firearms were too hard to come by and could gather unwanted attention, so the rebels used knives, hatchets, axes, and blunt instruments.

There was widespread fear as word of the rebellion spread, and white militias organized in retaliation against the slaves. Following the massacre, the community tracked down the suspects. Turner hid nearby successfully for six weeks until his discovery, conviction, and hanging, along with sixteen of his followers.

Nat Turner went to the gallows, saying he had nothing to add to his confession. The state ultimately executed fifty-six slaves accused of being part of the rebellion and punished many non-participant slaves in the frenzy. As well, approximately one-hundred-twenty slaves and free blacks were murdered in retaliation by militias and mobs in the area. Most were not involved in any way.

THE TRAIL OF TEARS: Jackson's hatred of Indians dated from his military expeditions, and perhaps this explains his merciless Indian Removal Act.

Jackson faced some legal problems from Indian issues in moving the so-called Five Civilized Tribes: Choctaws, Chickasaws, Cherokees, Creeks, and Seminoles. But Jackson did it anyway.

The Cherokees had a written constitution and a written language. Many lived a Christian life, but that did not matter to Georgians who wanted their land.

Cherokee Chief John Ross accepted George Washington's definition of a tribe as an independent nation. However, the state of Georgia ignored the national treaties and surveyed Cherokee land to sell it off by lottery.

In 1830, Jackson signed the Indian Removal Act leading to what became known as the Trail of Tears. The tribes were forcibly moved to Indian Territory (present-day Oklahoma) resulting in widespread death and sickness among the Indians.

CHEROKEE CENSUS ROLLS: There is no complete list of all persons involved in the movement of the Cherokees to Oklahoma. There is an 1835 microfilm titled: *T496 Census Roll of Cherokee Indians East of the Mississippi and Index to the Roll,* where you might find some names. The Cherokee Nation contained almost twenty-two-thousand natives plus some three-hundred-whites connected by marriage. The *T496* roll enumerates only sixteen thousand people, in five thousand different families.

There are more than thirty rolls (lists) of Cherokee people. The 1817 Reservation Roll is a listing of Eastern Cherokee Indians applying for a 640-acre tract in the East in lieu of removing to Arkansas. This was only good during their lifetime and then the property reverted back to the state. This roll is only an index of applicants. In most instances the people did not receive the reservation they requested. These microfilm rolls are available at many history research centers, and also through Ancestry.com and FamilySearch.com. For more information about the Cherokee Nation Rolls, go here:

   http://rootsweb.ancestry.com/~itcherok/genealogy/rolls-census.htm

MOVING TO INDIAN TERRITORY: In 1838 the War Department issued orders for General Winfield Scott to remove the Cherokees to Indian Territory.

Following the terms of the Treaty of New Echota, a Cherokee Indian removal treaty signed in New Echota, Georgia, they were forcibly removed. The treaty had been negotiated by a Cherokee leader, Major Ridge, who claimed to represent the Cherokee Nation when, in fact, he spoke only for a small faction.

Even though the treaty was fraudulent, the Cherokees were to be transported to "Indian Territory." The Cherokee National Council did not approve the treaty nor did Principal Chief John Ross sign it. However, this became the government's legal basis for their forcible removal.

The army herded the Cherokees into hastily built camps, where they endured the misery of a long hot, disease-plagued summer, but that wasn't the worst. During the fall of 1838 and winter 1839, an armed escort forced them on the twelve-hundred-mile trek. More than one out of four perished before reaching the end. A few found refuge in the Blue Ridge Mountains.

Many years later, a soldier recalled, "...*I have seen men shot to pieces, but the Cherokee removal was the cruelest work I ever saw.*"

BEATEN WITH A WALKING STICK: The first known attempt to assassinate a president was in 1835 when a mentally unbalanced house painter, Richard Lawrence, misfired at President Andrew Jackson outside the US Capitol. Lawrence quickly made another attempt with his second pistol, but it also failed. Jackson chased Lawrence and beat him with his walking stick.

At trial, Lawrence was found not guilty because of insanity and spent the remainder of his life in an insane asylum.

THE PETTICOAT AFFAIR: The 1829 to 1831 Petticoat Affair scandal involved members of President Andrew Jackson's Cabinet and their wives. Led by Floride, wife of Vice President John C. Calhoun, these women (the "petticoats") socially ostracized Secretary of War John Eaton and his wife, the former Margaret "Peggy" O'Neill. The group disapproved of circumstances surrounding Eaton's marriage, and what they considered Peggy's failure to meet the moral standards of a cabinet wife.

Peggy's father, William O'Neill, owned The Franklin House, a boarding house and bar in Washington, DC, only a short distance from the presidential mansion. This tavern became a frequently visited social center for politicians and military officials. Peggy was well-educated, spoke some French and was known for her ability to play the piano. However, the young girl's reputation was marred because she worked in her father's bar, which was frequented by men. Peggy often casually bantered with the boardinghouse clientele, violating local mores. When she was seventeen, she married John Timberlake, a sailor twice her age. He was deeply in debt with a reputation as a drunkard. When Timberlake died at sea soon after their marriage, Peggy quickly married John Eaton without waiting until the end of a respectful mourning period.

Floride (Mrs. John Calhoun) led the wives of Jackson's cabinet members, in an "anti-Peggy" coalition which shunned Peggy Eaton in public. They refused to pay courtesy calls on Mr. and Mrs. Eaton at their home, or receive them as visitors, and denied them invitations to parties and other social events. Jackson, no doubt remembering his late wife being a victim of gossip, sympathized with and supported his friend Eaton.

Subsequently, President Jackson appointed Eaton as his secretary of war, and Eaton's entry into a high-profile cabinet post intensified the opposition of Mrs. Calhoun's group.

Jackson took the opportunity to reorganize his cabinet by asking for the resignations of the anti-Eaton cabinet members. For the rest of Jackson's first term, his opponents used the Petticoat Affair to attack the president's moral judgment and his administration's policies and appointees as well.

THE ELECTION OF 1832: Jackson won a second term in 1832, with Martin Van Buren elected as Jackson's vice president. Historian Robert E. Remini said, *"The entire Eaton affair might be termed infamous. The situation ruined reputations and terminated friendships. And it was all so needless."*

LADIES FASHIONS: Hoop skirts went out of fashion in the 1830s to return ten years later, with fuller skirts held out by crinoline petticoats, a stiff cloth sometimes made of horsehair. The dresses came down within an inch of the ground. For a woman to expose her ankles was considered immodest and improper. The ladies often carried a silk parasol to hide their skin from the sun and protect their dresses from smoke and dirt. Hairstyles might be a Grecian knot at the back with false curls in front held on by hairpins and topped with a stylish hat. Instead of carrying a handbag, they deposited necessary items in the large pockets of their skirts. The ready-made clothing business began to come into existence. Before this, wives or other womenfolk ordered men's suits made to order as needed, and tailors created the outfits.

The ready-made suit trade was initially created to resolve the needs of sailors in seaport towns. Frequently the men could not remain ashore long enough to have their clothing prepared, so the ready-made industry came about. After the Civil War, some businesses previously making uniforms for the soldiers turned their energies into the new ready-to-wear clothing field.

THE GREAT AWAKENING: Historians and theologians identify three or four waves of growing religious enthusiasm between the early eighteenth century and the late twentieth century. Each of these several periods of religious revival was typified by well-attended revivals led by evangelical protestant ministers. The audience usually exhibited a sharp increase of interest in religion, and a profound sense of conviction and redemption. Communities saw an increase in church membership, and the formation of new denominations. The events had little impact on Anglicans and Quakers.

The Second Great Awakening took place in the early nineteenth century. The foundation of many Bible societies seeking to address the problem of a lack of affordable Bibles stimulated this event.

THE MILLERITES and the SEVENTH DAY ADVENTISTS: The Seventh Day Adventist Church formed out of a movement known today as the Millerite movement of the 1830s to the 1840s. In 1831, a Baptist convert, William Miller, was asked by another Baptist friend to preach in their church. He taught that the Second Coming of Jesus would occur somewhere between March 1843 and March 1844, based on his interpretation of a verse in Daniel. Many from the Baptist, Methodist, Presbyterian, and Christian churches gathered around Miller and followed him. More about this group in the next chapter.

BLACK HAWK WAR: A mixed-nation group of Native Americans, called the British Band, were commanded by Sauk leader Black Hawk who fought with the British during the War of 1812. About fifteen hundred men, women, and children of several Indian nations joined the group. Black Hawk, who had a history of being a thorn in the side of the US government, emerged as the leader. He agreed with other members of the tribe who felt the treaty giving their territory away was illegal because the entire clan had not been part of the agreement.

Black Hawk led more than four hundred warriors and their families back to the Rock River, where they planted their corn for the coming year. They crossed the Mississippi River from Iowa into Illinois in violation of several treaties as an attempt to reclaim their homeland.

Subsequently, both the Illinois and Michigan Territory militia were called up. General Winfield Scott was sent to defeat Black Hawk's Band. The war began in 1832. Battles raged from Illinois to Wisconsin from April through September and resulted in the deaths

Figure 23: Chief Black Hawk

The Sauk war chief and namesake of the Black Hawk War in 1832.

of several white settlers, militiamen, and soldiers. The relief force under General Scott suffered numerous deaths from cholera. Black Hawk and about half the Indian people who entered Illinois with him in 1832 died. Seventy settlers and soldiers, as well as hundreds of Black Hawk's band expired as a result of the combat.

By war's end, the military held Black Hawk and nineteen other leaders of the British Band as prisoners at Jefferson Barracks Military Post, located on the Mississippi River south of St. Louis. Black Hawk, then in his 60s, died in captivity in 1838. This Native American defeat signaled the end of battle between the pioneers and the Indians in Illinois and Wisconsin.

Jefferson Barracks, the oldest operating US military installation west of the Mississippi River, remained an essential and active US Army installation from 1826 through 1946.

JACKSON RE-ELECTED: Andrew Jackson defeated National Republican candidate Henry Clay in 1832. Martin Van Buren was elected the incoming VP.

President Jackson and his current Vice-President John C. Calhoun had a problematic relationship for several reasons, most notably the involvement of Calhoun's wife Floride in the Petticoat Affair, a problem continuing from Jackson's first term. As a result, Secretary of State Martin Van Buren and Secretary of War John Eaton resigned, and Jackson requested the resignation of all other cabinet offices as well, including Calhoun who only had a few months left to serve. Van Buren instigated the procedure as a means of removing Calhoun supporters from the Cabinet. Van Buren was then able to move into the vice presidency early.

MEANWHILE, DOWN ON THE FARM: Cyrus McCormick invented and demonstrated the first commercially successful reaper. He developed the machine over six weeks with the assistance of his black helper, Joe Anderson. The reaper, used in their 1831 harvest in the Shenandoah Valley of Virginia, revolutionized farming.

Cincinnati was the pork-packing center of the nation in 1836 and remained leader for years afterward. Chicago gained that distinction in the decade preceding the Civil War. The popular nickname for the city of Cincinnati was *Porkopolis* because herds of pigs traveled the streets. In the 1830s the plants could operate only four months a year because they had no method of refrigeration and the meat would not keep during the summer. An industry soon evolved using the greases and fats from the packing plants to make soap commercially.

HE SHUT DOWN THE BANK: Jackson, who disliked banks and paper money in general, vetoed the renewal of the charter for the Second Bank of the United States. He felt the bank did not support western expansion, which Jackson favored. The bank refused to give credit to those who wanted to adventure west.

Jackson's distrust in financial institutions led to what became known as the Bank War. The director of the Second Bank retaliated. He demanded repayments of loans, refused to offer credit and altogether made it difficult for people to get the money they needed to carry on business. Jackson removed all federal funds from the Second Bank of the United States, reallocating the funds to selected state banks. Jackson won the Bank War.

A NEW RELIGION: Joseph Smith, who saw the vision in 1820 of the two "personages" standing in the air, organized a church, later known as the

Church of Jesus Christ of Latter-day Saints (LDS), in Fayette, New York. He said he received an ancient record engraved on gold plates from an angel known as Moroni. He translated the plates and published the Book of Mormon on the twenty-sixth of March 1830 when he was twenty-four years old. While the book brought Smith regional notoriety, his congregation received threats of mob violence. Smith's "new religion" was not welcomed in New York, and he decided to go west.

First, Smith moved his followers to Kirtland, Ohio, during January 1831, where he encountered a religious culture including enthusiastic demonstrations of spiritual gifts including fits and trances, rolling on the ground, and speaking in tongues. Smith brought the Kirtland congregation under his authority and tamed their outbursts. By summer 1835, there were fifteen hundred to two thousand Mormons in the vicinity, many expecting Smith to lead them shortly to the Millennial Kingdom, as prophesied in the Bible. Headquarters of the church remained in Kirtland from 1831 to 1838. Under his charismatic leadership, membership grew to more than twenty-six thousand.

While Smith was in Ohio, a mob of residents incensed over Smith's political power beat him and his assistant unconscious, tarred and feathered them, and left them for dead.

THE MISSOURI MORMON WAR: Joseph Smith recovered from the beating, but a series of internal disputes led to the collapse of the Kirtland Mormon community. Building a temple in Kirtland had left the church deeply in debt, and creditors hounded Smith. They blamed him for promoting a church-sponsored bank that failed. They also accused him of engaging in a sexual relationship with his serving girl, Fanny Alger, who may have been his first plural wife.

Smith and his followers gradually migrated to northwestern Missouri, mainly settling in Jackson County, where tensions with non-Mormon residents led to episodes of violence. Jackson County evicted the Mormons in 1833. They resettled in surrounding counties. However, tensions grew again, and officials resumed attempts to remove them.

Three years later, the state created Caldwell County specifically for the Church of Jesus Christ of Latter-day Saints (LDS) to compensate for property losses in Jackson County. The town of Far West in Caldwell County, Missouri, became the county seat, and also headquarters of the church group in early 1838. However, this was still not a welcoming environment.

Having been threatened with extermination by the state governor, the LDS group fled Missouri during the winter, crossed into Illinois, and settled in a swampy area along the Mississippi River. Smith moved to a log house on the eastern bank of the river at Nauvoo, Illinois, later known as *The Homestead*.

During the summer of 1839, the Latter-day Saints in Nauvoo suffered from a malaria epidemic. Smith sent Brigham Young and other apostles on missions to Europe, where they made numerous converts, many of them impoverished factory workers. Over the next few years, an estimated sixteen thousand new Saints took up residence in Nauvoo and surrounding communities.

DON'T MESS WITH TEXAS: After a decade of political and cultural clashes between the government of Mexico and the increasingly large population of American settlers in Texas, a revolution began in October 1835. Delegates from fifty-seven Texas communities met at Washington-on-the-Brazos and declared they were an independent nation, free from Mexican rule. Hispanic soldiers tried to disarm the people of Gonzales, but the local militia defended them. A newly created Texian military under the command of Sam Houston went on the move. Texian became a term used by Texas colonists for all the people of the Republic of Texas, before it became a US state.

THIRTEEN DAYS IN SPANISH TEXAS: Military troops—first Spanish, then rebel, and later Mexican—occupied the Alamo during and after Mexico's successful war for independence from Spain in the early 1820s.

Later, the Alamo held fewer than two hundred American rebels fighting for Texas independence. In 1835, three thousand Mexican troops under General Santa Ana attacked the Alamo, formerly a Roman Catholic Franciscan mission and fortress. General Santa Ana warned opponents his Mexican Army would take no prisoners. The rebel Texans knew they had no hope of winning the assault and that death awaited all of them. After a thirteen-day siege, the Mexicans were victorious.

Captain Almaron Dickinson, the artillery officer of the Alamo garrison, was born in Tennessee where he learned the trade of blacksmithing. He later enlisted in the US Army as a field artilleryman. Captain Dickinson's young wife and child stayed with him. He served under commander Lt. Col. William B. Travis.

Figure 24: Remember the Alamo!

This is a drawing of the Alamo mission in San Antonio. It was first printed in 1854 in Gleason's Pictorial Drawing Room Companion.

REMEMBER THE ALAMO: Several civilian non-combatants such as women, children, and cooks were spared, including Almaron's young wife Susannah, and their baby daughter Angelina. Almeron was the last of the Texians to die, and Susanna was slightly wounded while hiding in the Mission Chapel. The eleven-man Texian team protecting the chapel were able to fire two twelve-pound cannon over the sandbags barricading the entrance. These brave men were among the last to be killed.

After the fighting, Susanna Dickinson, then about sixteen, was sent some seventy miles away to Gonzales with her baby, two dollars, and a pony. She was instructed to spread the news of the destruction awaiting those who opposed the Mexican government.

Ben, a black man accompanying her, is sometimes cited as a survivor of the Alamo, but this former seaman was actually a member of the Mexican army. He had been serving as Santa Ana's personal cook. Whatever conditions might have been like in *El Presidente's* service, Ben was perfectly willing to trade for a hike into slave territory.

Colonel Travis' slave, Joe, caught up with them on the road. A year later, Joe escaped from his new owners and became a free man.

Ultimately, Sam Houston led the Texas Army to victory over Mexican forces in the battle of San Jacinto. Santa Ana and his troops were taken prisoner along the San Jacinto River. Texas won independence from Mexico, becoming the Republic of Texas on the twenty-first of April 1836. In exchange for his life, Santa Ana ordered the Mexican army to retreat south of the Rio Grande.

The famous battle cry, *"Remember the Alamo,"* confirms the bravery and patriotism of the defenders in the old mission at San Antonio. They will never be forgotten, nor will their cause for liberty and the freedom of Texas.

ARKANSAS REPRESENTATION: The issue of representation brought up the topic of slavery again when southeast Arkansas proposed a three-fifths rule in order to count the numerous slaves held in the region. Northwest Arkansas wanted to proportion the congressional districts based on only free white men, which would give them a political advantage. Eventually a geographic compromise was struck. They would have eight representatives from the northwest, eight from the southeast, and one from a central district. After this compromise was approved, the Arkansas Constitution went to Washington for approval. After a twenty-five-hour session in the House over the slavery issue, the Arkansas Constitution finally passed. The President approved the bill creating the State of Arkansas on June 15, 1836.

THE CHEESE RIOT: *Toward the end of his term, Jackson and his staff hosted an open house to discuss issues of the day over a giant block of cheddar cheese in the entrance hall of the executive mansion.*

The story is bizarre. Jackson was popular with farmers and rural voters. Some of the wealthier ones decided to express their appreciation by delivering a wagon-size block of cheese, estimated to weigh about fourteen hundred pounds. Jackson realized this generous gift was more than he could handle, so he announced that anyone visiting could have a piece of cheese. However, Jackson had many enemies, and they decided to get even by spreading the word. The next day the lobby at the president's house experienced a cheese riot. Several thousand people lined up and pushed into the building. Some brought plates and knives. Most just dug out a handful of cheese. When the rush eventually subsided, and the doors closed, Jackson found he still had plenty of cheese left for himself.

BLUE LAWS LIMITED FUN: In 1835, P. T. Barnum's first circus tour hit the road. Later called "Barnum and Bailey's Greatest Show on Earth," and finally "Ringling Brothers, Barnum and Bailey Circus," the show was an instant hit. Barnum, who was rarely truthful or honest, ran a variety of businesses as a young man. He campaigned against the "Blue Laws" promulgated by rigid Christians (Calvinists) who sought to limit how much fun people could have. These "blue" laws persisted for decades such as "No liquor on Sunday," "No Hunting on Sunday," anti-gambling laws, and similar laws. In his own way, Barnum justified flim-flaming as long as the customer got a good value for his entertainment dollar.

BUSINESS PANIC OF 1837: Jackson became the only president to pay off the national debt, fulfilling a longtime goal. However, his refusal to renew the charter of the Federal Bank of the United States caused sharp business panics occurring in 1834 and 1837, and the currency shortage continued to cause problems.

The first signs came with crop failures. It became necessary to import wheat from Europe, but importers refused to extend credit to customers. Confidence in the nation's financial system disappeared, and Western banks began to close. By summer, businesses stumbled, and this period became known as *"The Panic of 1837."*

The financial crisis persisted for seven long years. Banks collapsed, businesses failed, prices declined, and thousands of workers lost their jobs. Unemployment may have been as high as twenty-five percent in some locales.

MARTIN VAN BUREN ELECTED: Martin Van Buren, who served as Andrew Jackson's vice president, won the presidency in late 1836 by promising to follow through on Jackson's policies. Van Buren was born to a Dutch family. He is the first president born in the new United States, although he spoke only Dutch growing up in New York.

His father was a patriot during the American Revolution. In addition to founding the Democratic Party, Martin Van Buren previously served as Governor of New York, US Secretary of State, and as the Vice President of the United States.

JACKSON RETIRES TO THE HERMITAGE: Jackson retired to the Hermitage but remained active in Democratic Party politics. One popular rumor is Jackson taught his pet parrot how to curse. It was all fun and games until they had to remove the parrot from Jackson's funeral in 1845 because it wouldn't stop swearing.

MARTIN VAN RUIN: Jackson was a tough act to follow, and Van Buren was just not equipped to compete.

Where Jackson was all rough edges and frontier attitude, Van Buren was a politician full of "street smarts" but he was not prepared for what happened after election. Shortly after taking office, the Panic of 1837 struck the nation, and the Dutch president got the blame for the economic problems.

Hostile newspapers called him "Martin Van Ruin."

THE SLY FOX AND THE WHIGS: The Whig Party emerged in the 1830s as the leading opponent of Jacksonians, pulling together former members of the Democratic-Republican party and the Anti-Masonic Party. Whigs also carried links to the upscale traditions of the Federalists. The Whigs, from the British party opposed to royal privilege and rights, formally organized in 1834. This party brought together a coalition of citizens united in their opposition to what they viewed as the executive tyranny of "King Andrew" Jackson. Van Buren had a lot of nicknames: "Sly Fox" because of his political prowess, "Little Magician" because he was only five-foot-six inches tall. He was also called the "Red Fox of Kinderhook" because of his red hair, and he came from a town in upstate New York called Kinderhook. The most long-lasting nickname goes to "Old Kinderhook," used during his 1840 election campaign with supporters carrying around signs

Figure 25: Martin Van Buren

Our eighth president served one term from 1837 to 1841.

Vice President: Richard M. Johnson

marked OK. The abbreviation became popular, and we continue using OK to this day.

Martin Van Buren's childhood sweetheart and later his wife, Hannah (Hoes) Van Buren, was also raised in a Dutch home. Her first language was Dutch, so English came with a distinct accent.

Martin and Hannah Van Buren had five sons, but Hannah contracted tuberculosis and died eighteen years before her husband was elected president. He remained single. Their four sons who survived infancy—Abraham, John, Martin Jr., and Smith—were all young bachelors when Martin became president in 1837. They moved into the White House with him.

A BEAUTIFUL GUEST: Dolley, the wife of former president James Madison, came to visit bringing her beautiful young niece, Angelica Singleton, who was visiting from South Carolina. President Van Buren's eldest son, Abraham, promptly fell in love with Angelica. They married and made their home in the presidential mansion where Abraham served as his father's private secretary, and Angelica assumed the duties of first lady.

Westward expansion was a dominant part of the American scene during the nineteenth century. The years 1837 to 1844 were challenging years for most Americans. You may find this reflected in your ancestors' financial status on the census.

Van Buren's inability to handle the economic crisis, combined with a growing political movement to the opposition Whig Party, led to his defeat in the 1840 election.

Chapter 5 in Summary from 1830 to 1840:

- ✓ Andrew Jackson continues as President
- ✓ The 1829-31 Petticoat Affair continues
- ✓ Nat Turner leads a slave rebellion
- ✓ Joseph Smith publishes his version of the Book of Mormon, 1830
- ✓ 1830, Jackson's Indian Removal Act resulted in the Trail of Tears
- ✓ The Black Hawk War raged from Illinois to Wisconsin
- ✓ The fifth US census of 1830 listed 24 states
- ✓ The fifth census Marshals in 1830 used printed schedules
- ✓ This census gave names of slave owners, but no names for slaves
- ✓ Census 1830 gives number of foreigners, and other info
- ✓ McCormick invents the reaper, revolutionizing farming methods
- ✓ Remember the Alamo 1836
- ✓ Martin Van Buren, a Dutchman, is elected president in 1836
- ✓ Panic of 1837 and economic depression is blamed on Van Buren
- ✓ 1837-1844 presented very difficult years.
- ✓ The Revolution of Texas ends with the Battle of the Alamo
- ✓ PT Barnum's first circus tours the United States in 1835
- ✓ The WHIG party emerges

> *"As to the presidency, the two happiest days of my life were those of my entrance upon the office and my surrender of it."*
>
> —Martin Van Buren

SIX—1840

A Nation on the Move

CENSUS OF 1840

From 1840 to 1850, many changes affected your ancestors' lives. Few, if any, records reveal as many details about individuals and families as the US Federal Census.

The sixth census, with thirty states and territories, includes information on the number of persons in each family engaged in occupations, names and ages of military pensioners, and the number of students, number of scholars in the public charge (not all students). Also, the number of free white persons over age twenty who could not read and write, and the number of deaf, mute and blind persons.

The census population of the United States had reached seventeen million, with results tabulated by twenty-eight clerks in the Bureau of the Census under President Martin Van Buren *(Takes a few hundred more clerks now!)*

Twenty-six states, as shown in the map, took part in the 1840 census, including the new ones; Arkansas and Michigan. The territories of Iowa, Wisconsin, and Florida also participated.

This was the first census attempting to count Americans who were "insane" or "idiotic." Published results indicated alarming numbers of black persons living in non-slave holding areas who were mentally ill, in striking contrast to the corresponding figures for slave holding states.

A report, submitted to the House of Representatives by John Quincy Adams, contended it demonstrated "a multitude of gross and important errors" in the published returns. On the contrary, Secretary of State John

C. Calhoun reported a careful examination by the supervisor of the census had certified its correctness. The report was not revised.

The 1840 census recorded the living pensioners of the Revolutionary War as well as other military services. The record notes an individual's age and the name of the head of the household where the individual lived. This military-related question was a first.

Records of all twenty-six states and three territories are available. The center of the nation's population, then sixteen miles south of current Clarksburg, West Virginia, continued to move slowly West.

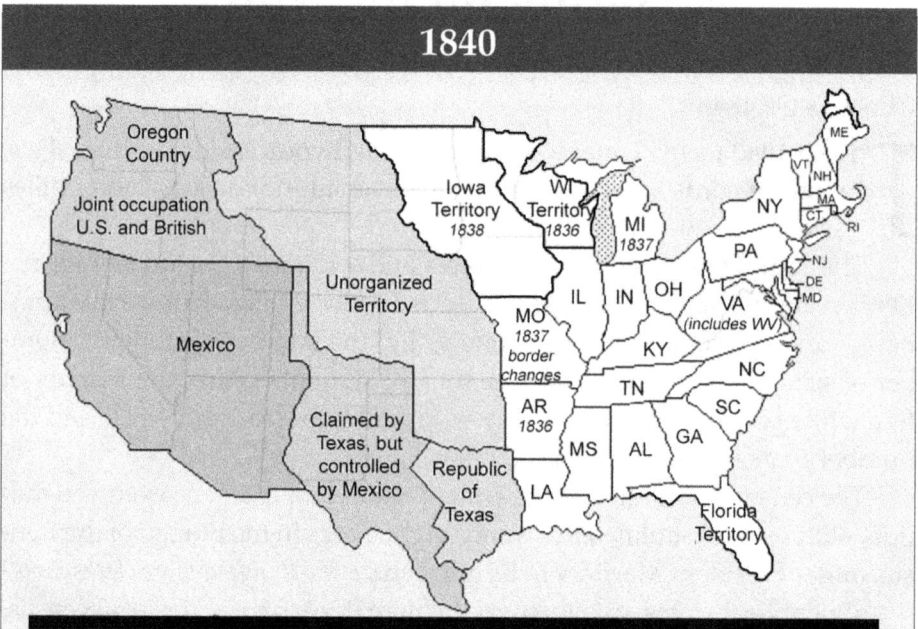

Figure 26: The 1840 census, Martin Van Buren president.

The 1840 census was the first that attempted to count Americans who were "insane" or "idiotic."

Twenty-six states included two new ones: Arkansas and Michigan. Arkansas achieved statehood in 1836 organized as a slave state. Twenty-five years later Arkansas became the ninth state to secede from the union and join the Confederate States of America. Missouri had a border change in 1837. New territories in 1840 were Iowa, Wisconsin, and Florida. Census schedules are available for only the white colored areas.

CONTINUING THE SEVENTH DAY ADVENTISTS: In the summer of 1844, some of William Miller's followers promoted the date of Jesus' second coming to be the twenty-second of October. By 1844, more than one hundred thousand people were anticipating what Miller called the *"Blessed Hope."* On the chosen day many of the believers stayed up late into the night watching and waiting for Christ to return. They were bitterly disappointed when both sunset and midnight went by and nothing predicted occurred. This event later became known as the *"Great Disappointment."*

After the fizzle of that October day, many of Miller's followers were upset and disillusioned. Most ceased to believe in the imminent return of Jesus. Some believed the date was incorrect. A few thought the date was right, but the event expected was wrong. This latter group developed into the Seventh Day Adventist world church.

The Adventist church is a Protestant Christian denomination which is distinguished by its observance of Saturday as the Sabbath, the seventh day of the week in Christian and Jewish calendars, and emphasis on the imminent second coming of the Christ. It is today one of the fastest-growing denominations in North America.

MORMONS AGAIN: Remember Joseph Smith? He led his congregation from New York to Missouri and on to Illinois. In 1841, Smith began revealing the doctrine of plural marriage to a few of his closest male associates.

Among them, John C. Bennett, an American physician and former surgeon in the US Army, briefly became a ranking and influential leader of the Latter-day Saints movement. He was also the first mayor of Nauvoo, Illinois.

Bennett used his status in the church as an excuse to seduce numerous women, both married and unmarried. While Bennett was mayor, he was caught having private sexual relations with some women in the city. He told the women the practice, which he termed *"spiritual wifery,"* was sanctioned by God and Joseph Smith. When discovered, he privately confessed his crimes, produced an affidavit declaring Smith had no part in his adultery and they disciplined him accordingly. Mormons look upon his life with sadness.

The New York Times on 10 Nov 2014 published a copyright story by Laurie Goodstein, saying Mormon leaders acknowledged the church's founder and prophet, Joseph Smith took as many as forty wives, some already married and one only fourteen years old. Smith probably did not have sexual relations with all of his wives because some were "sealed" to him only for the next life.

His first wife, Emma Smith, said polygamy was *"an excruciating ordeal."*

Joseph Smith introduced baptism of the dead in 1840, and the next year construction began on the Nauvoo Temple as a place for recovering lost ancient knowledge.

Earlier the Nauvoo Masons had initiated Smith into their lodge. Within months, Smith inaugurated a revised endowment or "first anointing," resembling rites of Freemasonry. Smith revealed a plan to establish the millennial kingdom of God, which would eventually create theocratic rule over the whole earth.

By mid-1842, popular opinion had turned against them. Smith and his brother Hyrum rode to Carthage, Missouri, to stand trial for inciting a riot. Once the Smiths were in custody, the charges increased to treason.

SMITH BROTHERS KILLED: On the twenty-seventh of June 1844, an armed mob with blackened faces stormed the Carthage Jail holding the Smith brothers.

Hyrum, who was trying to secure the door, was killed instantly with a shot to the face. Joseph went down soon after that. Church followers buried the brothers in the family cemetery near Nauvoo, Illinois. They are considered martyrs in the church. *The Homestead* exterior and grounds remain accessible to visitors.

In his brief thirty-nine years of life, the controversial Smith established thriving cities in Ohio, Missouri, and Illinois. He produced volumes of scripture, sent missionaries throughout the world, and orchestrated the building of temples.

Like Bennett, Smith served as mayor of Nauvoo, one of the largest cities in Illinois. He served as general of the Nauvoo Legion militia, and he was a candidate for president of the United States. Nominated in May 1844 by the new Reform Party, he was killed a month later.

Smith attracted thousands of devoted followers before his death, and millions in the century following. The Mormons regard him as a prophet on par with Moses and Elijah. Biographers, Mormon and non-Mormon alike, agree Smith was one of the most influential, charismatic, and innovative figures in American religious history.

BRIGHAM YOUNG ORDAINED LDS PRESIDENT: A few years after Smith's death, Brigham Young became president of the church. The constant conflict in Missouri and Illinois led Young to relocate the Latter-day Saints to the Salt Lake Valley, which was then part of Mexico. By the time Young arrived at the final destination, it had come under American control as a result of a war with Mexico, although US sovereignty would not be confirmed until 1848. Young's expedition was one of the largest and one of the best-organized westward treks. On the twenty-second day of August 1847, less than thirty days after arriving in the Salt Lake Valley, Young formed the Mormon Tabernacle Choir.

After Smith's death, his first wife and now widow, Emma, quickly became alienated from Brigham Young and the church leadership. When most Saints moved west, she stayed in Nauvoo and married a non-Mormon. She withdrew from religion until 1860, when she affiliated with the Reorganized Church of Jesus Christ of Latter-day Saints (RLDS), headed at one time by her son, Joseph Smith III.

FOUR PRESIDENTS IN ONE DECADE: Martin Van Buren lost his re-election bid to William Henry Harrison, who became the ninth president in 1841. The former Army commander famously led US military forces against Native Americans in the Battle of Tippecanoe.

WILLIAM HENRY HARRISON: The son of Benjamin Harrison, one of the Founding Fathers, and grandfather of another Benjamin Harrison who would be the twenty-third president in 1889, William was the last chief executive born as a British royal subject in the original thirteen colonies. His father, Benjamin Harrison, was a Virginia planter who served as a delegate to the Continental Congress, signed the Declaration of Independence, and held the office of fifth governor of Virginia

Figure 27: William H. Harrison

Our ninth president served only one month in 1841 before he was assassinated.

Vice President: John Tyler

during the Revolutionary War. William H. Harrison served as Governor of Indiana Territory from 1801 to 1812, briefly served as a major general in the Kentucky militia, The US government commissioned him to command the Army of the Northwest in the War of 1812.

During Harrison's campaign, the opposition tried to cast him as someone who'd rather *"sit in his log cabin, drinking hard cider."* Harrison accepted the lemons of criticism and made lemonade; he handed out whiskey in bottles shaped like log cabins in his campaign, and the public loved it.

Harrison, representing the Whig party, won the presidency as the hero of the Battle of Tippecanoe with John Tyler as his running mate.

The campaign slogan *"Tippecanoe and Tyler Too"* became famous.

DEATH OF A PRESIDENT: The old soldier took the oath of office on a cold, wet day in 1841. He wore neither an overcoat nor hat, riding on horseback to the ceremony rather than in a closed carriage. Harrison delivered the most extended inauguration address in American history, speaking for nearly two hours—almost eight thousand five hundred words.

Still coatless and hatless in the cold drizzle, Harrison rode proudly through the streets in the inaugural parade, and in the evening celebrated in three inaugural balls, including one fancy ball with about a thousand guests.

Within days, Harrison came down with a cold, his illness believed a result of the bad weather at his inauguration. He died thirty-two days into his presidency, apparently of pneumonia. His tenure of one month is the shortest in history and the first death in office of a US president. As a result, four presidents served within a single ten-year period.

SETTING A NEW PRECEDENT: Since a president had not died in office before, no one could agree on what power John Tyler should have as the surviving vice president. Tyler managed to convince everyone he should just become president, paving the way for the Twenty-fifth Amendment, which made the line of succession official.

Four years before the first census, John Adams had a vision of the possibilities of America. This led him to predict that the population of the United States would, at some time, exceed twenty million. Such a prophecy seemed little more than a wild flight of the imagination and was branded as utterly ridiculous.

John Tyler, as tenth President of the United States, was blessed with a similar vision. He made a similar prophecy and missed his guess by only a few years when he predicted that someday the population would reach a hundred million. In a letter addressed to his son-in-law's father in 1850, Tyler said, *"In a little more than half a century, a people who were regarded as little better than a host of murderers or sojourners among savage tribes have attained position among the first civilized powers."*

A NEW YOUNG PRESIDENT: At age fifty-one, John Tyler became the youngest person up till then to hold the office as president. His wife, Letitia (Christian) Tyler died in the White House in 1842. They were parents of eight children.

Two years later he married a second time to the much younger Julia Gardiner. Tyler was the first president to have a wife die while in office, and then he became the first president to marry in office. The general public had a field day over Tyler's choice of mates, but the May/December marriage proved a happy one, resulting in seven more children. The new first lady set about overseeing executive mansion repairs and ruled social and ceremonial affairs in high style. Julia

Figure 28: John Tyler

Our tenth US president served one term from 1841 to 1845. He was not popular.

Vice President: None

Tyler started the tradition of playing *"Hail to the Chief"* whenever a president appeared at a function.

NOT A POPULARITY CONTEST WINNER: Tyler stepped in to fill Harrison's unexpired term 1841 to 1845. He was expected to be only an acting president while he finished Harrison's term, but Tyler refused to be passive.

The new president vetoed the bill to re-establish the Second Bank of the United States, the bank that Jackson closed down. Tyler's veto caused an angry riot among his own Whig members. The brawl became the most violent demonstration on those grounds in US history up to then. Tyler made many enemies in Congress. He clashed with his own party, who later tried to impeach him.

Everyone pretty much hated Tyler and considered him a maverick. He butted heads with bigwigs like Henry Clay and Daniel Webster and vetoed acts they were trying to pass. The Whigs expelled John Tyler from his own party during his presidency. His entire cabinet, except one, resigned over his policies, and he was the first president to face impeachment. The effort failed in the House, and Tyler completed his term.

THE PRESIDENT NAMED AN ENEMY OF THE US: John Tyler at first sought a second nomination in 1845, but he had created too many enemies. He was not nominated.

Nearly bankrupt, Tyler retired with wife Julia to his Virginia plantation located on the James River in Charles City County. He named it *Sherwood Forest*, referring to Robin Hood, to signify he had been "outlawed" by the Whig party. His neighbors, largely Whigs, appointed him to the minor office of overseer of roads in 1847 to mock him. However, he treated the job seriously, frequently summoning his neighbors to provide their slaves for road work and continuing to insist on carrying out his duties even after his neighbors asked him to stop.

Although some have praised Tyler's political resolve, historians generally hold his presidency in low regard. One newspaper editor called him a "poor, miserable, despised imbecile." The feelings did not lessen after he left office.

Tyler owned forty or fifty slaves and was accused of having fathered children by at least one of the women. In August of 1999, Professor Darryl Cumber Dance of the University of Richmond, stated that Tyler fathered many children with women who were his slaves, including her own great-grandfather, but this accusation remains unproven. Although Tyler said he regarded slavery as an evil, he never freed any of his slaves.

After the Civil War began in 1861, Tyler was elected to the Confederate House of Representatives. When Tyler died the next year, President Lincoln did not issue the customary proclamation of mourning, and flags were not placed at half-mast. At Tyler's request a Confederate flag draped his coffin rather than the stars and stripes. He is the only former president who was not a US citizen.

In Tyler's own obituary the *New York Times*, referred to Tyler as "the most unpopular public man who ever held any office in the United States!"

THE OREGON TRAIL: Fur traders, trappers, and explorers laid the Oregon Trail about 1811 to 1840, but the path was only passable on foot or by horseback. By 1836, when the first migrant wagon train organized in Independence, Missouri, a wagon trail had been cleared to Fort Hall, Idaho, eventually reaching to the Willamette Valley in Oregon.

The first official wagon train to California left from Independence, Missouri, on the first day of May in 1841 with sixty-nine adults and several children. The journey would take six months, arriving in early November. Discarded supplies marked the trail. Broken down prairie schooners and dead draft animals scattered along the path, and often accompanied personal items like books, clothes, and even furniture.

There was never just one set of wagon ruts leading west. The wagons often spread out for several miles across the plains to avoid the choking dust clouds kicked up by other wagon trains. Enterprising settlers blazed dozens of new trails, with cutoffs allowing travelers to bypass stopping points and reach their destination quicker.

In what was dubbed "The Great Migration of 1843," an estimated one thousand emigrants left for Oregon. A year later the second organized wagon train on the Oregon Trail carried more than one hundred pioneers from Elm Grove, Missouri. They were not the first comers. The Hudson Bay Company had been operating its Canadian fur trade since 1670, and ten years later received an exclusive license to conduct business in the Oregon Country, comprised of the present states of Oregon, Washington, Idaho, British Columbia, and parts of Montana and Wyoming.

Hudson Bay Company policy discouraged immigration, so the emigrants were not welcomed in Oregon, which was then just a piece of land between the Pacific Ocean and the Rocky Mountains in the northwest portion of present-day United States. They were offered food and farming equipment at Fort Vancouver (now Vancouver, Washington). For many settlers, the fort at Vancouver became the last stop where they could get supplies, aid, and help before starting for their homesteads.

In truth, missionaries are the ones who blazed the Oregon Trail. Settlers of the Willamette Valley drafted the Organic Laws of Oregon organizing land claims within the Oregon country. As the group was a provisional government with no authority, these claims were not valid under the United States or British law at the time, but the US eventually honored them.

THE SOUND OF A RAILROAD WHISTLE: The first rail lines had begun operation in the 1830s but came into its own early in the next decade with the wind tearing smoke and steam out of the stacks and blowing noise of the engine warning everyone and everything out of their way.

Fewer than three thousand miles of track in 1840 increased ten times over in the next twenty years, then jumped to more than one hundred fifteen thousand miles by 1880. Those same years saw the growth of the far West, the start of an economic and political transformation as well as the conquest and dispossession of its native people. The two developments, westward expansion and the establishment of a national rail system, cannot be understood apart from one another. The consequences were especially sad for American Indians. Even before one mile of track was laid, the railroads began to undercut native independence.

TRAVELING IN THE SEVENTEENTH CENTURY: In 1806 when Henry Clay went to Washington from his home in Lexington, Kentucky, to serve in Congress, the trip took more than three weeks. The journey required boats, carriages, and horses. Forty years later, thanks to the railroad, he could get there in four days. Clay, an excellent orator, dominated American political life for much of his fourteen-year Senate career.

Figure 29: James K. Polk

Our eleventh president served one term from 1845 to 1849.

Vice President: George Dallas

JAMES K. POLK, POTUS NUMBER 11: John Tyler signaled the last gasp of the Old Virginia aristocracy in the top office. The 1844 presidential election boiled down to a fight between Tyler, James Polk, and Henry Clay. Fearing that he and Polk might split the vote, Tyler voluntarily withdrew. Once Tyler felt sure Polk would support the annexation of Texas, he became the first president not to seek re-election. Democrat James K. Polk won the election. Tyler had signed a bill to annex Texas three days before leaving office and under Polk, the process was completed.

FACIAL HAIR: All four presidents in this decade were cleanly shaven. By the end of the decade, beards began coming into popular favor again after having been out of fashion for seventy or eighty years. All the heroes of the American Revolution were beardless, as seen in their portraits. Side whiskers began to appear in the preceding generation and by the late eighteen-forties men in considerable numbers are seen in beards.

TALKING WIRES: Samuel B. Morse, inventor of the telegraph, sent the initial message in 1844 over the first telegraph line from Washington to Baltimore. His words were, *"What God hath wrought."*

MAILING A LETTER: Until 1847 the recipient of letters paid the postage. For a "single" message, written on a single sheet of paper, the postage rate was six cents for distances under thirty miles. The price rose, by gradual increases, to twenty-five cents for a single sheet letter sent for any distance over four hundred and fifty miles. Then the system was revised with rates significantly reduced.

A half-ounce message going under three hundred miles could pass for five cents, as compared with twenty cents for a single sheet under the old regulations. Postage stamps came into use in 1847. After that, the sender of a letter paid the postage.

THE TEX-I-CANS: Emigrants from the Southern states who planned to make it a slave state practically seized Texas. They overturned its constitution as part of the Mexican Republic, adopted a new law permitting slavery and proclaimed independence in 1836. The Congress of Texas voted for annexation to the USA in 1845 with the majority of voters in Texas approving a constitution. However, both Jackson and Van Buren refused to agree to the addition of Texas as a slave state.

President Tyler ignored those two and signed a bill authorizing the United States to annex the Republic of Texas. This bill led to the United States adding the Republic of Texas into the Union as the twenty-eighth state on December 29, 1845.

A Texican or a Texian were both mid-nineteenth century words for American colonists to Texas, residents of Mexican Texas and later, the

Republic. Today, the term is used specifically to distinguish early Anglo settlers of Texas, especially those who supported the Texas Revolution. Mexican settlers of that era are referred to as Tejanos, and residents of modern Texas are known as Texans.

A DARK HORSE IN THE CAPITOL: Democrat James K. Polk, president number eleven, was the first "dark horse" or little-known nominee to become president. His tenure occurred during the Mexican War, also known as the Mexican American War, which added Texas, California, and other territories to the United States. The war ended on the third of February 1848, although California was already firmly in American hands.

Born in a log cabin, Polk was the first of ten children born to a family of farmers. He became the ninth governor of Tennessee. A slaveholder for most of his adult life, he owned a plantation in Mississippi and continued to buy slaves while president.

Unlike John Tyler, who gave entertaining parties at the president's house, Polk had a reputation for hosting dull evenings. Stern, unsmiling Polk was a party-pooper. He banned from the Mansion all booze, card playing, and dancing.

SARAH CHILDRESS POLK: Beginning in early 1822, Polk courted Sarah Childress. They married two years later in Murfreesboro. Sarah Polk was from one of the state's most prominent families and she was educated far better than most women of her time, especially in frontier Tennessee. Her grace, intelligence, and fascinating conversation helped compensate for her husband's often austere manner. During his political career, Sarah assisted her husband with his speeches, gave him advice on policy matters, and played an active role in his campaigns. She very much enjoyed her social duties, but as a devout Presbyterian, she confirmed the ban on dancing, card games, and hard liquor at official receptions.

IMMIGRATION: In the 1830s and 1840s increasing numbers of immigrants, mostly Irish in the East, and Germans in the Midwest, began coming into the United States to settle. The Irish potato famine and economic instability in Germany brought nearly three million people, most of whom were Catholic, to the US.

Protestants, mostly in urban areas, felt threatened by the new arrivals. To many people, the Catholic Church represented tyranny and potential subjugation to a foreign power. The new laborers arrived and competition for jobs increased. Anti-immigrant and anti-Catholic feelings increased as nativist groups protecting the interests of native inhabitants against immigrants began to form in cities.

THE POTATO FAMINE: Thousands of Irish immigrants came rushing to America to escape their poverty in the 1846 potato famine in Ireland. They helped swell the population of the cities, operate the factories, build the railroads, and manage the households of wealthy industrialists.

A period between 1845 and 1849, known as the Great Famine or the Great Hunger in Ireland, created mass starvation, disease, and emigration. The famine caused by a blight infecting potato crops spread throughout Europe during the 1840s, precipitating some hundred thousand deaths in the worst affected areas and among tenant farmers of Europe.

THE CLOAK AND DAGGER KNOW-NOTHINGS: In 1849 a secret society named the Order of the Star-Spangled Banner came into being in New York City. When asked about their organization, members would give the canned answer: "I know nothing." Outsiders used this response as a nickname, which stuck.

As the Know-Nothings membership grew, they shed their clandestine nature and eventually became the American Party by the 1850s. The American / Know-Nothings Party reflected troubled times confronting the young United States. Primarily anti-Catholic, afraid of strangers and foreigners, and hostile to immigration, the Know-Nothings had rules about joining their secret society. They had initiation rites called "Seeing Sam," memorization of passwords and hand signs, a solemn pledge never to betray the order, and they rejected all Catholics.

Membership required a pure-blooded pedigree of Protestant Anglo-Saxon stock. They supported deporting foreign beggars and criminals. They also wanted to increase the naturalization period for immigrants to twenty-one-years. The group pushed mandatory Bible reading in schools and the elimination of all Catholics from public office.

With the nation facing growing conflict over slavery and westward expansion, unrest was prevalent. Dissent increased within the two major political parties, the Democrats and the Whigs. Conceived in fear and prejudice, the short-lived Know-Nothing Party's intolerance toward German and Irish immigrants led to violence across the nation.

HATERS IN THE CITY OF BROTHERLY LOVE: In May through July 1844 anti-immigrant violence rocked Philadelphia. Riots started over whether Catholic children should sing Protestant hymns at school and exploded after nativists demonstrated in an Irish Catholic neighborhood. Two Catholic churches burned and at least fourteen people died in the first riot.

Later, violence erupted at a Cathedral even though the state militia protected the structure. Feelings were high against the immigrants. Nativist rioters pelted them with rocks and bottles, and the militiamen opened fire. After the smoke cleared hours later, some fifteen to twenty people lay dead.

POLITICAL PARTIES: For a few years it seemed Know-Nothings were poised to topple the Whigs and take top place in the two-party system. However, the Know-Nothings collapsed under the pressure of having to make a firm position on the issue of slavery. Even today the United States continues to grapple with anxieties surrounding diversity and immigration. The attitudes are the same, but they may carry different names.

MEXICAN WAR: The War between the United States and Mexico from 1846 to 1848 helped to fulfill America's "manifest destiny" in expanding its territory. The conflict centered on the independent Republic of Texas which, under the leadership of Sam Houston, joined the United States after establishing independence from Mexico a decade earlier. President Polk wanted Texas as part of the US. His predecessor, John Tyler, started the admission process even before he left office. Polk and others saw the acquisition of Texas, California, Oregon, and other territories as part of the nation's Manifest Destiny.

During his four-year term, Polk met every major domestic and foreign policy goal. The Treaty of Guadalupe Hidalgo ended the US-Mexican War. Signed on the second of February 1848, it is the oldest treaty still in force between the United States and Mexico. As a result, the US acquired more than five hundred thousand square miles of valuable territory and emerged as a world power in the late nineteenth century. Mexico received a little more than eighteen million dollars in compensation from the United States as part of the treaty. The agreement created a border between Texas and Mexico. It also ceded to the US all of California, Nevada, Utah, New Mexico, most of Arizona and Colorado, and parts of Oklahoma, Kansas, and Wyoming. Quite a deal!

On the surface, the treaty seemed like a bonanza for the United States. But the unresolved issue of expanding slavery into new territory lit the fuse that would set off the war explosion a generation later.

LIGHTING THE WORLD: There were no kerosene lamps as late as 1849. Some of the cities used gas lighting while most depended on candles or lamps burning whale oil. Kerosene as an illuminant was unknown until late in the 1850s.

A FREE-SOIL PARTY: In Ohio, a group of men decided to form a new political party. They called it the Free-Soil Party, because they believed in free land for free settlers.

The Free-Soilers held a convention in Buffalo, New York, and ten thousand people attended. Their platform declared slavery was an institution of the states, not the nation, and Congress had no right to spread slavery by permitting it in the new western territories. The convention delegates then voted on candidates. The Free-Soilers chose former President Martin Van Buren as candidate for president.

CALIFORNIA OR BUST—THE GOLD RUSH: If you are unable to find your ancestors in the 1850 census, try looking in California. The discovery of gold nuggets in the Sacramento Valley sparked the Gold Rush.

Thousands of prospective gold miners rushed from all over the nation to reach San Francisco and the surrounding area. They were called the "forty-niners," referring to 1849 when the most massive influx arrived.

While gold mining itself was unprofitable for most diggers and gold-mine owners, some made huge profits, and the merchants and transportation facilities made vast fortunes. Enthusiastic new residents of California, whose population had mushroomed with the discovery, petitioned for admission to the Union as a free state.

OLD ROUGH AND READY, THE NEW PRESIDENT: General Zachary Taylor, twelfth president, won fame as a general in the Mexican War.

He served from March 1849 until his death during July 1850. Taylor grew up in a small woodland cabin on the Ohio River at Louisville, Kentucky. Later, with increased prosperity, his family moved to a brick house.

General Taylor, who had almost no education, served as an officer in the War of 1812. One of his lieutenants in the Black Hawk War was Jef-

Figure 30: Gen. Zachary Taylor
"Old Rough & Ready"

Our twelfth US President served only one year, 1849.

Vice President: Millard Fillmore

ferson Davis, future CSA president. Davis fell in love with his commanding officer's daughter, Sarah K. Taylor. Sarah's parents did not want her to be an Army wife and opposed the marriage.

SMOKING AND CHEWING IN THE WHITE HOUSE: Taylor and his wife were much more comfortable in a fort than at the presidential palace, so they treated the place as if it were part of a frontier fort. Zachary smoked and chewed—mostly he spit tobacco juice and rarely hit the spittoon, even if he tried. The capital city still had mostly dirt roads, so add the dust and mud and a general lack of consideration for the building and furniture and imagine the mess.

Many of the carpets were stained beyond hope, the walls coated with smoke and dirt.

MRS. TAYLOR IN THE WHITE HOUSE: Margaret "Peggy"(Smith) Taylor, served as hostess for the one-year term. With the rise in her husband's political career, his wife literally prayed for his defeat, for she dreaded the personal consequences of his becoming president.

By the time Taylor was elected, the hardships of following her husband from fort to fort and giving birth to several children had taken its toll. A semi-invalid, she remained in seclusion on the second floor of the executive mansion, leaving the duties of hostess to their daughter, Mary Elizabeth "Betty" Bliss. Mrs. Taylor chain-smoked a pipe, as many women did on the frontier.

RIDING THE RAILS MADE HIM SICK: A railroad trip took its toll on the health of President Taylor. When he made a railroad tour in 1849, it almost killed him. He was fairly old at the time and these trips were brutal. Before each stop on the route, the influential townspeople would get on the train and want to talk with the president. This meant thirty or forty people battled for the president's attention, trying to talk to him and wanting to shake hands until they reached the town.

The trip was scheduled to tour for a couple of months, but within two weeks, Taylor was sick and exhausted. They had to cancel further appearances and take him back to the White House.

THE PRESIDENT HELD SLAVES: Debate over the slave status of the extensive territories claimed in the war led to threats of secession from southerners. Taylor, a wealthy slave owner who held properties in the plantation states of Louisiana, Kentucky, and Mississippi, was the last president to own slaves while in office.

The House of Representatives was controlled by members of the Free-Soil Party, which opposed slavery. The Senate was controlled by southerners, who supported slavery. The two houses found it almost impossible to agree on anything.

Despite being a southerner and a slaveholder himself, Taylor did not push for the expansion of slavery—but he also did nothing to abolish the South's "peculiar institution." Taylor threatened to use force to prevent secession. Passions ran high everywhere, and tempers were at the boiling point.

Chapter 6 in Summary from 1840 to 1850:

- ✓ The 1840 census identifies the names and ages of pensioners of Revolutionary war
- ✓ Immigration rules expanded
- ✓ Mormons run into problems in Nauvoo, Illinois
- ✓ Joseph Smith and his brother Hyrum are killed
- ✓ Brigham Young relocates Latter-day Saints to Salt Lake City
- ✓ Four presidents serve in this 10-year period
- ✓ After only a month in office in 1841 William Henry Harrison, the ninth president, dies
- ✓ John Tyler, vice president stepped into office as number 10
- ✓ 1845 James K. Polk elected president number eleven
- ✓ 1849 Zachary Taylor, president number twelve, was a Veteran of War of 1812
- ✓ Taylor was called "Old Rough and Ready"
- ✓ The Know-Nothing party becomes powerful
- ✓ Immigration and Politics collide
- ✓ Violence stalked the City of Brotherly Love
- ✓ Explosive railroad expansion begins
- ✓ A generation of change: Gold Rush to California
- ✓ Debate grows over slave status, and southerners begin threats of secession
- ✓ The Oregon Trail wagons head northwest
- ✓ Annexation of Texas brings the American Mexican war

SEVEN—1850

A Continuing Crisis

THE SEVENTH CENSUS

This listing includes the color of each person (white, black or mulatto), their profession, occupation, or trade of each male over the age of fifteen, and the state or territory of birth for each person.

Genealogists love the 1850 census because so much new information appears. Names of all members of the household are given, including women, children, and slaves, making it much easier for researchers to identify a child's parents. Previous lists named the head of the family only.

Most people never notice column ten, where census takers made a mark or dash opposite the name of each person married before the first of June of that year. Other columns indicate if the person attended school within the year, persons over age twenty who could not read and write, and also notations for "deaf and dumb," blind, insane, a pauper, or a convict. The term "dumb" usually meant the person was unable to speak. If a person could read and write English or a foreign language, column twelve was left blank. The official enumeration day of this census was the first day of June. The population schedules are successive "snapshots" of Americans depicting where and how most people were living at particular periods in the past.

1850—The United States has grown to include thirty states by June 1. California was added a few months later without ever being a territory. Other new states added in this generation include Florida, Iowa, Wisconsin, and Texas; new territories were Minnesota, New Mexico, Oregon, and Utah.

AN EXCEPTION TO THE RULE FOR CALIFORNIA: Most newly acquired regions of the US went through long periods as territories before they had the sixty thousand inhabitants needed to achieve statehood. Prior to the Gold Rush, emigration to California had been so slow that it would have been decades before the population reached that number but with gold fever reaching epidemic proportions around the world, more than sixty thousand came to California in 1849 alone. Faced with such rapid growth, as well as a thorny congressional debate over the question of slavery in the new territories, Congress allowed California to jump straight to full statehood without ever passing through the formal territorial stage. Congress finally accepted California as a free-labor state under the Compromise of 1850.

- 31 STATES IN 1850: This census includes the following states and territories, broken up by bullets to make it easier to read:
- Alabama, Arkansas, California, Connecticut, Delaware, District of Columbia, Florida, Georgia, Illinois, Indiana, and Iowa;
- Kentucky, Louisiana, Maine, Maryland, Massachusetts, Michigan, and Minnesota Territory (includes Dakota area);
- Mississippi, Missouri, New Hampshire, New Jersey, New Mexico Territory (includes Arizona area), and New York;
- North Carolina, Ohio, Oregon Territory (includes Washington and Idaho areas), Pennsylvania, Rhode Island, and South Carolina;
- Tennessee, Texas, Utah Territory, Vermont, Virginia (includes West Virginia counties), and Wisconsin.

NEW INFORMATION: Every free person's name is listed, not just the head of the household. The marshals also collected additional "social statistics," including information on taxes, schools, crime, wages, estate value, and data on mortality. Beginning with the 1850 census, a person's state or country of birth is known, and that helps narrow the geographic search for the specific town of birth.

While the person's age is not an exact date of birth, it does provide a "ballpark" figure useful for tracking the person from one census to the next, especially if other people have the same name. It is also helpful in locating the person in any existing vital records.

Each marshal was also responsible for subdividing his district into "known civil divisions," such as counties, townships, or wards, and ensuring that his assistants completed their returns correctly. Marriage "within the year" means during the year before the official census day, for instance for the 1850 census, the wedding date would be between June 1, 1849, and May 31, 1850.

AGRICULTURE AND INDUSTRIES: This record includes farm and industry schedules to gauge the productivity of the nation's economy. The agricultural census contains data on all free persons who operated farms

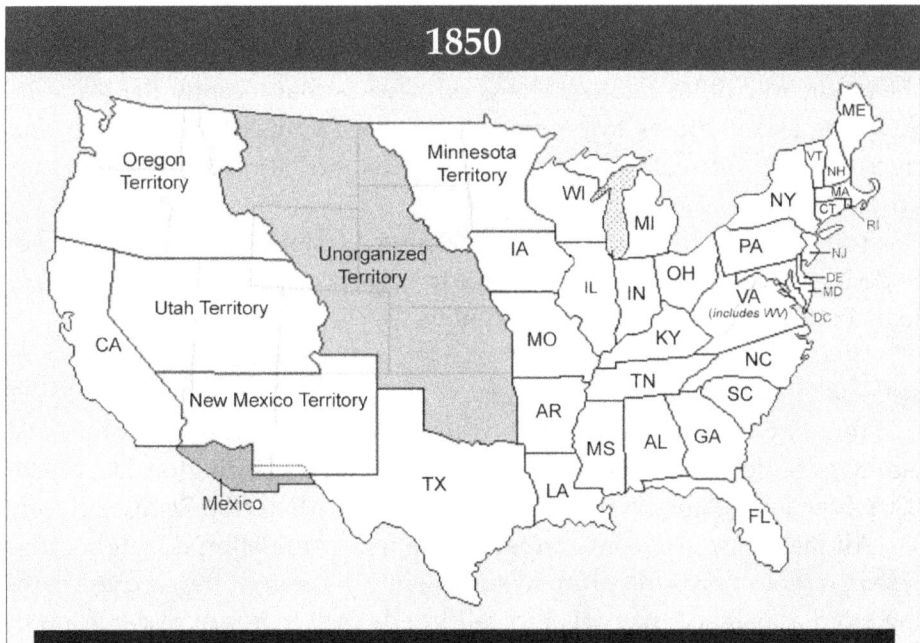

Figure 31: 1850 Census, President Zachary Taylor.

By September 1850, there were a total of thirty-one states in the Union, with Florida, Texas, Iowa, Wisconsin, and California being the latest editions. The four new territories of Oregon, Minnesota, New Mexico, and Utah were also enumerated. There were no substantial losses of state- or district-wide census records. Schedules exist for all the white colored areas.

producing goods valued at more than a hundred dollars a year. The agriculture schedule is two pages long with forty-six columns. These "farm schedules" list US farms and ranches and the farmers who owned and operated them, but do not include every farm in the United States. The first agricultural census in 1840 was somewhat limited in scope, recording numbers of familiar farm animals, wool and soil crop production, and the value of poultry and dairy products. The information collected generally increased by year but may include such items as the value and acreage of the farm, whether it was owned or rented, the number of livestock owned in various categories, the types and value of crops, and the ownership and use of various farm implements.

NON-POPULATION SCHEDULES: National Archives and Records Service deposited the agriculture schedules in a variety of archives, so they are not easy to find. Most are not indexed but searchers should still check the online microfilm catalog. The good news is that recently the National Archives asked copies to be made available for historical research and microfilming. Agriculture lists are known as the "non-population census schedules."

You may have to go where the microfilms are stored, or hire a researcher to do it for you, or it might be possible to borrow a roll through interlibrary loan, or at the LDS family history centers.

Hint: As keywords, use mortality, manufacturing, non-population, or the census year.

You may hire a searcher or do your research in person at the National Archives Building, 700 Pennsylvania Avenue, NW, Washington, DC 20408-0001. Staff is available to answer questions in the Microfilm Reading Room.

All microfilmed records are available for examination during regular research room hours, no prior arrangement is necessary. Researchers coming from a distance may wish to call in advance to verify research room hours and to have any additional questions answered. Some National Archives and Records Administration (NARA) Regional Records Service Facilities around the country have non-population census records. You can check their microfilm catalogs online or call the consultant's office at 202-501-5400.

STATE ARCHIVES: If the schedules in which you are interested are not available from NARA, then you should contact the historical society research libraries or state archives. They may make microfilmed records available through interlibrary loan.

When you find the microfilm you need, the main census search page provides fields to search for the agricultural census. Click the box of the area you want to explore and then enter the words or numbers you want to find. Searching on the "last name" field will be a useful place to start for users seeking data on specific farm operators. For each farm, enumerators noted the name of the individual residing there and having control of the farm. Consequently, the agricultural census contains the names not only of farm owners but also managers, agents, and tenants. This farm schedule could provide invaluable data about your ancestor's farming interests.

At this time, Ancestry.com does not appear to include these agriculture and industry schedules.

SLAVE SCHEDULES IN THE CENSUS: The bureau created a special census for slaves in 1850 and 1860. By 1870 the practice of slavery was outlawed. The slave's name is usually not entered, so these schedules are not

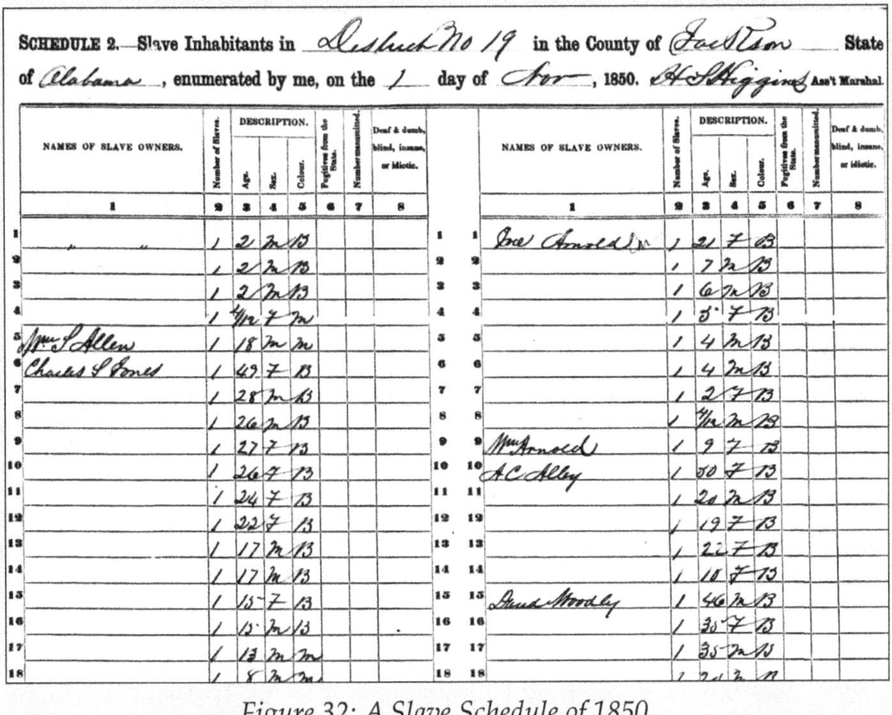

Figure 32: A Slave Schedule of 1850.

too helpful in tracing black history. Still, the form does have some value in slave research as it does show the name of the slave owner, the number of slaves owned, and the number of slaves freed.

Under a slave owner's name is a line for each slave giving age, sex, color, whether handicapped or fugitive, but they remain unnamed—and they still only counted as three-fifths of a person until long after the Civil War.

THE MISSOURI COMPROMISE OF 1820: The Missouri Compromise of 1820, introduced by Senator Henry Clay, meant to keep the number of slave-holding states equal with the non-slave-holding states, and it did keep the peace for the moment. Missouri could come in as a slave state, but only if the northern portion of what was Massachusetts could become the new non-slave state of Maine. Those senators in 1820 would see this issue again and have to deal with it later.

And so it was thirty years later, the Compromise of 1850, also introduced by Henry Clay, consisted of five laws dealing with the issue of slavery. California had requested permission to enter the Union as a non-slave state. If permitted, that would again upset the balance between the free and slave states.

THE COMPROMISE OF 1850: Congress debated the contentious compromise issue well into the summer. Clay's new Compromise bill was defeated every time they called the vote. Heated discussions escalated on the future of slavery in the territories. California had never been a territory and had only been part of the US less than two years, but the minerals discovered the previous year at Sutter's Mill brought on a gold rush. Sixty thousand "forty-niners" came flooding in.

Congress allowed California to jump straight to full statehood without ever passing through the formal territorial stage. Utah and New Mexico joined as territories with no decision on the slavery topic.

The dispute continued. But unexpected events were about to cause a drastic change in history.

DEATH OF A PRESIDENT: President Zachary Taylor, "Old Rough and Ready," had opposed the new Compromise, but he died suddenly after only sixteen months in office leaving behind a country sharply divided.

Taylor died suddenly after eating a snack of cherries and milk. The doctor listed the cause of Taylor's death as gastroenteritis, or "cholera morbus," a term commonly ascribed in the nineteenth century to those who died from an undetermined cause.

MILLARD FILLMORE, NUMBER THIRTEEN: The vice president, Millard Fillmore, supported the Compromise of 1850. He was sworn into office 10 July 1850, a day after the death of Zachary Taylor. Fillmore quickly signed the Compromise and admitted California as the sixteenth free state.

Millard Fillmore came from poor, uneducated beginnings as the son of tenant farmers to become a New York lawyer. He rose from poverty through study and became a lawyer with little formal schooling. In 1833, he won election to the US House of Representatives. After serving in Congress, Fillmore, a Whig, became Zachary Taylor's vice president.

Taylor had pretty much ignored Fillmore, so he was not at all prepared to become president, yet when the

Figure 33: Millard Fillmore

Our thirteenth US president served out the unexpired term of President Taylor from 1850 to 1853.

Vice President: None

president died in office Fillmore was sworn in. As was customary when a new president took over, all the cabinet officers submitted their resignations expecting Fillmore to refuse but he did not. Fillmore dismissed the cabinet and changed administration policy.

A CLASSROOM ROMANCE: Abigail Powers' widowed mother had moved her family to western New York, believing her insufficient funds would go further in a less settled region. She was right. Although impoverished, she educated her small son and daughter beyond the usual frontier level with the help of her late husband's library.

As a teenager, Abigail began to teach at the private New Hope Academy, where her oldest pupil was nineteen-year-old Millard Fillmore. The

world of knowledge and Fillmore's steady progress drew them together, and gradually, the relationship between teacher and student evolved into a romantic attachment.

Millard and Abigail wed in 1826 and became parents of two children, long before his presidential years.

When Abigail Fillmore first moved into the White House, she was reportedly appalled at the fact there was no library inside. With a special appropriation of two thousand dollars from Congress, she spent many happy hours selecting books. Abigail taught herself how to play the piano. Her music, along with volumes of Shakespeare, history, and geography books, soon filled the rooms of the mansion. She essentially created a literary salon. Abigail invited writers such as William Thackeray, Charles Dickens, and Washington Irving to meet there, as well as performance artists like Jenny Lind.

Every Friday night the white house hosted a reception, where the first lady stood for hours greeting and socializing with guests, in spite of a painful broken ankle that never healed. While his wife created music and laughter, Fillmore added a cooking stove and running water to the presidential manor. His policies on slavery did not appease either abolitionists or slaveholders. Although he opposed slavery, Fillmore saw the Compromise as necessary to preserve the Union. Congress debated the contentious issues well into the summer, but by September, Clay's Compromise became law.

A COMPROMISE THAT SATISFIES NO ONE: The Compromise of 1850, which admitted California as a free state, effectively nullified the Missouri Compromise of 1820. That contract had kept a balance of slave and free states for thirty years. In exchange, no federal restrictions on slavery would extend to Utah or New Mexico. The balance of free and slave states was now utterly destroyed.

THE LARGEST SLAVE MARKET: As for Washington, DC, not only did the nation's capital allow enslavement, it was base to the largest slave market in North America. They were buying and selling human beings like cattle within earshot of the nation's Capitol.

Long before the Civil War, the District of Columbia operated as an active and profitable slave auction depot. Slave pens dotted the area around the National Mall in the early 1800s. Groups of chained captives passed the Capitol and the president's house daily.

For instance, sites of slave auctions included the house across from the Smithsonian Castle, the United States Hotel down the street from the Capitol, and numerous nearby taverns.

The blatant presence of open slavery in the capital of a nation where "all men are created equal" angered abolition advocates and reassured bondage supporters. The situation was an embarrassment with foreign visitors.

MARKET CLOSED BUT SLAVERY CONTINUES: Under the new Compromise of 1850, the slave trade was prohibited in the District of Columbia, although slavery was maintained. That meant citizens could own slaves, but they could not legally sell them. Not until the next decade would all enslaved persons in the nation's capital be set free.

THE HATED FUGITIVE SLAVE LAW: Finally, and most controversially, a Fugitive Slave Law passed, requiring northerners to return runaway slaves to their owners under penalty of law. A person who gave food to a runaway slave could go to jail.

Yanks claimed the law was unfair, and they refused to enforce it. However, President Fillmore insisted on enforcing the unpopular Fugitive Slave Act, and the many flagrant violations set the scene for the tempest coming later in the decade.

DRED SCOTT DRAWS ATTENTION: Landmark decisions made at this time led to many conflicts in the future. The Dred Scott case held that blacks, whether free or slave, could not be US citizens so they could not sue in federal courts. Dred Scott was a slave in Missouri. His owner took him from Missouri, a slave-holding state, to the "free" territories of Illinois and Wisconsin from 1833 to 1843, where the Missouri Compromise of 1820 forbade enslavement.

After returning to Missouri, Scott filed suit for his freedom, claiming his ten-year absence made him a free man. He lost the case in Missouri, so Scott brought a new lawsuit in federal court.

Scott's master maintained that no Negro or descendant of slaves could be a citizen in the sense of the Constitution because, in the opinion of the justices, blacks were not really people. In 1857 the Court held that the US Constitution was not meant to include American citizenship for black people, regardless of whether they were enslaved or not. The Supreme court held because Scott was not a person under the US Constitution, he was not free based on his residence no matter where he lived. Scott remained a slave.

While the decision was well-received by slaveholders in the South, the opposition was outraged. The nation increasingly became distinctly divided. People living in the new territories in the westward expansion movement wanted to achieve statehood, and it was hard to know on which side of the slave-or-free divide their land would occupy.

HARRIET TUBMAN AND THE UNDERGROUND: If you are observant while researching in this time frame, you may discover your ancestors involved in a secretive humanitarian organization. The Underground Railroad, a network of secret routes established to help slaves escape to freedom, became more active in this period, reaching its peak between 1850 and 1860.

Harriet Tubman, born into slavery, became a "conductor" on the Underground Railroad. She escaped and helped more than three hundred slaves to freedom before the war, all while carrying a bounty on her head. Although only five feet tall, this young black woman was also a nurse, a Union spy, and a women's suffrage supporter. Born in Maryland in 1822, she was also known as *Black Moses* or *Grandma Moses*.

Ms. Tubman is remembered as an African American freedom fighter in the struggle for liberation from slavery and racism. She

Harriet Tubman (1823– 1913)
nurse, spy and scout

Figure 34: Harriet Tubman

An escaped slave, Ms. Tubman became a conductor on the Underground Railroad.

personally led at least seventy slaves to freedom, including her elderly parents, and instructed dozens of others on how to escape on their own.

In later years Harriet was quoted, *"I never ran my train off the track and never lost a passenger."*

A head injury caused by a cruel overseer in her youth continued to cause her painful problems, and she endured brain surgery to help relieve her symptoms.

UNCLE TOMS CABIN: In the summer of 1852, Harriet Beecher Stowe published a little book, *Uncle Tom's Cabin*, influencing more people than all the legislative acts. The book's success was unprecedented in the history of American literature and increased the unrest. Stowe wrote this work of anti-slavery fiction in response to the Fugitive Slave Act. It sold three hundred thousand copies its first year. A story circulated just after the battle of Bull Run, claiming President Lincoln met Mrs. Stowe for the first time and greeted her as *"the little woman who caused this great war."*

Uncle Tom was indeed a significant influence in those events, although whether or not the meeting really happened is in doubt. The Compromise of 1850 did not address the issue of slavery in the vast unorganized territory in the Great Plains, but with California clamoring for construction of a transcontinental railroad link to the East, the question required an answer.

IMMIGRATION RULES: During the 1850s, immigrants could become naturalized in any court performing naturalizations, including city, county, state, and federal courts. As an example, this naturalization record of the author's second-great grandfather appears as one line in an old record book in Chillicothe, Ohio. "Thomas Bahr, Naturalized, 15 Mar 1852, Chillicothe Probate court."

> *1852: 15 March, Naturalization of Thomas Bahr; Chillicothe, Ross Co, Ohio; Court of Common Pleas, Chancery and Partition Records. Vol 13, Page 442. On motion of Thomas Bahr and it appearing to the satisfaction of the Court he has complied with the laws of Congress in such case made and provided this day declared on oath he would support the constitution of the United States of America and renounce forever all allegiance and fidelity to every foreign prince potentate, state, or sovereignty, whatever and particularly to the* **Grand Duke of Baden** *of whom he was*

*late a subject. Whereupon the said Thomas Bahr was naturalized
and declared a citizen of the United States of America.*

From that one brief record, we learn the original spelling of his name, that he was from Baden, Germany, and now living in Ross County, Ohio, where he became a naturalized citizen of the US.

ANOTHER EXAMPLE: By finding the ship manifest, it appears the Bahr family immigrated from Ortenberg, Germany, to Le Havre, France, and from there to New York on the *Oneida* packet ship. Passenger list of the *Onieda* from Havre to New York dated the twenty-seventh of February 1847 shows:

Birthplace: Baden. Destination: New York. Occupation: Farmer.
BAHR: Thomas age 46

> J. Baptist 19
>
> Ann Marie 16
>
> Wendel 12
>
> Elizabeth 10
>
> Cecile 9
>
> Georg 6

The name was later found Americanized to Barr. Three Barr children are missing from the list. They show up in America later. If they are not on this ship, then how and when did they get here? Their mother Maria Ann had died, probably in childbirth, three years earlier. Missing are the oldest son William, age twenty-three, Martin, age thirteen, and Mathaus, age three. No explanation here, only speculation about creating another family history mystery to be solved someday. The family is scattered west in the 1850 census and beyond.

THE FIRST ELEVATOR: Elisha Ottis invented the first safety elevator and demonstrated it at the New York World's Fair in 1853. Ottis was standing on the platform and had someone cut the rope holding it. The elevator fell only a few inches before stopping. That sudden stop gave people the courage to try out his new invention.

MORTALITY SCHEDULES: Four mortality schedules captured a snapshot of life spans and causes of death throughout the country, and are available for the federal census years of 1850, 1860, 1870, and 1880. If one of your ancestors died in the right place at the right time, you might benefit from this unique listing. Free county-by-county typescripts of most states and mortality schedule years are also available on the Internet here: http://www.mortality-schedules.com/

The Mortality Schedule reported each person who died in the twelve months before the census. These are listed separately on Ancestry.com like the 1850 and 1860 slave schedules, and the 1890 special veteran's census, so you may have to search for them. In the state listings, mortality schedules were generally also recorded for the years of 1855, 1865, and 1875.

FILLMORE AND THE WHIGS: Upon becoming president in July 1850, Millard Fillmore dismissed Taylor's cabinet and carried out his policy priorities.

In August 1850, the social reformer Dorothea Dix wrote to Fillmore, urging support of her proposal in Congress for land grants to finance asylums for the impoverished mentally ill. Though her plan did not pass, the two became friends, meeting in person and corresponding, continuing well after Fillmore's presidency. His pressure for compromise on the slavery issue left him with few fans on either side, as a result his stay in the executive mansion would be brief.

Fillmore's stance on the brutal and unpopular Fugitive Slave Law alienated him from voters in the North. He was the last Whig president. In 1852, he sought election to a full term but was passed over by the Whigs in favor of Winfield Scott, who was then defeated by Democrat Franklin Pierce.

ABIGAIL FILLMORE: she served as hostess during her husband's presidency, but when attending the outdoor ceremonies for his successor's inauguration, she caught a cold. The next day she came down with a fever, which turned into bronchitis, and then developed into pneumonia. Abigail died just twenty-six days after the Fillmore family left the presidential mansion. Fillmore was bereaved again a few months later when his only daughter Mary died of cholera, a bacterial disease usually spread through contaminated water.

THE KNOW-NOTHINGS: The newly-organized American Party, better known as the Know-Nothings, reflected the troubled times confronting the young United States. The nation faced growing conflict over slavery and westward expansion, which led to dissent within the two major political parties, the Democrats and the Whigs. As slavery's expansion became the primary issue of American politics, the Whigs suffered a drastic decline in popularity; it wasn't long before they were willing to give up the ghost.

THE WHIGS DISAPPEAR: The much-embattled Whig Party broke up after Fillmore's presidency ended. Fillmore joined the Know-Nothings. He retired from politics and later married a wealthy widow, Mrs. Caroline C. McIntosh.

...And meanwhile, back in Washington, the beat goes on.

Figure 35: Franklin Pierce

Our fourteenth president served one term from 1853-1857.

Vice President: William King

FRANKLIN PIERCE at age forty-nine in 1853 became the youngest man to be elected president. Pierce was the first president born in the nineteenth century. He chose to affirm his oath of office on a law book rather than swear it on a Bible. That did not find favor with his wife Jane who remained devout, although timid and reserved.

Jane Appleton's family had opposed the marriage due to Pierce's political ambitions. Jane married Franklin anyway, perhaps thinking he would change. However, Franklin Pierce became a member of the House of Representatives and then a US Senator in 1837. Jane Pierce was forced to become the political wife she never wanted to be.

Jane hated Washington so much she fainted when she learned her husband was a nominee for president, but the President-elect convinced his wife the office would be an asset for their son Benny's success in life. She begged her husband to resign his Senate seat and return to New Hampshire, which he did at the end of his term.

He served as an officer in the Mexican War but stayed mostly out of public life for the next decade. Pierce attained the rank of brigadier general in the Army during the Mexican war. After the war, he worked with Alden Partridge, president of Norwich University in Vermont, to improve recruiting and training for the militia.

Shortly after Pierce's triumph in the 1852 election, the couple had a tragedy that took them to the depths. Benny was killed and nearly beheaded when a train car they were traveling in derailed and careened down an embankment. Pearce and his wife watched in horror. Their two older sons also died early in life.

Jane believed God was punishing them for her husband's political ambitions. She was always quiet and prone to deep depressions. She relied on help from her aunt Abigail "Abby" Means and her older sister, Mary Appleton Aiken. Pierce allowed Jane to visit her sister as much as she wanted, and her aunt often acted as a political hostess for him when Jane could not.

MELANCHOLIA: Jane Pierce blamed politics for all the troubles in her life, including the deaths of her children and her husband's excessive alcohol consumption, for Pierce did have a reputation as a drunk. The two gradually drifted apart.

On March 4, the presidential inauguration took place. Jane was not present for the ceremony. She distanced herself during her husband's presidency, wrapped in melancholia. For the first two years of her husband's term, she remained in the upstairs living quarters of the president's house, spending her days writing letters to her dead son. She left the social duties to her Aunt Abby. Finally, two years later in 1855, Jane Pierce seemed to recover and made an official appearance as first lady at a New Year's Day reception. After that Jane occasionally served as hostess for the remainder of her husband's term.

THE FIRST WORLD'S FAIR IN US: 1853—President Pierce opened the first world's fair held in the United States, the "Exhibition of the Industry of All Nations," seen by more than a million visitors before it closed. Located on Sixth Avenue in New York in a large palace on the site of the current New York Public Library, twenty-three foreign nations and colonies participated in the show.

SENATOR DOUGLAS CREATES A BLOODBATH: Senator Stephen Douglas of Vermont authored the Kansas-Nebraska Act. He favored a northern rail route to California to benefit Chicago. The two territories of Kansas and Nebraska made the Missouri Compromise null and void; popular vote would decide the matter of slavery in the new territories.

The Kansas-Nebraska Act of 1854 created far more problems than it could ever solve as the two opposing factions fought for supremacy.

While trying to prevent secession by pacifying the southerners, Douglas's compromise unintentionally caused more violence and helped push the United States over the brink and into Civil War.

Passage of the 1854 Kansas-Nebraska Act became the most significant challenge during the Pierce administration. The Act provided for organizing the two territories and permitting them self-determination on the slavery question. This controversy caused much of the rancor culminating in the action that followed, called "Bleeding Kansas." Although Pierce was morally opposed to slavery, the president saw federal action against slavery as an infringement on southern states' rights.

BLEEDING KANSAS: The Kansas-Nebraska Act allowed the settlers to vote whether they would come in as a slave or free state. Senator Douglas did not anticipate the violence to accompany the creation of Kansas Territory, when both pro-slavery and anti-slavery settlers rushed in to gain control of the new state government.

JOHN BROWN: At age fifty-four John Brown was a failed businessman, an impoverished farmer with a few cattle in Ohio, some land in upstate New York at North Elba that he had not yet paid for, and mostly he was known as a militant abolitionist.

Brown's first wife died during childbirth with their eighth child. His second marriage to teenage Mary Ann Day added a total of thirteen more. Brown's surviving sons were among his most trusted lieutenants, and the entire Brown family was involved in abolitionist work.

When several of his sons and his son-in-law moved to Kansas, John Brown followed. They went partly to improve their economic status and find new, virgin soil for farming, but they also wanted to spread freedom in the West. Of his seven sons: John Jr, Jason, Owen, Frederick, Watson, Salmon, Oliver, five went to Kansas with him in 1855, bringing a wagonload of weapons along.

Brown participated in the Underground Railroad and helped protect fugitive slaves from slave catchers. John Brown's half-sister Florella and her husband, the Reverend Samuel Adair, a chaplain at Fort Leavenworth, lived in a cabin near Osawatomie, Kansas, which was a frequent stop on the Underground Railroad.

In 1856 pro-slavery forces under Sheriff Samuel J. Jones in Lawrence, Kansas, burned the Free-State Hotel, destroyed two anti-slavery newspapers and other business places. This dangerous situation saw both groups struggling to gain control.

CAPTURED AND KILLED: Three days later, John Brown, five of his sons, and three other associates seeking revenge for the sack of Lawrence, retaliated by brutally capturing and killing five Southern pro-slavery settlers along Potawatomi Creek, decapitating some of them with swords.

The Potawatomi Massacre marked the beginning of bloodletting in "Bleeding Kansas." Both sides of the slavery issue embarked on a campaign of terror, intimidation, and armed conflict that lasted throughout the summer. Many people say these incidents were the first shots of the War between the States. Depending on who was speaking and where they stood on the issue, the event might be called the Civil War, the Rebellion, Southern War for Independence, or the War of Northern Aggression.

Later that summer a pro-slavery minister who worked as a scout for the US Army murdered Brown's unarmed son, Frederick, shooting him in the heart at close range. His body, when discovered, was riddled with bullets. Brown's group left Kansas and went back East, but the fight was not over. We will hear from John Brown again.

THE BLOODHOUND LAW IN RETURN FOR LAND: Pierce wanted a transcontinental railroad with a link from Chicago to California, and the trade-off to get his railroad became a despicable law. His support for the Kansas-Nebraska Act and his determination to enforce the Fugitive Slave Act polarized the nation. This Act required all escaped slaves upon capture returned to their masters. All officials and citizens of free states were required to obey the law no matter their personal opinion.

Abolitionists nicknamed it the Bloodhound Law for the dogs used to track down runaway slaves. Abolitionists resented Pierce's attempted expansion of slavery through Kansas and Nebraska.

Pierce was hard-working and his administration mostly untainted by graft, yet the legacy from those four turbulent years contributed to the tragedy of secession and the impending civil war. Like presidents before him and those coming after, Pierce confronted hundreds of job applications for government "spoils."

Pierce said launching the *USS Merrimac*, one of six newly commissioned steam frigates, was one of his happiest days in office.

RIDING THE ORPHAN TRAINS: The Orphan Train Movement was a supervised welfare program transporting orphaned and homeless children from crowded Eastern cities of the United States to foster homes located mainly in rural areas of the Midwest, beginning in the mid-1850s. Orphan homes and other facilities were overflowing with homeless or abandoned children, mostly offspring of impoverished, down-on-their-luck immigrants. City fathers agreed, one solution could be the Orphan Trains.

WANTED
Homes for Children

A company of homeless children from the East will arrive at

TROY, MO., ON FRIDAY, FEB. 25th, 1910

(O. H. Avery   E. B. Woolfolk   H. F. Childers
     Wm. Young   G. W. Colbert
Applications must be made to, and endorsed by, the local committee.

An address will be made by the agent. Come and see the children and hear the address. Distribution will take place at the

Opera House Friday, Feb. 25, at 1:30 p. m.

B. W. TICE and MISS A. L. HILL, Agents, 105 E. 22nd St., New York City.
RUY. J. W. SWAN, University Place, Nebraska, Western Agent.

Figure 36: An Orphan Train advertisement

A young Congregational minister, Rev. Charles L. Brace, age twenty-six, an assistant minister in one of the most impoverished neighborhoods in New York, was concerned about conditions. For instance, in 1850, New York City's population was five hundred thousand, but an estimated thirty thousand homeless children lived on the streets or in more than two dozen orphanages.

A small group of clergymen and social reformers formed the New York Children's Aid Society (CAS) in 1853 because of concern for homeless, neglected, and delinquent children. Brace came up with the idea to resettle poor orphaned children with farm families in the West.

When the orphan train movement began, all these abandoned children were living on the streets of New York City, hungry, cold, alone in the world. The children survived by begging, selling matches, stealing, or sweeping streets. So, if slum children needed work and farmers lacked workers, the economic solution sounded simple: transport idle young people to the country.

Brace sent his first orphan train to Dowagiac, Michigan, in 1854. The move was so successful that other orphanages quickly followed suit, first in New York and then in other cities.

"A car full of homeless children will be taken next week by the Children's Aid Society of Chicago to a village in the northwestern portion of Kansas, where homes are being procured for them," the *Tribune* reported in 1891.

"Orphan train riders" ranged in age from infants to older teenagers. The farm families agreed to treat them like members of the family and send them to school, and in return they expected the children to help work on the farm or in the house.

Field agents made regular visits to homes where children had been placed and wrote reports after each visit. Children were frequently removed from homes and transferred to other homes if the situation was not harmonious.

SEEING THE OUTSIDE WORLD: For better or worse, waifs from the big city could get a glimpse of the wider world.

The sad part is that to speed their assimilation, many children were stripped of information about their birth families, ethnic identities, and religious heritage as they boarded the trains.

Children who had known only slums and crowded streets experienced the thrill of seeing the open countryside through the windows of an orphan train.

The intent of the program was not adoption as it is now known, but foster care. Families acted from various motives, and not all children found happy homes. Some suffered abuse, others were treated like hired help, or were never entirely accepted. Officials knew their placements were not perfect, and they tried to carefully screen inappropriate families. Despite problems, the system provided the best chance for many children.

Soon, thousands of children were riding the rails to new homes. Once a child became selected for the train, the Children's Aid Society (CAS) agent dressed each child in new clothing, gave them a Bible and accompanied them on the way west.

Fliers posted in towns announced a train was coming. Most children thought the train ride, which could last from days to weeks, an exciting adventure. Few understood what was happening. Once they knew, their reactions ran the gamut from delight at finding a new family to resentment at being duped. The towns where they stopped, naturally, had to be along a railroad line. The screening committee (mostly men) usually consisted of a town doctor, clergyman, newspaper editor, store owner, or a teacher.

The committee selected possible parents who would choose a child on the day the train arrived. They assigned some children to specific families in advance. Most lined up at train stops, and families picked the one they wanted. Local committees approved applications of families wanting children, and society agents followed up with yearly visits, often removing children from unfit homes.

Mr. Brace believed street children would have better lives if they left the poverty of their lives in New York and grew up in morally upright farm families. Recognizing the need for labor in the expanding farm country, Brace believed farmers would welcome homeless children, take them into their homes and treat them as their own, and for the most part, they did.

FINDING FOSTER FAMILIES: Brace's program would turn out to be a forerunner of modern foster care. His system put its faith in the kindness of strangers. The Children's Aid Society agent placed orphan train children in homes for free, where they could serve as an extra pair of hands to help with chores around the farm. Families agreed to raise them as they would their natural-born children, provide them with decent food and clothing, provide a "common" education, and give them a hundred dollars when they turned twenty-one. Older children placed by the CAS were supposed to receive pay for their labors. Legal adoption was not required. Many children placed out west had learned to survive on the streets of New York, Boston, or other large eastern cities, and did not behave as the grateful, obedient children many families expected.

If you think your ancestor may have been an Orphan Train Rider, you can find more information at the National Orphan Train Complex in Concordia, Kansas. This museum and research center each contain a great deal of information about the Orphan Train Movement, the various institutions participating, and the children and agents who rode the trains.

TRAVEL IN THE LATE 1850s: While the nation's network of iron and steel rails grew more extensive and accessible, stagecoach connections to small and isolated communities continued to supplement passenger trains well into the second decade of the twentieth century. However, stagecoach travel across the vast expanse of the American West attracted the most attention. Mostly the attention came because of inordinately long distances involved, as well as the Herculean effort required to maintain regular service across the dry and sparsely populated landscape.

Stagecoach lines in the East tended to connect preexisting centers of population, and passengers took regular meals at the established inns and taverns along the way. Nothing of the kind existed in the West in 1858, when John Butterfield started up an overland stage line for passengers and mail connecting St. Louis and San Francisco by way of El Paso, Texas, a trip that would take about twenty to twenty-five days. The route also ran through Tucson and Los Angeles, but neither was more than a village of a few hundred residents at the time.

No outlaw or Indian ever killed a passenger on a Butterfield stage, but some died in accidents caused by not-well-trained mules or by mustangs running wild.

NO MONEY ON BOARD: Butterfield's stages did not carry shipments of valuables. Butterfield's instructions to his employees were: *"No money, jewelry, banknotes, or valuables of any nature, will be allowed to be carried under any circumstances whatever."* For this reason, Butterfield did not require a "shotgun" rider next to the driver. However, when in Comanche or Apache territory, guns were ready.

In October 1859, a passenger heading east on a Butterfield stage wrote the following:

> *"After leaving Arizona's San Pedro River Stage Station, the conductor asked how many of us were armed and requested those who had arms to have them ready for use, as we now were in the Apache country. Guns and pistols were produced, and we rode all night with them in our hands."*

Butterfield's Overland Mail Company made two trips a week from September 1858 to March 1861. The difference between a stagecoach and a mail coach is all about the mail. Butterfield coaches often had window openings, but the western models designed for rougher conditions had no glass panels. The roof was strong enough to support luggage, and sometimes seating as well. Luggage and mailbags went in the canvas-covered boot at the back. On a mail coach, a sizeable compartment below the driver's seat held mail as did a roomy rear boot.

Butterfield's operations on the Southern Overland Trail ended in March 1861 with the start of the Civil War.

JAMES BUCHANAN, THE BACHELOR PRESIDENT: James Buchanan moved into office as the fifteenth president. Buchanan, of Scottish descent, was the only bachelor ever to serve in the presidential office, although he may not have been genuinely single. Many people speculated about his sexuality and close relationship with Alabama Senator William Rufus King. The two lived together for more than ten years, despite being rich enough to each have their own home. Andrew Jackson called them "Miss Nancy and Aunt Fancy" behind their backs.

When Senator King left for France in 1844, Buchanan wrote: *"I am now solitary and alone, having no companion in the house with me. I have gone a-wooing several gentlemen but have not succeeded with any one of them."*

There is also a legend about a broken heart. Anne Caroline Coleman, daughter of the wealthy iron manufacturer and protective father Robert Coleman, was also the sister-in-law of one of Buchanan's colleagues from the House of Representatives. By 1819, James and Anne were engaged but spent little time together. James Buchanan

Figure 37: James Buchanan

Our fifteenth president served one term from 1857 to 1861.

Vice President: John C. Breckinridge

stayed busy with his law firm and political projects during the financial panic, and this took him away for weeks at a time.

Soon after Anne broke off the engagement, she died suddenly. Some believe Anne's death served to deflect awkward questions about Buchanan's sexuality and bachelorhood. Buchanan was a good lawyer but not a great president. He alienated both Republican abolitionists and northern Democrats and started the Panic of 1857. Buchanan tried in vain to find an agreement to keep the South from seceding. The question of slavery and a compromise that was not satisfying to anyone marred his tenure.

HURRICANE CAUSES BANK FAILURES: A violent hurricane lashed at *Central America*, a sailing vessel carrying passengers and a big shipment of gold from California.

The year was 1857, and US banks needed that gold to reach its destination safely.

The ship full of gold lost its battle with the hurricane and sank to the bottom of the ocean.

The US banks could not gather all the gold their customers demanded, and as nervous depositors demanded their money, banks began to fall like dominoes.

That summer ushered in the collapse of fourteen hundred state banks and five thousand businesses. While the South escaped mostly unscathed, northern cities saw numerous unemployed men and women take to the streets to beg. Many financiers believed Europe's declining purchase of US agricultural products caused this first worldwide economic crisis.

Buchanan agreed with the southerners who attributed the economic collapse to over-speculation when talk of secession and disunion reached a boiling point.

THE DRED SCOTT DECISION: The landmark Dred Scott decision essentially stated the federal government had no right to exclude enslavement in the territories. The decision inflamed more regional tensions, which burned ever higher for another four years. By the end of Buchanan's presidency, the slavery issue reached a boiling point that threatened the imminent destruction of the entire country.

MORMON HANDCARTS: The Mormon handcart movement began in 1856 and continued until 1860 for the Church of Jesus Christ of Latter-day

Saints, also known as the LDS Church. Early members of the church often encountered hostility, primarily due to their practice of withdrawing from secular society and gathering in locales to practice their distinct religious beliefs. Their neighbors felt threatened by the group's rapid growth in numbers, its tendency to vote as a bloc. They acquired political power, held claims of divine favor, and continued to practice polygamy.

Violence directed against the members caused the church body to move from Ohio to Missouri, to Illinois, and finally to Salt Lake City. In 1838, the Missouri Governor delivered an extermination order against all Mormons living in the state. Brigham Young said he received divine direction to organize the church members and head beyond the western frontier of the United States.

The handcart pioneers, participants in the migration to Salt Lake City, Utah, walked and pulled two-wheeled handcarts to transport their belongings from the railroad terminus at Iowa City, Iowa. Motivated to join their fellow church members in Utah but lacking funds to purchase full ox teams, nearly three thousand Mormon pioneers made the journey to Utah from Iowa and Nebraska in ten handcart companies.

HEADED FOR HEAVEN IN A HANDCART: Built to Brigham Young's design, the handcarts resembled a large wheelbarrow, with two wheels five feet in diameter, a single axle four and a half feet wide, and weighing sixty pounds. The handcarts generally carried up to two-hundred-fifty pounds of supplies and luggage, though they were capable of handling loads as heavy as five hundred pounds. Carts used in the first year's migration were made entirely of wood, actually green timber, which caused some problems.

Groups organized into companies with five persons per handcart. Each person was limited to seventeen pounds of clothing and bedding, children allowed only ten pounds. The handcart pioneers slept each night in round tents supported by a center pole. Four companies per tent, and the twenty occupants per tent slept with their feet to the center, like spokes on a wheel. Every hundred pioneers had a wagon to haul provisions, drawn by three yoke of oxen.

The companies made good time, and their trips were mostly uneventful. Emigrant companies included many children and elderly individuals. Pushing and pulling handcarts was exhausting work. Journals and recollections describe periods of illness and hunger.

One journal recorded this:

"People made fun of us as we walked, pulling our handcarts, but the weather was fine, and the roads were excellent. Although I was sick and we were very tired at night, still we thought it was a glorious way to go to Zion."

Two of the companies started their journey dangerously late and were trapped in heavy snow and severe temperatures in central Wyoming. Despite a dramatic rescue effort, more than two hundred in these last two companies died along the way. John Chislett, a survivor, wrote, *"Many a father pulled his cart, with his little children on it, until the day preceding his death."*

Figure 38: The Handcart Pioneers

The monument stands on Temple Square in Salt Lake City, Utah.

Although fewer than ten percent of the emigrants made the journey west using handcarts, the pioneers who did go with that group have become a meaningful symbol in LDS culture, representing the sacrifice of the pioneer generation.

JOHN BROWN'S PLAN FAILS: The abolitionist John Brown, who had participated in "Bleeding Kansas" and his anti-slavery sympathizers, raided the federal arsenal at Harpers Ferry, Virginia (now West Virginia) in 1859. He believed armed rebellion was the only way to overthrow the institution of slavery in the United States.

Brown left Kansas and moved east. Four years after the Kansas incident, twenty-one men under Brown's leadership planned to seize the United States Armory at the confluence of the Shenandoah and Potomac Rivers. Although the townspeople soon began to fight back, Brown's men succeeded in capturing the armory. Jason and Salmon did not take part in the assault on Harper's Ferry, but the rest of the family did.

Army workers discovered Brown's men early in the morning. Local militia, farmers, and shopkeepers surrounded the armory. When a company of militia captured the bridge across the Potomac, they cut off any route of escape for Brown's raiders. During the day, four townspeople were killed, including the mayor.

Only five of Brown's twenty-one men escaped the raid and its aftermath. John Brown's son Watson, age twenty-four, was mortally wounded while carrying a white flag and trying to negotiate with the responding militia. One of Brown's men, William H. Leeman, panicked and tried to flee by swimming across the Potomac River, but he was shot and fatally injured. During the intermittent shooting, Oliver Brown, at age twenty-one the youngest of John Brown's three sons to participate in the action, was mortally wounded and died the next day. Of all Brown's twenty children, only half survived their childhood, and two more were killed during the raid on Harper's Ferry.

Brown hoped this action would cause an uprising of slaves. His plan failed when federal troops under the command of Colonel Robert E. Lee killed several of the raiders and captured their leader.

The immediate aftermath of the Harpers Ferry raid and trial proved especially tricky for son Owen, daughter Annie, and daughter-in-law Martha because they were involved. Owen escaped during the attack and remained in hiding for months. In January 1860, his sister Ruth wrote, *"Owen is wandering somewhere, our anxiety for him is very great."*

Because of his leadership role in raiding the federal armory, the state of Virginia sentenced John Brown to be hanged for treason.

To millions of enslaved black people and many whites, John Brown's body hanging on a gallows in 1859 symbolically became the crucified Christ. To southern slave owners, his figure was more like the devil himself.

John Brown's Body, a 340-page narrative poem about the Civil War by Stephen Vincent Benet, won the Pulitzer Prize in 1929. The town of Harpers Ferry is now a spectacular national park.

In the 1970s, a descendant, Nell Brown Groves, said: *"I'm very proud of what my grandfather, John Brown, did. Slavery was wrong. What he stood for was right."* Groves, listed in *Who's Who Among American Women* for her musical and artistic accomplishments, continues to perpetuate the name. *"We're proud of what he did,"* she said, *"and we're loyal to the cause."*

Chapter 7 Summary from 1850 to 1860:

- ✓ 1850 census names all members of the household, includes 30 states, 4 new territories, a separate slave census, agricultural and industrial schedules and offers the first mortality schedule
- ✓ Slaves count as 3/5 of a person on the census
- ✓ Four presidents served in this ten-year period
- ✓ 1850 President Taylor dies of unknown causes
- ✓ Millard Fillmore is sworn into office after Zachary Taylor's death
- ✓ City of Los Angeles and San Francisco incorporated in April 1850
- ✓ First safety passenger elevator installed on March 23, 1857 by Elisha Ottis
- ✓ 1853 Franklin Pierce, 49, took office as the youngest man to be elected president
- ✓ The Dred Scott decision caused much conflict
- ✓ The Underground Railroad, helped slaves escape, reaching its peak between 1850-60
- ✓ Washington DC was home to the largest slave market in North America
- ✓ 1857 James Buchanan becomes the fifteenth president
- ✓ To get land for a transcontinental railroad, Pierce enforced the Fugitive Slave Act
- ✓ Panic of 1857 saw collapse of 1,400 state banks and 5,000 businesses, worldwide
- ✓ Abolitionist John Brown seizes the armory at Harper's Ferry, loses fight
- ✓ By the end of Buchanan's presidency, the slavery issue is tearing the country apart
- ✓ Orphan trains bring children west
- ✓ Butterfield stage line carries mail and passengers from Memphis to San Francisco

EIGHT—1860

The Civil / Uncivil War

THE PONY EXPRESS: 1860

Overland mail between Sacramento, California, and St. Joseph, Missouri, begins with mail carried over the Oregon Trail by a series of riders on horseback called the Pony Express. Previously, letters bound for California had to go overland twenty-five days by stagecoach or on a long sea voyage by ship. The Pony Express, meanwhile, had an average delivery time of just ten days.

The owners set up a string of nearly two hundred relief stations across what is now Missouri, Kansas, Nebraska, Colorado, Wyoming, Utah, Nevada, and California. Lone riders would ride between stations at a breakneck pace, switch mounts every ten to fifteen miles and then hand their mailbags off to a new courier after seventy-five or a hundred miles. They made their runs in extreme weather conditions, harsh terrain, and in spite of the threat of attacks by bandits and Indians.

Their primary goal being speed, the Pony Express went to great lengths to keep their loads as light as possible. They used a particular type of mailbag like a knapsack. Most of the riders were small, wiry men about the same size as a modern horse racing jockey. It wasn't unusual for them to hire young teenagers. During the frontier days, a boy of fourteen was considered a man with responsibilities.

In his autobiography, which might or might not be true, the folk hero Buffalo Bill Cody claimed he rode for the Pony Express as a carrier at the age of fourteen. He said he once rode three hundred eighty-four miles on a single run.

In spite of becoming a romantic legend, the Pony Express was not a successful enterprise. The company never turned a profit during its year and a half history. When Western Union completed the transcontinental telegraph in 1860, the Pony Express became obsolete and service ended in October 1861.

THE LAST CENSUS BEFORE WAR: James Buchanan, the only president ever elected as a native of Pennsylvania, ordered the last census before the civil war.

Two new states in this census are Minnesota and Oregon making thirty-three in the union before succession.

Territories include Kansas, New Mexico, Nebraska, Utah, Washington, Indian, and the unorganized Dakota territories. The War was beginning

1860

Figure 39: The 1860 census, James Buchanan, president.

The eighth census of USA numbered thirty-three states,and was the last census where slaves counted as a big part of Southern wealth. Slaves were legally considered property in 1860. Schedules exist for all except Indian Territory.

by the time the 1860 data was ready for tabulation, so the staff could only produce abbreviated reports. No significant loss of records occurred. More than one hundred eighty clerks in the Bureau of the Census tabulated more than thirty million residents in the US Census of 1860. Census takers collected information including the name of each member of the household as well as age, sex, color, the occupation of persons over age fifteen, the value of their real and personal estate, place of birth, whether the person married during the year, and whether handicapped or a convict.

Personal estates information might be helpful to a researcher. However, many people at that time gave false information to avoid paying high taxes on their property holdings.

This census also gave more specific birthplace information about foreign-born residents. Just as US residents had to list a specific state or territory of birth, this might say "Wales" or "Scotland" instead of "Great Britain." At the time the census takers submitted the returns, the country was galloping at breakneck speed toward war. The data collected served as useful information for Union field commanders. For example, maps could show important population information as well as transportation routes.

INDIANS FINALLY COUNTED: This was the first census that officially counted American Indians, even though only those who "renounced tribal rules" were included. The 1860 form does not include "Indian" as a choice in the column for "color." However, enumerators recorded more than forty thousand American Indians. Using specially designed forms, agents enumerated Indians living near military reservations in California, Dakota Territory, and Washington Territory. The count of taxed Indians includes many persons of mixed Indian and white heritage.

SLAVE SCHEDULES: As in previous censuses, the new slave schedules are separate, but they can be searched just like any other part of the record. The slave's name is usually not entered, yet the table does loudly proclaim the name of the slave owner, the number of slaves owned, and the number of slaves freed. Sometimes the listings for large slave holdings take the form of family groupings. However, slaves are usually listed from eldest to youngest with no apparent effort to portray family structure.

BUCHANAN FALLS SHORT: President James Buchanan was forced to address the slavery situation in his final message to Congress. His inability to handle the sharply divided pro-slavery and anti-slavery partisans with a unifying principle led to his consistent ranking by historians as one of the worst presidents in American history. By 1860, it was apparent that Buchanan wasn't going to be a candidate for re-election.

Figure 40: Abraham Lincoln Daguerreotype 1863

LINCOLN WINS ON ANTI-SLAVERY: The brand-new Republican Party offered Abraham Lincoln, a former Whig, as a candidate on an anti-slavery platform. He defeated three opponents in the November election of 1860, leading to fervent cries of potential rebellion in slave states. Although Lincoln claimed the electoral college vote by a considerable majority, the popular vote revealed just how split the nation was.

Abraham Lincoln—uneducated, middle to lower class, a lawyer for the common man—was such an outcast socially, economically, and physically that in some respects he was perhaps better suited to empathize with the plight of those people struggling to survive those terrible times. The pursuit for equality was not only something he believed in but something he felt personally, because of his hardships.

Abe Lincoln was first a Whig, then a Republican, and finally a member of the National Union party. Lincoln later became a War Democrat, a combined group of Democrats and Republicans, but division still reigned.

Southern Democrats thought slavery should expand, but northern Democrats opposed the idea. Both groups hotly debated states' rights, a continuing conflict over the proper allocation of power between the states and the federal government.

READY TO RUMBLE: The election proved to be the breaking point for an already unstable nation. Six weeks later on the twentieth of December

1860, South Carolina called for a vote to secede. Within three months, state by state in the South held their convention and counted the votes. With Lincoln elected on an anti-slavery platform, the South felt all hope of compromise gone. The house was not only divided, it was on fire.

There were attempts to bridge the differences between North and South, yet Lincoln's election victory ultimately prompted the slave states to secede. Before Lincoln took office, six more states said goodbye—Alabama, Louisiana, Mississippi, Florida, Georgia, and Texas; seven states in seven weeks.

While the fate of the nation hung in the balance, James Buchanan remained a lame-duck president until Lincoln could be installed. Buchanan left the Capitol on the third day of March while the nation teetered on the brink. Abraham Lincoln became the sixteenth president during this national crisis that would tear states and families apart. The challenge would test Lincoln's leadership skills, as well as his resolve. It was all anyone talked about everywhere in the country.

WHY DO WE NEED A WAR? America's southern states became the economic engine of the nation with cash crops of tobacco, cotton and sugar cane.

Slaves represented the bulk of the planter's wealth. By the start of the war, the South was producing three-fourths of all the world's cotton. Cotton was king, creating more millionaires per capita in the Mississippi River valley than anywhere in the nation.

The open markets where humans were inspected like animals, bought, and sold to the highest bidder proved an increasingly lucrative enterprise. No matter how wide the gap between rich and poor, whites eased their class tension by the belief they belonged to the "superior white race." Many convinced themselves they were doing God's work by providing homes for what they considered an inferior people. Many southerners believed by seceding they were actually doing the right thing to preserve their independence and protect their slaves.

CONFEDERATE PRESIDENT ELECTED: In Montgomery, Alabama, the convention to form the Confederate States of America (CSA) opened in February. Four days later, after electing Jefferson Davis as president, the seven southern slave states officially set up the CSA. The new government

Figure 41: Jefferson and Varina Davis

hastened to form an army from scratch, practically overnight, as states volunteered militia units.

Four more slave states, Virginia, Arkansas, Tennessee, and North Carolina declared their secession and joined the Confederacy when the war started in April. Missouri and Kentucky divided on the issue, sometimes standing on one side or the other. Neither of those two states declared secession so the Confederacy did not control them. Maryland and Delaware also never declared for either side.

JEFFERSON DAVIS. WHO? Named for Thomas Jefferson when he was born in Kentucky, the Davis family soon settled on a plantation called *Rosemont* in Woodville, Mississippi. Young Jefferson attended a Dominican boys' boarding school in Kentucky, and at age thirteen entered Transylvania College at Lexington. He later spent four years in the military academy at West Point. Another cadet in the class behind him was Robert E. Lee, who would become his most famous Confederate general.

Davis served as a lieutenant in the Black Hawk War under the future president, Zachary Taylor. Davis fell in love with Taylor's daughter, Sarah. Gen. Taylor admired Davis for his soldiering skills but opposed the romantic match. Because her father was opposed to the marriage, Davis resigned his military post before the wedding. Sadly, Sarah died of malaria just a few months later, and for several years Davis avoided the public. Ten years after the loss of his first wife he married Varina Howell.

THE CSA PRESIDENT'S LADY: Varina Howell Davis, as first lady of the Confederacy, quickly became consumed by heavy responsibility. Varina had family on both sides of the conflict and held unconventional views for a woman in her public role. She never forgot the ponderous weight on her husband's shoulders, and she stayed close by in case he needed to talk with her, which he frequently did.

She supported the Confederacy position on slavery and states' rights, but she was ambivalent about the war.

In her role, Varina visited hospitals regularly, delivered supplies, wrote letters for wounded men, and advised women in authority positions within the hospitals. Varina found a way to get needed supplies to them. Her dark side presented itself on rare occasions, including the ability to spew wounding sarcasm at a moment's notice.

Varina showed forthrightness and a candor considered destructive at times. Still, her friends remained supporters.

After his election, Davis moved into the CSA office on the second floor of the Custom House on Main Street in Richmond. The Cabinet room and the State and Treasury Department were there also.

The city leased the Brockenbrough house for the CSA presidential mansion. It was referred to as the Grey House, and now features the Confederate Museum. In 1864, several of the Davises' domestic slaves escaped. James Dennison and his wife, Betsey, who had served as Varina's maid, used saved back-pay of eighty gold dollars to finance their escape.

In another version of the story, Betsey stole the money along with two thousand in Confederate bills. Betsey also supposedly revealed accounts of the CSA First Lady's vicious temper. Another slave, the butler named Henry, left one night after allegedly building a fire in the mansion's basement to divert attention.

Davis's first presidential act was to send a peace commission to Washington to prevent an armed conflict. Lincoln refused to see the CSA emissaries and sent armed ships to Charleston, South Carolina, to resupply the Union garrison at Fort Sumter.

WHO IS THIS ABRAHAM LINCOLN? Lincoln, also a Kentucky native, was the first president born outside the original thirteen colonies. Lincoln was born in a log cabin and learned early to struggle for a living. He was the first president to have a beard, and he was an outstanding wrestler. He won all but one of approximately three hundred wrestling matches.

In 1861 this fifty-two-year old son of a Hardin County frontiersman became president of the United States with Hannibal Hamlin as vice president.

The presidential Lincoln usually appeared in a Prince Albert coat, a long cylindrical black wool cutaway named for Prince Albert, the husband of Queen Victoria. The Prince Albert remained fashionable among men of the upper classes until the first decade of the twentieth century. The style went out with whiskers, sideburns, and beards. However, the distinctive coat continued to be worn by men whose calling in life demanded a certain definite sedateness of manner, such as undertakers, ministers, physicians, and various public officials.

As for the top hat, Lincoln would remove the somewhat battered stovepipe, revealing his usually messy hair, and often out dropped the paper from which he would deliver his speech. When he finished, the president deposited his papers back into the lid, put the hat on his head, and away he went. At six-foot-four, Lincoln would stand out even today, and he certainly towered over the men and women of his era. The top hat made him appear even taller still.

By the time of his presidency, Abraham Lincoln's habit of using his hat as a briefcase was well-established and he was a messy person. Papers, briefs, letters, and notes scattered to the four corners of his office as a lawyer in Illinois. The tall hat didn't entirely solve his chaotic problem, but at least it separated essential documents from the untidy whirl of papers on his office desk. He wore the top hat in war and peace, on the stump, and in Washington on occasions both formal and informal.

James Buchanan, when he was president, deliberately chose men like himself, those who would not question his authority.

Conversely, Lincoln picked a team of independent, strong-minded men, all more experienced in public life, with more education, and better known. He placed his three chief rivals in the top three positions. Each of the three thought they should have been elected instead of that unknown prairie lawyer. William Seward, Salmon Chase, and Edward Bates would head the State Department, the Treasury, and the Justice Department.

MARY TODD LINCOLN: Lincoln's wife, Mary Todd arrived as the fourth of seven children of Robert Smith Todd, a banker, and Elizabeth "Eliza" (Parker) Todd in Lexington, Kentucky. Mary was born into comfort and refinement. When Mary was six, her mother died in childbirth, her father remarried, and they had nine more children. Mary never got along well with her stepmother, so she went to live with her married sister in Springfield, Illinois, and there she met her future husband.

In Illinois, the rising young lawyer and Democratic politician Stephen A. Douglas courted her, yet she chose Abraham Lincoln, a fellow Whig. They became parents of four sons: Robert "Bob," Edward "Eddie," William "Willie," and Thomas "Tad." Lincoln is described as an affectionate, though often absent, husband and father. Only the first son, Robert, would survive childhood. In later years, when he had become quite wealthy, he would have his mother committed to a mental institution.

During her Washington years, Mary Todd Lincoln faced many personal difficulties caused by the political divisions. Most of her family sided with the Confederacy so the while the north accused her of treason, yet the south condemned her for not being more loyal to the South. The war was not only the worst political crisis in American history up to then, but for the Lincolns and many other families, it was a painful and tragic family quarrel as well.

Figure 42: Mary Todd

Mary was courted by Stephen A. Douglas, but she chose Abraham Lincoln.

Kentucky permitted slavery but never joined the Confederacy, though many of its sons fought for it. Mary's family kept slaves, and several of her half-brothers and brothers-in-law served in the Confederate Army.

David Todd, a commissioned officer at Libby Prison, treated the Prisoners of War (POW) badly. His reputation for brutality to Union prisoners outraged the nation and deeply embarrassed the Lincolns.

Four of Mary's brothers were in the Shiloh battle. Samuel was the first to die, only four weeks after he enlisted. He died from an abdominal wound—gut-shot, they called it.

The newspapers of the day were not kind to the president. *"He was a gallant private in the Crescent regiment and died in defense of his country against the hireling invaders whom the husband of his sister, Abraham Lincoln, sent to desolate our country and dishonor our people....*" (The Charlotte NC Democrat, 06 May 1862)

Mary's half-sister Emilie's husband, General Benjamin Hardin Helm, a West Point graduate, commanded the famed Kentucky "Orphan Brigade." The name came from how the Confederacy viewed its soldiers from Kentucky which remained in the Union, but was represented by a star in both flags, US and Confederate.

Gen. Helm fell in battle on the twentieth of September 1863 at Chickamauga, Georgia. A grieving Emilie arrived at the White House that December, accompanied by her daughter Katherine. Northerners widely criticized the president for entertaining the "rebels."

Mary's brother George Rogers Clark Todd served as a surgeon in the Confederate Army under Robert E. Lee. Although he was in the profession of one who would heal and relieve suffering, George was better known for his cruelty to prisoners from the north.

Probably Mary's favorite sibling, Alexander "Aleck" Todd, was the youngest and seemed to be loved by everyone.

Aleck Todd joined the Orphan Brigade, the most significant Confederate force raised in Kentucky. He was killed by friendly fire near Baton Rouge, Louisiana, in August 1862. Aleck served at Shiloh and the first siege of Vicksburg—much of that time as an aide to his brother-in-law, General Helm. Mary did not mourn her fallen brothers publicly. She told one visitor that in joining the Confederates, they *"made their own choice."*

Mary worked hard to serve as first lady in a city dominated by eastern culture. Critics considered Lincoln as the first "western" president, and they regarded Mary's manners as coarse and pretentious. She had difficulty negotiating social responsibilities and rivalries, spoils-seeking solicitors, and avoiding baiting newspapers in the climate of high national intrigue. She refurbished the presidential house, including extensive redecorating of all the public and private rooms, and even purchased new china dishes. Newspaper criticism of Mrs. Lincoln's extensive overspending habits would continue throughout the Lincoln administration.

The president was angry about the cost, even though Congress eventually passed two additional appropriations to cover these expenses.

The Lincoln's two young sons, Tad and Willie, became friends with the domestic staff. Tad Lincoln's boyish presence also provided relief, not only for President Lincoln but also for the soldiers camped around the executive mansion. They grew fond of the lad's humor and energy.

Physically, Mary suffered from migraine headaches as well as depression, especially after the deaths of her sons. Their second son Eddie died as a three-year-old in 1850 before the Washington years, probably of diphtheria. The third, Willie, succumbed to typhoid at age twelve while living in the executive mansion. The youngest son, Tad, died of heart failure at the age of eighteen in 1871. Mary held several séances in the white house seeking to communicate with her dead children. Abraham probably attended at least one of these.

In 1863 Mary told her sister, Emilie Todd Helm, that Willie and Eddy visited her, coming to the foot of her bed. She claimed the spirits of her sons took actual ghost form and manifested in her bedroom.

There are twenty-six known photographs of Mary. They are all in a booklet entitled *The Photographs of Mary Todd Lincoln* by Lloyd Ostendorf. There are no known photos of Mary and Abraham together.

THE WAR BEGINS: April 12, 1861, Lincoln was hardly settled in the mansion when the first shots exploded in South Carolina. The Confederates requested the US Army to evacuate Fort Sumpter in the harbor of Charleston. The commander refused. Confederate forces bombarded the fort, thus initiating four terrible blood-soaked years of conflict.

April 15, 1861—The new US President called for seventy-five thousand volunteers to fight the secessionist activities in the south. A year later the Army of the Tennessee, under General U. S. Grant, repulsed the Confederate advance at the Battle of Shiloh, in southwestern Tennessee, one of the most significant battles in the war. This campaign, along with the unconditional surrender of Fort Donelson to General Grant on February 16, signaled the first small successes of the Northern Army.

From the beginning, Lincoln asserted the North was fighting solely to preserve the Union, not to interfere with slavery. After firsthand conversations with soldiers and their commanders, he came to realize the importance of slavery to the South's military. The slaves were the ones who dug the trenches and built up forts for the Confederate army. They were the ones who cooked, worked in the hospitals, and drove the teams to haul supplies. At home, they planted and harvested the crops and kept the farms in operation. That freed up Confederate soldiers to focus on fighting.

In late July, Lincoln gathered his cabinet to read his legal brief for emancipation to take effect six months later, giving the states in rebellion a chance to end the war.

Three and a half million slaves in the South would be free, but the order did not cover the slaves in the loyal border states. Since they had not joined with the rebels, the president's war powers could not be used to liberate their slaves. The hundred days between the time he signed the proclamation and when it took effect became a critical time to test the fragile unity in his cabinet.

BATTLE OF ANTIETAM: In the foggy dawn hours of September 17, 1862, at Antietam Creek in Maryland, Confederate General Robert E. Lee's Army of Northern Virginia and Union General George B. McClellan's Army of the Potomac, prepared for battle near Sharpsburg. It would be the bloodiest day in United States history. General Robert E. Lee guided his Army across the Potomac in early September 1862, in his first invasion of the northern states.

Civilians generally hid inside their houses as the armies passed through their towns; northern Virginia's farms had been stripped bare of food. Major General George B. McClellan was responsible for defending against Lee's invasion. Over September 15 and 16, the Confederate and Union armies gathered on opposite sides of Antietam Creek not far from the town of Sharpsburg.

The great general Lee daringly divided his men, sending half of them under the command of his trusted commander, Thomas "Stonewall" Jackson. All Lee's troops were worn-out, hungry, and many were sick, yet they fought bravely.

MILLER'S CORNFIELD AND A CHURCH: Beginning in a cornfield owned by a man named Miller near the Dunker German Baptist church, the battle changed the course of the nation. Dunkers, more commonly known as the German Baptist Brethren, practiced modesty in their dress and general lifestyle. Other Christian principles which the Dunker's stress are pacifism. Both North and South members refuse military service. They practice total abstinence from alcohol and are opposed to slavery. Dunker services are simple. The worshipers sing hymns with no musical accompaniment. Men sit on one side and women on the other. The churches are simple with no stained-glass windows, steeple or crosses.

Figure 43: After the Battle of Antietam.

Bodies on both sides could be seen scattered, silent, and cold on the sprawling Antietam battlefield near the Dunker church.

Yet hour after hour after hour, the men and guns blaze back and forth along Antietam Creek near the church. The savage and bloody combat continued for twelve hours of intense and often close-range fighting with muskets and cannons across the region, and finally, all those fine young men lay dead.

When darkness came, estimates of twenty thousand bodies on both sides could be seen on the desolate Antietam battlefield, not counting the wounded and missing. Both Yanks and Rebs regrouped to claim their dead and wounded.

Finally, Lee retreated. The North claimed a victory. The Confederates were pushed back but still not beaten.

The families at home read the casualty reports, fingers sliding down the columns of one, two, even three pages of fatalities and injuries, calling out names for neighbors who could not read for themselves. It was a sad day everywhere. Many parents, mothers, and wives were grief-stricken. Many children had become fatherless.

Figure 44: Lincoln and son Tad in 1863.

THE DEATH OF LITTLE WILLIE LINCOLN: The war took a terrible toll on President Lincoln, but the most crippling blow he suffered in the presidential mansion was the death of his eleven-year-old son, Willie. Lincoln and his wife grieved deeply over Willie's death.

The actual cause of death is not known, but a lack of proper sanitation could have been a factor. During the 1860s, Washington sewers were open, and a filthy canal brought the city's drinking water. Garbage was dumped into the ditch just a short distance from the president's house.

Willie grew sicker over the next two or three weeks. Lincoln never left the boy's side, sleeping and eating in a chair next to his bed. Doctors gave up hope for the child.

Death took Willie on the afternoon of the twentieth of February 1862. The East Room was the site of his funeral.

Lincoln accepted an offer from a friend, William Thomas Carroll, to place the body of Willie in one of the Carroll family tombs until Lincoln retired from the presidency and returned to live in Springfield. Lincoln returned to the cemetery the next day to watch as they moved the boy's body to the crypt in a remote area built into the side of a hill. It was a beautiful and peaceful spot. Lincoln returned to the tomb on at least two more occasions and had Willie's coffin re-opened. The President claimed he had to look upon his son's face just one last time. Lincoln tried to go on about his work, but his spirit was crushed. One week after the funeral, he closed himself up in his office all day and wept.

WATCH OUT! HERE COMES THE TRAIN: In the dark hours of the war, President Lincoln signed the Pacific Railroad Act. Fearing that the western states, led by California, might form a separate and independent coalition made it seem urgent. The act was the political plum of the age. Subsidies were generous: sixteen thousand dollars per mile for track laid in flat country and forty-eight thousand in the mountains. Land grants went to the railroad of six thousand four hundred acres per mile, later raised to more than twelve thousand acres for every mile of track laid. The networks linked every city before the war.

Railroads had a massive impact on the economic, social, and political development of the United States and on Americans. In the South, most railroads in 1860 were local affairs connecting cotton regions with the nearest waterway. Shipment previously was by boat, not rail. After the Union blockaded the ports in 1861 and seized the critical rivers in 1862, long-distance travel was difficult. While most of the fighting happened in the South, Yank raiders (and sometimes Confederates too) systematically destroyed bridges and rolling stock. They sometimes even bent the rails to hinder the logistics of their enemy.

THE WAR DRAGS ON: While North and South tore the country apart over state's rights, another war caused by empty soup pots began to brew.

ON THE VERGE OF STARVATION: The Sioux represent a confederacy of several tribes speaking three different dialects, the Lakota, Dakota, and Nakota. Throughout the late 1850s, treaty violations by the United States coupled with late annuity payments by Indian agents caused increasing hunger and hardship, especially among the Dakota.

Civil War expenses saw the government fall even more behind on its debts and delivery of food, leaving the Dakota on the verge of starvation. In turn, traders refused to provide any more supplies to the Dakota on credit, and negotiations reached an impasse. The Dakota had no way of feeding themselves. Their children were hungry.

The situation came to a head in Minnesota in the summer of 1862.

By August all the Sioux bands were famished and restless. They were angry at the US government over late payments of annuities and other empty promises. Called the Dakota Indian War of 1862, the natives made extensive attacks on hundreds of Minnesota settlers and immigrants, which resulted in settler deaths and caused many to flee the area. The Governor appointed Henry Sibley as a colonel in the state's military forces and commander of the army. He was assigned to march against the Dakota with four armed companies.

The five-week conflict had a profound impact on not only the Dakota tribe, but Native Americans across the nation. An intense desire for immediate revenge smoldered when soldiers captured hundreds of Dakota men and held almost sixteen hundred women, children, and elderly noncombatants.

They kept the prisoners in a stockade of two or three acres on the river bottom below Fort Snelling (Michigan). Many died in the harsh conditions. The next year, the army put the surviving Dakota captives from the Fort Snelling camp aboard steamers and took them to an even more desolate reservation at Crow Creek, in Dakota Territory.

A KANGAROO COURT: More than one thousand Dakota, also known as Teton or eastern Sioux, were jailed for their parts in the uprising. The defendants were not allowed legal representation. The trials were brief, some lasting less than five minutes. A military tribunal quickly tried the men, sentencing more than three hundred to death.

PRESIDENT LINCOLN INTERVENES: When President Lincoln learned of the number of condemned people, he took a step that outraged many. He requested transcripts of the trials, so he could personally review the evidence.

After reviewing more than three hundred records, the President commuted the sentences of all but thirty-eight of the condemned warriors. Minnesota officials hanged those Dakota men in the largest mass execution in US history. Lincoln and his lawyers concluded the other cases failed to meet reasonable standards of evidence or procedure. He upheld death sentences only when evidence showed the prisoners had either raped (two cases) or killed civilians (thirty-six), as opposed to merely having participated in the battle. Neither side felt happy with the result. The Indian people were bitter about the hangings, and many Minnesota settlers and voters elsewhere viewed Lincoln as forgiving unforgivable violence.

Lincoln wrote to Bishop Henry Whipple, *"If we get through this war, and I live, this Indian system shall be reformed."*

Next, Congress passed legislation making it illegal for the Dakota to live in Minnesota. It remains a law to this day. To ensure they drove the Dakota from Minnesota, officials created a bounty awarding money for every Dakota scalp turned in. How could that happen in our land of the free?

The aftermath of the US-Dakota War of 1862 also engulfed another tribe called the Ho-Chunk, also known as the Winnebago Indians, who were living along Blue Earth River at the time of the war. The desire of colonists to remove all Indians from Minnesota led to a similar bill to evict the Ho-Chunk. Although uninvolved in the conflict, this tribe resided on prime agricultural land that colonists wished to obtain.

HOMESTEADS IN THE WEST: May 20, 1862—The Homestead Act is approved, granting to settlers the family farms of one hundred sixty acres.

The land carved from Indian territories was up for grabs. Practically any adult over twenty-one, the head of a family, or a citizen who had never taken up arms against the US Government could apply. Women and immigrants who applied for citizenship were eligible.

The law required only a three-step procedure: file an application, improve the land, and register for the patent (deed). Some six hundred thousand farmers would soon receive a clear title to their own land.

LAND GRANT AGRICULTURAL COLLEGES: The first colleges established in America were to prepare ministers and to educate the upper classes. Examples of these early colleges are Harvard, William and Mary, Yale, and Princeton. The study of agriculture at these colleges was a rarity. Fathers taught their sons how to farm in the same manner their fathers had taught them. They needed different colleges to teach scientific agriculture.

On the seventh of July 1862, the Land Grant Act was approved, calling for public land sales to fund agricultural education and this eventually led to establishing state university systems. Congress donated thirty thousand acres of public land to each state for colleges; primary subjects would be agriculture and mechanics.

These land-grant colleges trained young people in farming methods, as well as agricultural experiment stations and an array of service agencies, all designed to further the education and welfare of independent farmers. However, farmers did not always trust the colleges and didn't see much value in what they were doing.

TURNING POINT OF WAR: By late 1862, the course of combat changed, taking on characteristics of total war where armies demoralize the enemy by destroying their resources.

In this type of conflict, troops make no distinction between civilian and military. The Union and Confederate forces moved toward total war, both sides at times crossing the lines between military and civilian targets.

BUYING AN ARMY SUBSTITUTE: with enlistments ending and fewer joining, Congress passed the Conscription Act, creating the first wartime draft of US citizens in American history. The act called for registration of all males between the ages of twenty and forty-five, including aliens who intended to become citizens.

Black men were excluded from the draft because they were not considered citizens, and wealthier white men could afford to pay for substitutes. It was becoming a poor man's war. Exemptions could be bought for three hundred dollars, or by hiring a substitute draftee. This clause led to bloody draft riots in New York City, where outraged citizens protested the exemptions as unfair.

Life was tense. People opened the morning papers with dread, for after every battle the long list of killed and wounded brought sadness to thousands of families on both sides of the Mason-Dixon line. Then came the flood of wounded and sick pouring back from the front to be cared for by an impoverished nation; thousands died in the hospitals, and thousands more were injured and maimed for life.

"A soldier's life," one veteran said, *"consisted of marching and misery."*

Most men on both sides were unaccustomed to the rigid nature of being a soldier, and the loss of personal freedom that came with being in the military proved to be an obstacle for most of them. Both armies were plagued by deserters, whose absence depleted the strength of their respective forces. Cowardice was defined as deserting in the face of the enemy.

Historians traditionally distinguish between stragglers—those soldiers who leave with the intention of returning—and deserters, who are absent without leave, or AWOL, for thirty days or more. By Christmas 1862 desertion rates were extremely high.

SOME SLAVES ARE FREE: Finally, in 1862, Lincoln signed the District of Columbia Emancipation Act freeing all enslaved persons in the nation's capital.

However, the war was far from over, and it was not going well for the North. Lincoln searched for a remedy. He thought about how the southern states used slaves to support their armies on the field and managed the home front so more men could go off to fight.

Up until then, the main focus of the war had been to preserve the nation. Lincoln presented an idea to his secretary of state, William Seward. The secretary agreed it was worth a try, but persuaded Lincoln to wait until the Yankee forces enjoyed a military victory.

And then it came. Fresh on the heels of the Union victory at Antietam (also known as the Battle of Sharpsburg), President Lincoln issued the preliminary Emancipation Proclamation. The legal paper stated all slaves in places of rebellion against the federal government would be free as of January 1, 1863. It changed the status under federal law of more than three and a half million enslaved African Americans in the Confederate states from slave to legally free.

With that proclamation, freedom for slaves became the legitimate war aim.

The decree only applied to the states in rebellion, and those states were not obedient to the US government, so it did not free a single slave. Still, this was a critical turning point, transforming the fight to preserve the nation into a battle for human freedom.

The proclamation authorized the recruitment of freed slaves and free blacks as Union soldiers. More than one hundred eighty thousand African Americans signed up for the army, and ten thousand in the navy. They made a vital contribution to Union victory while securing their freedom.

BATTLE OF GETTYSBURG: July 3, 1863—Anxious to move the war into northern territory, Lee's CSA forces invaded Pennsylvania where he faced the blue uniforms of Brigadier General John Buford. After three days of battle surrounding what was then the tiny town of Gettysburg, Union defenders turned back the infantry assault. Known in journals as Pickett's Charge, the battle is named after Major General George Pickett, one of three Confederate generals leading the assault.

WOMEN IN THE WAR: Wives in both the North and the South carried the responsibility of keeping the family together, running the farm, and operating a family business. Their spouses either volunteered or drew the military draft. In the northern states, women organized ladies' aid soci-

Figure 45: A little girl in a mourning dress.

This Daguerreotype is from about 1864, and the girl is holding a photo of a soldier in uniform, probably her deceased father.

eties to supply their troops with everything they needed. They baked and canned and planted fruit and vegetable gardens for the soldiers. They sewed and laundered uniforms, knitted socks and gloves, mended blankets and embroidered quilts and pillowcases. They organized door-to-door fundraising campaigns, county fairs and performances of all kinds to raise money for medical supplies and other necessities.

Almost one-third of all the soldiers who engaged at Gettysburg became casualties. In hospitals across the country thousands of women stepped in to serve as nurses. The treatment they provided to sick and wounded soldiers saved countless lives.

Women also ventured onto the battlefield, many changing their appearance so they could fight incognito for the cause they believed in. Others didn't want to be separated from their husbands, so they followed the Army, some working as laundresses, cooks, nurses, and even spies. They also acted as mothers and housekeepers—"havens in a heartless world"—for the soldiers under their care.

At field hospitals around Gettysburg, amputated limbs lay in heaps. Survivors collected bodies on the field and buried them near where they fell. Staggering losses injured both sides but hit hardest on the Confederates because the north possessed more money, hardware, and men. The numbers overwhelmed and numbed the citizens' capacity to respond.

White women in the South threw themselves into the war effort with the same zeal as their northern counterparts. The Confederacy had less money and fewer resources, so they did much of their work on their own or through local auxiliaries and relief societies. They, too, cooked and sewed for their boys. They provided uniforms, blankets, sandbags and other supplies for entire regiments. They wrote letters to soldiers and worked as untrained nurses in makeshift hospitals. They even cared for the wounded soldiers in their homes.

Many southern women, especially wealthy ones, relied on slaves for everything and had never had to do much work. However, they were forced by the exigencies of wartime to expand their definitions of "proper" female behavior.

THE ANGEL OF GETTYSBURG: Everyone in almost every occupational or social status found themselves affected by the war. For instance, Elizabeth Thorn's husband, Peter, became caretaker of Evergreen Cemetery in Gettysburg soon after their marriage. An archway with interior living space on each side for the caretakers formed a gateway into the cemetery grounds.

Elizabeth's parents lived on one side of the archway while Peter and Elizabeth lived on the other. When the war began, Peter was called into the 138th Pennsylvania Infantry, leaving cemetery duties to Elizabeth and her father. The burials were usually only a few each month, until the terrible battle that day on Cemetery Ridge. Elizabeth and her parents were told to leave, so they walked away with only the clothes on their backs to find somewhere to stay. At a farmhouse, Elizabeth pitched in to help bake bread to feed the hungry refugees coming through the area. When Peter's family returned the next day to the gatehouse, they found their hogs killed, windows shattered by gunfire, trunks they had carried to the cellar for safety now empty of belongings, the house filled with wounded men begging for water.

Figure 46: The Gatehouse at Gettysburg cemetery.

Outside, the townspeople had dumped "collateral damage" bodies of civilians killed in Gettysburg needing burial.

Elizabeth and her family left again to search for food. They had gone hungry for a couple of days when the family made their way back to the cemetery again. On arrival, they saw vast numbers of bodies stacked at the cemetery waiting for interment. Fifteen dead horses lay near the house, and nineteen other horses rotted on property nearby. The putrid smell of animal and human decay overpowered them. The house was in shambles. In her document Elizabeth described the scene this way: *"The beds and a dozen pillows we brought from the old country were not fit to use again. The legs of six soldiers had been amputated on the beds in our house and they were ruined with blood. We had to throw them away."*

The work of digging holes and burying the dead in the July heat came to Elizabeth, who was six months pregnant, and her aged father. Ultimately, they interred one hundred five war casualties. The Thorns received no compensation for damages. Elizabeth became known as the "Angel of Gettysburg," and a statue of her stands today in the cemetery.

THE GETTYSBURG ADDRESS: About fifty thousand soldiers from both armies were casualties in the three-day battle, the costliest fight in US history. The Battle of Gettysburg proved to be the "high watermark of the Confederacy." It was the last major push of Confederate forces into Union territory. Gettysburg remains a tribute to the men who fought and died on its fields. The battle played a significant part in retaining the character of the USA.

President Lincoln delivered his most memorable speech on this field. The Gettysburg Address begins: *"Fourscore and seven years ago, our fathers brought forth on this continent a new nation, conceived in liberty and dedicated to the proposition that all men are created equal. Now we are engaged in a great civil war ... ."*

And still, the war dragged on, and although all people may have been created equal, they were not treated equally.

SADNESS IN THE SOUTH: 1863 through 1864 was a sad and mournful year for the South. During the year, the Confederate cities of Vicksburg and Port Hudson were captured. Yanks held complete control over the Mississippi River while forcing Confederates out. In Richmond about five thousand people, mostly poor women, led a riot to protest the exorbitant price of bread.

General Thomas "Stonewall" Jackson, one of the South's most successful generals, was accidentally shot by friendly fire from the Eighteenth North Carolina Infantry Regiment. At a nearby field hospital, the surgeons amputated General Jackson's arm. They moved him to a second field hospital in Virginia, where he died at the age of thirty-nine.

CONFEDERATE TEARS: These years were especially difficult for CSA First Lady Varina Davis. She first faced the death of her father, followed by the death of her husband's close friend, General Jackson. She thought sadly of his unfortunate wife and infant daughter Julia. But the most profound blow was the loss of their son Joseph, age five, who climbed over a balcony railing and fell to his death on the bricks below. The loss of Joseph was just another tragedy in the life of Jefferson Davis, whose four sons all preceded him in death.

In almost every village and city on both battlefronts the Ladies Aid Society women scraped cotton to make lint for packing wounds and knit socks to keep a soldier's feet warm and dry. They made bandages, found clothing, knitted mittens, collected provisions, clothing, and blankets for the soldiers. Two large charitable societies, the Sanitary Commission and the Christian Commission, moved donations to the front and distributed them to the needy.

ARLINGTON NATIONAL CEMETERY: On a Virginia hillside rising above the Potomac River and overlooking Washington, DC, stands Arlington House. The nineteenth-century mansion seems out of place amid the more than two hundred fifty-thousand military grave sites that stretch out around it.

The mansion, intended as a living memorial to George Washington, was owned and constructed by his adopted grandson, George Washington Parke "Wash" Custis.

Wash's only child, Mary Anna Randolph Custis, married her childhood friend and distant cousin, Robert E. Lee. Mary Anna inherited the mansion and lived there with her husband and children until the war changed everything.

Once Virginia seceded and became a Confederate state, US Army soldiers took possession of the mansion, and Mary Anna had to leave.

Throughout the war, federal troops used the land as a camp. They turned it into a headquarters with forts, incorporated into the defenses of Washington, DC. They appropriated the grounds for use as a military cemetery, as a purpose to render the house undesirable should the Lee family ever attempt to return. They never did.

LADIES' FASHIONS: Patterns for ladies' dresses were first manufactured in 1863, by Ebenezer Butterick of Massachusetts. He sold them through the stores and also by mail. Previously, dressmakers and sewing ladies had to create their own patterns by trying to imitate dresses shown in pictures of stylish women or on the miniature dressmaker dolls.

WORTHLESS GREENBACKS: The federal government began issuing paper currency during the Civil War. As photographic technology of the day could not reproduce color, they decided to print the back of the bills in some color other than black. Because the color green stood as a symbol of stability, it was selected. These "greenbacks" started a tradition of printing the back of US paper money in green.

People had to get accustomed to new kinds of money. The banks suspended money in coin in December 1861; gold and silver went out of circulation. For a few months, the only "money" was sticky postage stamps. In 1862 the new legal tender appeared, yet the greenbacks quickly began to drop in value. Of course, the Confederate currency was worthless also.

PRISON CAMPS IN THE SOUTH: The North ended prisoner exchanges because the Confederates refused to acknowledge black troops as soldiers. They refused to treat them as POWs or exchange them, so the camps were overfilled and under-supplied. The Confederate commissary was so poorly managed, a lack of supplies prevailed everywhere. Everyone was hungry, especially in the prisons where prisoners starved.

Andersonville, or Camp Sumter as it was known officially in Georgia, became the most notorious Confederate prison. That one held more prisoners at any given time than any of the other southern prison camps. Overcrowded to four times its capacity, Andersonville had an inadequate water supply, inadequate food rations, and unsanitary conditions. In the fourteen months of its existence, more than thirteen thousand Union captives died. The chief causes of death were scurvy, diarrhea, and dysentery.

PRISON CAMPS IN THE NORTH: Conditions at prisoner-of-war camps weren't much better. Camp Rathbun at Elmira, NY, saw nearly three thousand rebel soldiers die of disease and cold. Known among its inmates as "*Hellmira,*" the camp posted a mortality rate of almost twenty-five percent. Both sides were short of food. Even at the front, food for the troops was chiefly cornmeal, sometimes with the cob ground in with the corn for filler.

SHERMAN'S MARCH TO THE SEA: In an attempt to cut the railroad supply route, in the summer of 1864 General William Tecumseh Sherman led some sixty thousand soldiers on a two-hundred-fifty-mile march from Atlanta to Savannah, Georgia. His forces followed a "scorched earth" policy, destroying military targets as well as industry, infrastructure, and civilian property, disrupting the Confederacy's economy and its transportation networks.

ATLANTA BURNING: By the end of September 1864, Sherman held Atlanta. On November 15, 1864, Union forces led by Sherman destroyed three thousand buildings, including businesses, hospitals, homes, and schools. As Atlanta still lay smoldering, Sherman and his troops began their audacious march to the sea. The fall of Atlanta increased the odds that Abraham Lincoln would be re-elected president on the Republican Party platform to preserve the nation and abolish slavery.

Sherman's purpose in his infamous March to the Sea was to frighten Georgia's civilian population into abandoning the Confederate cause. The Yankees stole food and livestock, burned the houses and barns of people who tried to fight back. They "drove old Dixie down," wrecking three hundred miles of railroad, numerous bridges, uncounted miles of telegraph lines. The Yankee soldiers seized five thousand horses, four thousand mules, and thirteen thousand head of cattle from the farmers. They confiscated close to ten million pounds of corn and ten million pounds of fodder. The army destroyed uncounted cotton gins and mills belonging to the southerners and left them desolate.

Sherman's army reduced their need for traditional supply lines by "living off the land" when they ran out of rations. Foragers seized food from local farms for the Army. They left a starving citizenry in the South. The March attracted a massive number of refugees. One historian estimated ten thousand liberated slaves followed Sherman's army, while hundreds died of hunger, disease, or exposure along the way. The operation broke the back of the Confederacy and helped lead to the eventual surrender.

MARCHING SONGS: Soldiers sang many tunes during the march, such as "John Brown's Body," and "The Battle Hymn of the Republic," with soldiers improvising and adding verses as they went along. One ballad written afterward came to symbolize the campaign: "Marching Through Georgia." Written from the point of view of a Union soldier, the lyrics detail freeing slaves and punishing the South for starting the war.
The chorus went like this:

> *Hurrah! Hurrah! We bring the Jubilee.*
> *Hurrah! Hurrah! The flag that makes you free,*
> *So, we sang the chorus from Atlanta to the sea,*
> *While we were marching through Georgia.*

SAVANNAH AS A CHRISTMAS GIFT: By the end of the year, the Yanks held Savannah. Sherman telegraphed President Lincoln, *"I beg to present you as a Christmas gift the City of Savannah, with one hundred and fifty guns and plenty of ammunition, also about twenty-five thousand bales of cotton."*

The South has long reviled Sherman's memory. He may have been a hero up North, but they cursed his name below the Mason-Dixon line. The southerners considered this the War of Northern Aggression while the Yanks called it the War of Southern Rebellion. Even the battles had different names recorded in military records for each side. Like everything else in this life, it all depends on perspective.

THE SLAVES ARE FREE: By the eighteenth of December 1865, the required three-quarters of the states ratified the Thirteenth Amendment, which ensured "neither slavery nor involuntary servitude ... shall exist within the United States." While the blacks were now free and offered equality, at least on paper, such treatment did not extend to the Native Americans nor women. And still, the war went on.

THE WORST OF TIMES: Citizens expressed their anger and resentment in many destructive ways, from "draft riots" in the north, to savage mobs hunting down and stoning to death dozens of harmless Negroes and white people in the south. They senselessly burned asylums, attacked police stations and armories. Federal troops put down the mobs by musket and bayonet, killing at least a thousand citizens. It was a distressing time for everyone.

Circumstances were worse in the South, where citizens lived in dire poverty. They had drafted every able-bodied man between sixteen and seventy into the army. General Grant said, *"They robbed both the cradle and the grave."*

LONG WALK OF THE NAVAJO: January 1864—While citizens were continuing to kill each other in the War, the US Army relocated bands of Navajo people from their traditional lands in eastern Arizona Territory and western New Mexico Territory to Fort Sumner in the Pecos River valley, now in New Mexico. At least two hundred Navajo died along the mournful three-hundred-mile trek, requiring almost three weeks travel on foot.

SAND CREEK MASSACRE: November 29, 1864—Meanwhile, Black Kettle's band of Cheyenne and Arapaho Indians had been promised safety at their camp between the Arkansas River and Sand Creek in southeastern Colorado Territory near Fort Lyon.

Black Kettle flew a US flag, with a white flag tied beneath it, over his lodge to show he was friendly, just as the Fort Lyon commander had advised him. Only about seventy-five men, mostly too old or too young to hunt, plus all the women and children remained in the village with twenty to thirty warriors to protect them. The natives, lacking artillery, were not prepared to offer resistance.

Some atrocities are simply too horrifying to understand. Army Colonel John Chivington, a Methodist preacher more than six feet tall, a Freemason, and an opponent of slavery, led more than four hundred men of the Third Colorado Cavalry in an attack on the sleeping camp. A few months before the attack while addressing a gathering of church deacons, Chivington dismissed the possibility of making a treaty with the Cheyenne: *"It simply is not possible for Indians to obey or even understand any treaty. I am fully satisfied, gentlemen, that to kill them is the only way we will ever have peace and quiet in Colorado."*

Chivington gave the order. Two officers refused to obey and told their men to hold fire, but the rest ignored the white flag and murdered as many Cheyenne as they could. The number killed varies from seventy-five to five hundred, depending on whose report you read. Black Kettle, the Cheyenne chief who had raised the flag in a futile gesture of fellowship, survived the massacre, carrying his badly wounded wife from the field and straggling east across the wintry plains.

During the attack, Indians took shelter in the high banks along Sand Creek. As they fled, many were killed and wounded by artillery fire. Some of the natives managed to slip horses from the camp's herd and flee up Sand Creek to a nearby Cheyenne camp on the headwaters of the Smokey Hill River. Most, on foot, were shot down.

In testimony before a congressional committee investigating the massacre, Chivington claimed he killed as many as five to six hundred Indian warriors alone.

Before Chivington and his men left the area, they plundered the teepees and killed the horses. After the smoke cleared, Chivington's men went back and murdered many of the wounded. They also scalped many of the dead—women, children and infants. Chivington and his men decorated their weapons, hats, and gear with scalps and other body parts, including human fetuses and male and female genitalia. Chivington escaped court-martial because he had already resigned from the military. But his once-promising career was over.

Sand Creek was the My Lai of its day, a war crime exposed by soldiers and condemned by the US government. It fueled decades of war on the Great Plains. The site on Sand Creek is now a national historic site in Colorado.

After the brutal slaughter of those who supported peace, many of the Cheyenne, including the great warrior Roman Nose, joined the Dog Soldiers. Several Arapaho men joined them. They sought revenge on settlers throughout the Platte valley, including an 1865 attack on what later was known as Fort Casper, Wyoming.

A SUDDEN REPLACEMENT: In 1864, Lincoln faced the challenge of re-election with the war still raging. He decided, unbeknownst to his first-term vice president, Hannibal Hamlin of Maine, to replace him with a southern War Democrat. He picked Andrew Johnson.

THOSE PESKY POLITICAL PARTIES: During the Civil War, the Democratic Party in the North split into two factions: War Democrats and Peace Democrats, often called Copperheads.

Copperheads opposed the war and advocated a negotiated peace with concessions to the South.

The War Democrats demanded a more aggressive policy toward the Confederacy. To attract War Democrats to their side, the Republican Party and some Democrats created the National Union Party before the general election of November 1864.

LINCOLN'S SECOND TERM: This presidential campaign happened in the middle of the Civil War. Lincoln, elected to his first term as a Republican, ran for his second term under the National Union banner. He won against his former top Civil War general, Democrat George B. McClellan.

By the time of Lincoln's second inauguration, the war was winding down. For four

Figure 47: Abraham Lincoln campaigns for a second term.

heart-breaking, hellacious years, more than seven hundred thousand citizens of the United States of America perished to solve the state's rights issues surrounding slavery.

They fought all across the nation at battlefields like Gettysburg and Vicksburg, with the Confederacy finally losing the contest because of attrition, and by Abraham Lincoln's bold decision to emancipate the slaves.

The 1860s witnessed first the tearing apart and then the binding together of a nation that seemed forever torn in two. School children later learned the rhyme:

> *In '61 the war had begun,*
> *In '62 'twas halfway through,*
> *In '63 the slaves were free,*
> *In '64 the war was almost o'er.*

A STILLNESS AT APPOMATTOX: April 9, 1865—CSA General Robert E. Lee, as commander-in-chief of Confederate forces, surrendered his twenty-seven-thousand-man army to USA General Ulysses S. Grant. They conducted the surrender at a private home in a rural town named Appomattox Court House, Virginia, effectively ending the conflict. The two men had not seen each other face-to-face in almost two decades.

Well-dressed in a new gray uniform with a red sash around his waist over which he buckled a sword with ornate scabbard and handle, General Lee wore boots spit-shined to a mirror polish as he waited for Grant to arrive.

In contrast, Grant arrived at the McLean house in a mud-spattered uniform; a government-issue sack coat with trousers tucked into muddy boots, no sidearms, and with only his tarnished shoulder straps showing his rank.

This is still how Grant is remembered—as a general, not as a president. He might have strength in his soul, but no grace, little culture, and no evidence of self-doubt.

When Grant arrived, he and Lee greeted each other. Then Lee returned to the chair where he had been waiting near an unlit fireplace. Grant chose a chair in the middle of the room.

Grant found it hard to get to the point of the meeting. The two generals briefly discussed their only previous encounter, back during the Mexican American War. Lee brought the attention back to the issue at hand. The historic meeting lasted only about an hour and a half.

CONDITIONS OF SURRENDER: The officers were allowed to keep their sidearms, private horses, and baggage. Each officer and every man received permission to return to their homes not to be disturbed by United States authority so long as they observed their paroles and the laws in force where they lived.

One of the officers said he remembered it like this: *"Before us in proud humiliation stood the embodiment of manhood: men whom neither toils and sufferings, nor the fact of death, nor disaster, nor hopelessness could bend from their resolve; standing before us now thin, worn and famished but erect, and with eyes looking level into ours, waking memories that bound us together as no other bond."*

Within a month of Lee's surrender, the remainder of Confederate forces gave up the fight. Anticipating the war's conclusion, Lincoln pushed a moderate view of Reconstruction. He hoped to reunite the nation speedily through a policy of reconciliation in the face of lingering and bitter divisiveness.

Polls show Lincoln is the most admired president, but those four traumatic years of his presidency significantly changed the course of the country's history as well as our ancestors' lives.

LINCOLN'S RE-ELECTION: Abraham Lincoln built the Republican Party into a strong national organization. Further, he rallied most of the northern Democrats. Lincoln chose Andrew Johnson as a running mate because of his loyalty to the Union and his success in serving as Tennessee's wartime military governor. Lincoln and Johnson ran as a team on the National Union ticket in 1864, the only time a Republican and a Democrat ever shared an election ballot.

Lincoln never used the ruthless tactics of modern campaign managers, but he could play hardball when he had to. He needed all the help he could get in his faltering re-election bid. His primary support came from soldiers and those who continued to believe in the war. Fourteen states allowed soldiers to vote where they were stationed. Eleven states did not, and one of those was Indiana, where Lincoln was strong.

He sent a letter to General William Tecumseh Sherman asking him to allow any soldiers he could spare to go home to vote. One week before the election, officers granted leave to all enlisted men in hospitals or otherwise unfit for field duty. The men were transported to and from their homes. The soldiers knew they were voting against their own self-interest; prolonging their personal risk, and length of wartime service. Still, they voted for the man they had come to respect.

Lincoln was re-elected by a wide margin of two hundred twenty-one to twenty-one electoral votes, with fifty-five percent of the popular vote.

Abraham Lincoln was the first president to be photographed at his inauguration. Oddly enough, his future assassin, John Wilkes Booth, can also be seen in the same photo.

LINCOLN'S ASSASSINATION: On the fourteenth of April in 1865, less than two months after his second inauguration, and five days after the surrender of General Robert E. Lee, Lincoln was filled with joy. The day was Good Friday. The war was ending. The killing could finally stop. He thought it was a very good Friday.

He put on his silk top hat, recently purchased from Washington hat maker J. Y. Davis. Lincoln had personalized the hat with a black silk mourning band in memory of his son Willie. With the president and his wife were their guests, Major Henry Rathbone, and his fiancée, Clara Harris. The two couples went to the Ford Theatre to see the comedy play, *Our American Cousin.*

Lincoln, with his wife and guests, arrived a few minutes late and came up the stairs to the president's box. The orchestra broke into a performance of *"Hail to The Chief."* The actors suspended the play a moment and gave a tribute to Lincoln before continuing.

In the balcony, the President and his guests laughed at the show along with the audience—not suspecting a fiend lurked just behind their balcony door armed with both a gun and a knife.

At a moment of laughter, actor John Wilkes Booth, a Confederate sympathizer, quietly pushed open the door and fired his Derringer at the back of the President's head. Rathbone jumped up to grapple with Booth and felt a Bowie knife slicing deep into his left arm from shoulder to elbow, opening an artery.

Booth leaped from the balcony onto the stage, an eleven-foot drop, for his final appearance on the Ford Theatre stage. He held his bloody dagger high in the air and cried out, *"The South is avenged."* He escaped through the stage door, in spite of having injured his leg in the jump. A boy waited just outside, holding Booth's horse.

A doctor in the audience rushed over to examine the paralyzed president. Friends carried Lincoln across the street to Petersen's Boarding House, where he died early the next morning.

The president was no stranger to death threats. Later, they found a folder in his desk, labeled "A" for assassination and filled with the notes. Still, the entire country grieved the death of Abraham Lincoln. As the nine-car funeral train carried him home for burial in Springfield, Illinois, people showed up at train stations all along the way to pay their respects.

WHAT ABOUT BOOTH? Booth belonged to one of America's most renowned families of actors. His brother Edwin was widely regarded as the country's leading actor, as was their father, Junius Brutus Booth. John Wilkes Booth was an acclaimed performer in his own right, celebrated for his charisma, athleticism, and dashing good looks and he had been featured at Ford's Theatre more than once. He promised his mother he would not fight for the Confederacy, although he passionately supported slavery.

A CONSPIRACY TO KILL: Washington, DC, stands on the north bank of the Potomac River that once separated the North from the South, and lay closer to the Confederate capital of Richmond than to northern cities like Philadelphia or New York. Many southern sympathizers lived there, several of Ford's Theatre employees among them. Booth was not performing that night, but no matter. He had played Ford's Theatre so often he knew the layout backstage very well.

Booth was disappointed that General U. S. Grant did not join Lincoln that night. The General had accepted Lincoln's invitation, but declined at the last minute. According to a descendant, Julia Grant had recently been the victim of Mary Lincoln's acid tongue, and Mrs. Grant wanted no part of a night on the town with the first lady. Grant backed out, citing the couple's desire to travel to New Jersey to see their children.

Booth did not act alone. "Wanted" posters appeared everywhere, offering a reward for the arrest of Booth and his accomplices. Booth and his conspirators plotted to kill not only Lincoln, but Grant, Secretary of State William Seward, and Vice President Andrew Johnson that night.

At the same moment Booth was shooting Lincoln at the Ford Theatre, Lewis Powell stormed Seward's house and repeatedly stabbed the cabinet member, who was bedridden after a near-fatal carriage accident. Seward somehow survived the savage attack. VP Johnson's would-be killer spent the evening getting drunk and eventually lost his nerve. He never made it to the vice president's rooms in the Willard Hotel, so Johnson was not harmed and was sworn in as president a few hours after Lincoln's death.

The conspirators were all captured, including Dr. Samuel Mudd, who had treated Booth's injured leg but may not have known he was the assassin.

THE AFTERMATH: US soldiers shot and killed Booth twelve days later at a farm in rural northern Virginia. A military tribunal in Washington, DC, tried and found guilty eight others implicated in Lincoln's death.

Four were hanged, including Mary Surratt, the first woman executed by the federal government. Mary's husband, a drunk who died of a stroke in 1862, had left the family in financial difficulty, so she opened her home to lodgers. A devout Catholic, the widow and her adult children were known to be Confederate sympathizers. Some claimed the Surratt boarding house was a safe house for Confederate spies. They found Mary Surratt guilty of abetting, aiding, concealing, counseling, and harboring her co-defendants.

Historians have conflicting views regarding Surratt's innocence. She repeatedly insisted she was not guilty, but more than a thousand people, including government officials, members of the US armed forces, friends and family of the accused, official witnesses, and reporters, watched her die by hanging.

ANDREW JOHNSON, PRESIDENT: Vice President Andrew Johnson became the seventeenth president on the assassination of Abraham Lin-

Figure 48: The Hanging of Mary Suratt

The suspected conspirators in the Lincoln Assassination trial are hanged in the south Arsenal yard in Washington DC. Ticketholders came to watch the deaths of Mary Surratt, Lewis Powell, David Herold, and George Atzerodt on 7 July 1865.

coln. When he was in Tennessee, Andrew Johnson was the only sitting senator from a Confederate state who did not resign upon learning of his state's secession. Johnson remained firmly with the Union. However, after Abraham Lincoln's election in 1860, he was threatened with ruin when Tennessee seceded. The state confiscated Johnson's property, and drove his wife and two daughters out of the state.

Johnson didn't have an easy time in childhood either. His father had died young, leaving the family penniless. Because of poverty, few written records exist of his early life.

Andrew and his brother William were apprenticed to a local tailor where they learned the trade as well as essential reading and writing skills. The boys were not happy in servitude, so they ran away. The pair dodged authorities who sought to return them to their employer.

They found work as itinerant tailors. Andrew moved to Greeneville, Tennessee, and established a very successful tailoring business.

Later he made all of his own suits as president.

RECONSTRUCTION: The process to bring the seceded southern states back is known as Reconstruction.

US troops occupied the former Confederate states under supervision of federal governors from *1865 to 1877*. If you had family living in one of the former Confederate states, this is good to know.

In the twelve years after the Civil War—the era of Reconstruction—massive changes appeared in American culture, economy, and politics.

Born in a log cabin in Raleigh, North Carolina, Johnson was the only president to have truly come up from poverty, and he was also the first president impeached.

As president, in a strange twist often found in history, the racist Johnson had to oversee Reconstruction of

Figure 49: Andrew Johnson

Our seventeenth president completed the unexpired term of Abraham Lincoln from 1865 to 1869.

Vice President: none.

the South, including giving the vote to former black slaves and other civil rights. Johnson, known for his uncontrollable temper, had to put a divided country back together with no support from either side.

There are only a few times in American history, other than during Reconstruction, where lasting hatred of another group of the same culture of people has occurred. Johnson pardoned thirteen thousand five hundred former Confederates, more pardons than any president offered before or since. He favored quick restoration of the seceded states to the Union, but his plans did not protect former slaves.

The Confederacy attempted to appease many of the requirements set forth by Congress to become states in good standing again. The southerners were not willing, though, to grant rights to former slaves. This unwillingness culminated in the impeachment of President Andrew Johnson and the beginning of a period called Radical Reconstruction in 1867, which was controlled by the Radical Republicans and by Congress.

RADICAL RECONSTRUCTION: Radical Republicans wanted to enact sweeping transformations of southern social and economic life, permanently ending the old planter-class system.

EXCEPT FOR TENNESSEE: The first Reconstruction act divided the states of the former Confederacy, except for Tennessee, into five military districts under the rule of former Union generals. Johnson's home state of Tennessee had many Union supporters and met most of the demands.

The districts effectively put those states under military control from March 1867 until January 1877. During the military rule, white men, most of them native Virginians, filled nearly all the public offices.

- First Military District (Virginia)
- Second Military District (North Carolina, South Carolina)
- Third Military District (Georgia, Alabama, and Florida)
- Fourth Military District (Arkansas and Mississippi)
- Fifth Military District (Texas and Louisiana)

Although Kentucky was not subject to reconstruction as such, the period of readjustment following the Civil War was a troubled one for them also. Violence begun by guerrillas continued for years. Also, white "Regulators" tried to terrorize the new freedmen and keep them in a perpetual state of fearful submission that would assure the agricultural labor supply.

TAKING CARE OF WIDOWS AND ORPHANS: Union soldiers were covered for pensions under the federal system, while each former Confederate state had to create and fund its own pension system. In a change from previous conflicts, African American veterans became eligible for pensions from the very beginning.

Later, the pensioners included women, both as widows and as veterans (primarily nurses). Orphaned children could receive assistance, although the process was daunting and time-consuming. Each category had its own set of eligibility rules. Benefit limits changed dramatically over time and amounts were affected by politics on both sides of the Mason-Dixon Line.

THE PENSIONS FOR YANKS: For Union soldiers, the pension system began in 1862. Soldiers disabled as a result of their service could apply for a pension; the amount of allowance depended on their rank and their injury. Dependents (widows and children) of soldiers killed on duty were also eligible.

No one got rich from these early pensions. A "totally disabled" private received just eight dollars a month from the first pension system, but amounts increased as the country needed to recruit soldiers to a war that was no longer popular or easy. Pensions served as recruiting tools. Under this system, pension money could be collected from the date of discharge if they filed their claim within one year. However, if they waited for some time to file, pension payments could only begin on the date of application. The federal government began paying pension payments as early as 1861 to Union veterans.

NO PENSIONS FOR REBS: Ex-Confederate soldiers had to apply to the individual states in which they served during the war, even though pensions paid to former veterans were to be paid by the state in which the vet resided. It was not until the 1890s that all former Confederate states created and funded their own state pension programs. Before that, veterans' homes for the indigent and artificial limbs were all the states had to offer these former soldiers.

A NEW PARTY IN THE MAKING: When Congress convened in December of 1865, the southerners elected representatives including Alexander Stephens of Georgia, the former vice president of the Confederacy, along with four former CSA generals, eight colonels, six cabinet members, and numerous lesser-known rebels.

The furious northern congressmen removed the southerners from the roll call and denied seats in Congress to all representatives from the eleven former Confederate states. President Johnson made matters worse by attempting to form a new political party, the National Union Party, to include the southerners. However, his rude, gruff behavior toward his political opponents alienated those who heard him. Many began to believe Johnson's supporters were all ex-rebels.

JOHNSON'S IMPATIENCE: President Johnson favored granting full citizenship to former slaves, including voting rights. The war was over and he wanted it done immediately. However, the Radicals took control, passing a series of Acts—each one over the president's veto—adding restrictive requirements for southern states. Andrew Johnson was no Abraham Lincoln. The graceless Johnson was a heavy drinker, and his peers said that even during his rare stretches of sobriety, he was still a cantankerous loudmouth.

THE IMPEACHMENT OF PRESIDENT JOHNSON: As the conflict between the branches of government grew, Congress passed the Tenure of Office Act, restricting Johnson's ability to fire cabinet officials. When he persisted in trying to dismiss Secretary of War Edwin Stanton, the House of Representatives charged the president with "high crimes and misdemeanors," and impeached him. He escaped removal from office by a single vote short of the required two-thirds after his trial in the Senate, but he was so disgraced he was denied his party's nomination that year.

Impeachment is only a formal statement of charges. Not convicted of any crime, the temperamentally tumultuous Andrew Johnson remained in office to finish his term.

THE POWER OF A POCKET VETO: Both the Senate and House of Representatives met in separate, large "chambers" on the second floor of the Capitol Building. The Constitution mandates that both houses meet jointly at least once a year. Each Congress usually has two sessions, since members of the House of Representatives serve two-year terms. Congress' vacation traditionally comes in August, when representatives adjourn for a month-long summer break.

If a president receives a bill within ten days of Congressional adjournment and does not sign it, he has issued a pocket veto. The bill may or may not be reconsidered by Congress when it reconvenes. In a final move to outmaneuver President Johnson, Congress voted to remain permanently in session. Lack of adjournment deprived Andrew Johnson even of the power of the pocket veto. He became a powerless president.

KU KLUX KLAN: December 24, 1866—As civil rights for freed slaves emerged from the Civil War Era, the Ku Klux Klan formed secretly to discourage blacks from voting. The Klan, as an American white supremacist hate group, brought in a brutal and shameful era of terror and crime in the war-ravaged southern states. The despicable Klan has existed in three distinct periods during the history of the United States. First, in the late 1860s, second in 1915, and third after 1950. In each era, membership was secret and estimates of the total were highly exaggerated by both friends and enemies.

WELCOME TO ALASKA: March 30, 1867—Secretary of State William H. Seward completed the purchase of Alaska from Russia for seven point two million dollars, approximately two cents per acre.

PRESIDENTIAL ELECTION OF 1868: Amid Johnson's impeachment trial in May, the Republicans held their national convention. They unanimously selected Ulysses S. Grant, an immensely popular military man. As a commanding general in 1865, Grant led the Union Armies to victory over the Confederacy. He continued his service under Lincoln's successor President Andrew Johnson, who promoted Grant to General of the Army in 1866.

Disillusioned by the president's conservative approach to Reconstruction, Grant drifted toward the Radical Republicans, a faction committed to the emancipation of the slaves and later to equal treatment.

The Radical Republicans unanimously nominated Grant as their candidate for president on the first ballot at the convention. Their platform supported black suffrage in the South as part of the passage to full citizenship for former slaves. As a concession, they decided to let the northern states decide for themselves whether to give the vote to people of color.

Grant's opposition, Horatio Seymour, governor of New York, became the Democratic candidate for president. However, Seymour received only eighty electoral votes to Grant's two hundred fourteen.

GRANT IS IN, UNDER A FAKE NAME: A new president with a false name, U. S. Grant, won the presidency in 1868. The congressman who introduced Grant believed, mistakenly, that the candidate's first name was Ulysses and his middle name was Simpson (his mother's maiden name). Grant, born Hiram Ulysses, never amended the error and went on to accept Ulysses S. Grant as his real name. At 46, he was the youngest president of the nineteenth century in 1868.

THE BATTLE OF THE WASHITA: Grant had been elected but not yet sworn in, when trouble erupted again on the plains. The peace chief Black Kettle and others of his Southern Cheyenne tribe who managed to escape the 1864 massacre at Sand Creek in Colorado were camped in Indian Territory (later Oklahoma). By early November 1868, Black Kettle's camp of about sixty lodges joined other tribal bands at the Washita River. Black Kettle's village was the western-most of a series of winter camps of Cheyenne, Arapaho, Kiowa, Comanche, and Apache bands, running ten to fifteen miles along the Washita River in western Indian Territory.

On November 26, the tribal council decided they would send out runners to talk with the soldiers once the foot-deep snow cleared. They wanted to clear up any misunderstandings and reaffirm that Black

Figure 50: General U.S. Grant is nominated for president.

Kettle's people wanted peace. Meanwhile, they decided to move downriver the next morning to be closer to other tribal camps.

However, General Philip Sheridan, in command of the US Army's Department of the Missouri, had already decided upon a winter campaign against the Cheyenne. While challenging, a winter campaign offered chances for decisive results. If the Indians' shelter, food, and livestock could be destroyed or captured, not only the warriors but also their women and children would be at the mercy of the Army and the elements. The tribe would be forced to surrender.

Sheridan recalled General George A. Custer, who had been court martialed, and suspended from the army for a year for disobeying orders. Sheridan wanted Custer to lead the campaign in driving the Southern Plains tribes onto reservations. Sheridan's standing orders to Custer were, *"To kill all the warriors, capture all the women and children, destroy all camps and material goods, and kill all the ponies."*

CUSTER ATTACKS AT DAYBREAK: Custer commanded Seventh Cavalry forces against the various bands on the Washita River. Custer's troops followed a trail to Black Kettle's village, where Custer divided his army into four parts, moving each into position so at first light of morning they could simultaneously converge on the camp.

At daybreak, Double Wolf awoke and heard the horses' hoofbeats as the Army columns began their attack. Wolf fired his gun to alert his people, but he was among the first to die in the charge. The Cheyenne warriors stumbled out of their lodges to take cover behind trees and in deep ravines. They tried to draw the soldiers away from women and children.

But the Indians were no match for the sudden charge of well-armed soldiers. This time the soldiers killed Black Kettle and his wife, and most of the villagers, too.

"Ben" Clark, the highly regarded scout and guide attached to the Seventh Cavalry, recalled seeing women and children murdered at the Washita: *"The regiment galloped through the tepees ... firing indiscriminately and killing men and women alike,"* he said. One cavalry unit was seen pursuing *"a group of women and children,"* shooting and *"killing them without mercy."*

Lieutenant Edward Godfrey also observed soldiers made no effort *"to prevent hitting women during the attack."* About fifty women and children survived, were taken captive, and marched through the snow to Fort

Dodge in Kansas and on to Fort Hays where they were held as prisoners in an "Indian corral" until the Cheyenne nation surrendered the next year.

Sensing trouble on the plains, a group of New York pastors met with Grant and advised him not to abandon his "peace" policy to satisfy a money-starved public. That *"would be a blow to the cause of Christianity throughout the world,"* they said. The *New York Herald* reported the president assured the clergymen he would never abandon the peace policy. That was quite a contradiction to actuality.

THE BLACK HILLS GOLD: Grant engineered the breach of the treaty signed in 1868 between the Lakotas and the United States, to accommodate miners seeking gold in the Black Hills. It was not a good thing to do to the Lakota and would be the cause of an issue in the next decade.

THE GOLDEN SPIKE: On the tenth of May in 1869, at Promontory, Utah, Governor Leland Stanford pounded in a ceremonial golden spike to celebrate the nation's first transcontinental railway.

Former President Franklin Pierce's 1855 dream of a transcontinental railroad had come true.

The railroad companies had a difficult time finding semi-skilled labor. Most Caucasians in California preferred to work in the mines or agriculture. The railroad experimented by hiring local emigrant Chinese as manual laborers, many of whom were escaping the poverty and terrors of what was happening in their homeland.

When they proved themselves as workers, the Central Pacific (CPRR) from that point forward preferred to hire Chinese, and even set up recruiting efforts in Canton. Despite their small stature and lack of experience, the Chinese laborers were responsible for most of the heavy manual labor since only a very limited amount of that work could be done by animals, simple machines, or black powder. Most of these Chinese workers were represented by a Chinese "boss" who translated, collected salaries for his crew, kept discipline, and relayed orders from an American general supervisor.

The railroad also hired some black people escaping the aftermath of the Civil War. Most of the black and white workers were paid thirty dollars per month and given food and lodging. Most Chinese were initially paid thirty-one dollars a month and provided lodging, but they preferred to cook their own meals.

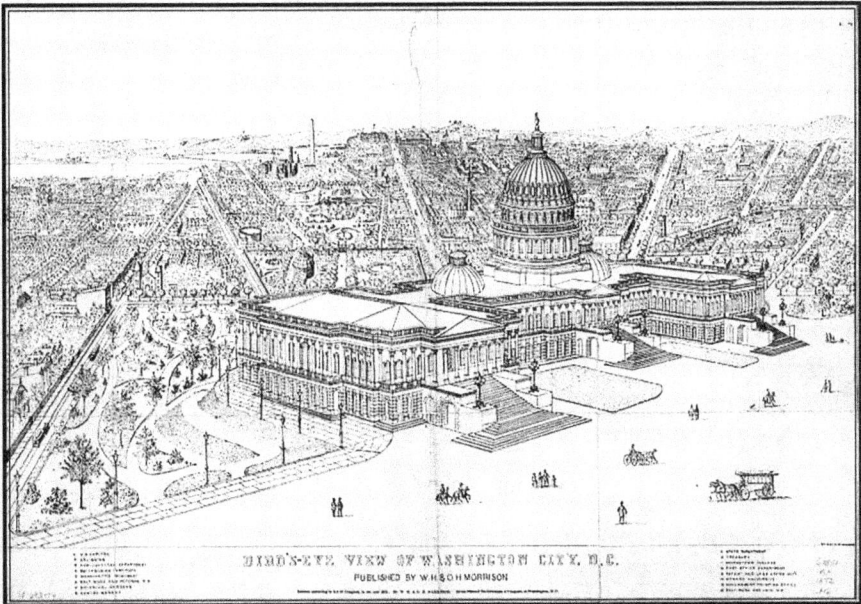

Figure 51: Washington, DC, in 1872.

The original building was completed in 1800 and was subsequently expanded, particularly with the addition of the massive dome. Both its east and west elevations are formally referred to as fronts, though only the east front was intended for the reception of visitors and dignitaries.

By 1850, it became clear the Capitol could not accommodate the growing number of legislators arriving from newly admitted states. Two new wings were added—a new chamber for the House of Representatives on the south side, and a new chamber for the Senate on the north.

The majority of the Union Pacific track across the Nebraska and Wyoming territories was built by veterans of both armies, as well as many recent immigrants. Almost all of the roadbed work had to be done manually, using shovels, picks, axes, two-wheeled dump carts, wheelbarrows, ropes, scrapers, etc., with initially only black powder available for blasting. Carts pulled by mules and horses were about the only labor-saving devices available. Lumber and ties were usually provided by independent contractors, woodcutters who cut, hauled, and sawed the timber as required.

The Union Pacific (UPRR) equipped several railroad cars to serve as portable bunkhouses for the workers and gathered men and supplies to push the railroad rapidly west. Along with the bunkhouses, they added a galley car to prepare meals, and even provided for a herd of cows to be moved with the railhead and bunk cars to provide fresh meat. Hunters were hired to provide buffalo meat from the large herds of American bison.

One of the most significant technological achievements of the nineteenth century, the completion of the first transcontinental railroad across the United States made cross-country travel much easier. Previously a journey to the western states meant a dangerous six-month trek over rivers, deserts, and mountains. Or, a traveler could hazard a six-week sea voyage around Cape Horn. The Central Pacific's engine Jupiter and the UPRR's engine No. 119 met at Promontory Summit, Utah, on that date. This is now the location of the Golden Spike National Historical Park.

RECONSTRUCTION CONTINUES: Reconstruction was the primary focus of Grant's administration. He worked to reconcile the North and South, while also attempting to protect the civil rights of newly freed slaves.

While Grant was personally honest, some of his associates were corrupt, and his administration became tarnished by scandals. Grant offered no vision for a country still shattered by the Civil War.

Chapter 8 in Summary from 1860 to 1870:

- ✓ 1860 is the first census counting American Indians who "renounced tribal rules"
- ✓ Information in this census includes names, places of birth and more
- ✓ Again, a separate slave census, same as 1850, gives only names of the owner
- ✓ Abraham Lincoln elected 16th president, Nov 6, 1860
- ✓ Pony Express leaves Sacramento, CA for St. Joseph, MO
- ✓ Lincoln changed the course of history
- ✓ Travel was mostly by stagecoach or horseback
- ✓ Confederates bombard Fort Sumter in Charleston Harbor, April 12, 1861
- ✓ 1861 the war begins, four turbulent years follow
- ✓ 1862 the president signs the Pacific Railroad Act
- ✓ 1862 some pensions are approved for Union vets
- ✓ 1863 Congress passes the Conscription Act, the first wartime draft of US citizens
- ✓ 1864 the war ends, though surrender was still four months away
- ✓ 1865 Lincoln is assassinated five days after the Confederate surrender
- ✓ Vice President Andrew Johnson becomes 17th President.
- ✓ Johnson oversees the South's reconstruction
- ✓ American culture, economy, and politics is changed
- ✓ Johnson endures much conflict with the Republican dominated Congress
- ✓ Johnson is impeached
- ✓ 1868 General U. S. Grant, elected the 18th president
- ✓ Grant was a Civil War hero with a counterfeit name

NINE—1870

The Nation's Centennial

LIFE IN THE CENTENNIAL YEAR

What was it like to live in the United States when it was just a hundred years old, and the industrial revolution had begun to change people's lives?

Furnaces, gaslights, and indoor plumbing arrived, but families still arranged their lives around sunup and sundown. Chores took most of a child's time; games and entertainments were scarce, and few books existed for children. People did most of their own doctoring, often with patent medicines containing habit-forming narcotics. Wildcatters discovered petroleum in Pennsylvania, but people did not know what to do with it. The new kerosene lights were much better than lighting with whale oil and didn't gum up machinery like whale oil.

There were no thermostats to turn up the heat when it was cold. Men braved the icy outdoors to put another log on the fire or stir coals in the furnace and bring the heat up. People who did not have bathtubs took their baths standing in cold bedrooms, and that was serious business. The bather had to work fast undressing; then they filled the basin with rainwater, preferably warmed from the teakettle on the stove. Washing face and hands first, the bather used a soapy sponge to rub over his body. With the basin sitting on the floor, water would be poured over soapy skin, then rinsed and dried. Most houses did not have closets for clothing. Of course, most people only had one or two changes of clothes, so not much storage was needed.

The kitchen was the most overworked room in the house. Cooking happened not in a microwave oven but on an enormous iron range burning coal and wood. Families usually kept the fire going all day long. The kitchen ruled the back of the house or in a separate building, so cooking smells and cooking heat would not go into the living areas. Easily cleaned oilcloth was used on kitchen tables rather than linens. Roots and herbs hung in the kitchen for medicine or seasoning.

Usually, the mother performed as the family doctor with knowledge of how to use the bag full of ancient remedies. A spring "tonic" of sulfur and blackstrap molasses cleansed the blood after a long, cold winter; sassafras tea restored strength from blood loss. Stepping on a rusty nail was dangerous, so a careful person picked up the object, greased it, and carried it in his pocket to prevent sickness. If a cut became infected and inflamed, they might make a poultice of old bread or biscuit soaked in milk to relieve the pain and draw out the poison. Germs and vitamins were unknown in 1876. There were no laws regulating medicine at all. A self-appointed medicine man (or woman) decided what had to happen. They were indeed "practicing" medicine.

Monday was always wash day, no matter the weather, outdoors with a big washtub or iron pot, heavy stirring stick, homemade soap, and buckets of water carried from the pump. After a tumble in the tub and rinsing, clothes were spread on bushes to dry, or on a clothesline if the home was lucky enough to have one.

BLACKS CAN VOTE: In 1870, the Fifteenth Amendment passed, giving Negro men the right to vote in the North as well as the South. Race, color, or previous condition of servitude could not prevent a citizen from voting. However, women still could not vote, no matter their color.

President Grant signed legislation aimed at limiting the activities of white terrorist groups, such as the Ku Klux Klan, whose members used violence to intimidate blacks and prevent them from voting. The president even stationed federal troops throughout the South to maintain law and order at times. Critics claimed Grant's actions violated states' rights, while others contended the president did not do enough to protect freedmen.

THE CENSUS EXPANDS: Ulysses S. Grant was president for the ninth census with thirty-seven states ratified. You may find many young men missing from this census, particularly in the South, because this was the first census after the war and the end of slavery. It was also the first census to list all persons, including former slaves, as individuals. For the first time, researchers can see each person's place of birth and the month, if born within the year. No matter when the enumerator may have visited the home, the count remained based on who was living there on the first of June. Citizens were offered five different forms to complete for the 1870 census: general population, mortality, agriculture, products of industry, and social statistics.

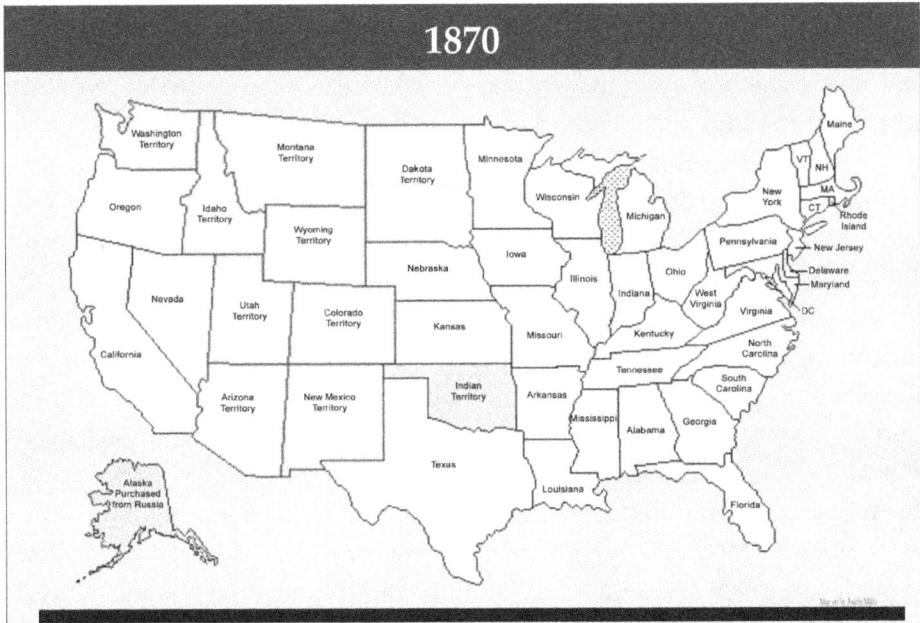

Figure 52: The 1870 Census, Ulysses S. Grant, president.

This was the first census after the Civil War ended slavery, and the first one to list all persons, including former slaves, as individuals. The total of 37 states included four new states in the 1870 Census: West Virginia, Nebraska, Kansas, and Nevada. New territories included New Mexico, Colorado, Idaho, Arizona, Utah, Wyoming, Montana, Washington, Dakota, and Indian Territory. Although Alaska was purchased in 1867, the US government did not record an 1870 census. Schedules are available for all the white colored areas.

The territory of Alaska, purchased from Russia in 1867, got its first census, an unofficial count by the US Army at Sitka. Alaska was variously under the jurisdiction of the US Army (until 1877), the US Treasury (from 1877 until 1879), the US Navy (from 1879 until 1884), and finally, Alaska gained statehood in 1959.

The 1870 count estimated a total US population of more than thirty-eight million. Although this census schedule is the first to list "Indian" as a choice in the column heading for color, they had been counted before.

Information to be found in this census includes: name, age at last birthday, sex, color (W=White, B=Black, M=Mulatto, C=Chinese, I=Indian), profession, occupation or trade, value of real estate, personal property, place of birth (state, territory or country), whether father or mother is of foreign descent, month of birth and month of marriage if either happened within the year, whether attended school, whether can read or write, whether deaf, dumb, blind, insane, or idiotic.

New states in this census include West Virginia 1863, Nebraska 1867, Kansas 1861, and Nevada 1864. Territories include New Mexico, Colorado, Idaho, Arizona, Utah, Wyoming, Montana, Washington, Dakota, and Indian Territory.

There is an unusual checkbox on the 1870 census asking about male citizens aged twenty-one years and up whose right to vote was denied or abridged on grounds other than rebellion or crime. Confederate veterans and civil servants of the rebellious states were prevented from voting or holding elected office during the reconstruction period. Penalties applied for refusing to reply to questions asked on all questionnaires.

General Francis A. Walker, head of the census, didn't get paid. Congress failed to appropriate funds for him. Walker resigned in 1871 but continued working without compensation until he finished the job.

U. S. GRANT, AMERICAN HERO, AMERICAN MYTH: Ulysses S. Grant, as a war hero and the symbol of Union victory, became the Republican's logical candidate for president.

He arrived at West Point as a young seventeen-year-old, five feet one inch tall, weighing a hundred seventeen pounds. By 1863 he was still slender at five feet seven weighing a hundred thirty-five. It was not his dream, but his father's dream for him that brought young "Sam" Grant to the prestigious military school.

Cadet life was austere, disciplined, controlled, unremitting; and living conditions were spartan. Not an outstanding student, Grant loved fast horses. He was a fearless rider with phenomenal endurance and speed.

On graduation from West Point, Grant moved to Jefferson Barracks a few miles south of the city of St. Louis, Missouri. From there, he went to fight in the war with Mexico, even though Grant felt the conflict was wrong.

William Conant Church, soldier and journalist who wrote a biography of Grant, said, *"Grant was more noticeable for his horse racing. The town was full of lively fellows, and there were many horses whose owners considered them fast. (Grant) was always in the forefront of any racing that was going on. On Saturdays the whole town seemed to get out on Fort Avenue and every man who had a horse took part. Grant had that little black mare, and it was a horse of tremendous speed. He was the best horseman I ever saw. He could fly on a horse, faster than a slicked bullet."*

He could ride, but Grant could not hold much liquor. After a single drink, his fellow officers said he stumbled and slurred his words. He did indulge in heavy drinking during the years when he was stationed on the West Coast, and he drank more when separated from his family during the war while serving under a difficult commanding officer in California.

JULIA DENT GRANT: Sam Grant was a student at West Point when a fellow student, Fred Dent, wrote his sister Julia about how impressed he was with Grant.

Frederick Dent Sr., the father of Julia and Fred, owned about thirty slaves on a Missouri plantation. A planter and merchant, he refused to consider freeing them on moral ground, doing so only when compelled by the law of emancipation. No doubt some stimulating conversations happened around the dinner table when Dent's future son-in-law talked about his Civil War experiences.

Ulysses Grant fell hard for Julia. When her pet canary died, Ulysses crafted a small yellow coffin and summoned eight fellow officers to conduct an avian funeral service. Ulysses asked Julia to wear his West Point class ring as a sign of their exclusive affection. She agreed, and they wed in 1848. The bride's veil was trimmed with jasmine blossoms as she floated downstairs to the parlor where her young Army officer waited. Julia wore an elegant watered silk white wedding gown and veil of fringed white tulle. They served a lavish wedding cake, with music and other refreshments. Among the groomsmen were several men who would later fight against Grant as Confederate officers.

The newlyweds enjoyed a three-month honeymoon excursion by riverboat and stagecoach, stopping in Louisville and then traveling through Ohio to the home of his parents and other relatives.

Julia was born with strabismus, or "crossed eye," which prevents both eyes from lining up in the same direction. After her husband became president, Julia considered surgery. She said, *"I never had the courage to consent, but now my husband has become so famous I really thought it behooved me to try to look as well as possible."*

Ulysses objected, *"Did I not see you and fall in love with you with these same eyes? I like them just as they are, and now, remember, you are not to interfere with them. They are mine and let me tell you, Mrs. Grant, you had better not make any experiments, as I might not like you half so well with any other eyes."*

Because her crossed eyes remained uncorrected, Julia almost always posed in profile for portraits. The general urged his wife to bring their children to live with him whenever it was deemed reasonably safe. He deeply missed his wife. Grant drank very little later in life and never imbibed when Julia was around. Knowing how much Grant needed his family nearby, Julia allowed their twelve-year-old son Fred to live in the army camp at times. He looked out for himself and was in almost every battle of the campaign. During the 1863 battle of Vicksburg, young Fred not only witnessed the fighting, he also dodged a bullet.

After four years of war, an assassination, and an impeachment trial, Washington was ready for a little happiness and laughter, and Julia obliged. She became a popular hostess, planning lavish state dinners, where guests enjoyed expensive wines and liquors. Although Julia did spend a great deal of money, she avoided the criticism of being a spendthrift like Mary Lincoln.

As first lady, Julia presided over Tuesday afternoon receptions for the general public. Her only requirement for these receptions was asking ladies to wear hats and the men to leave their weapons at home. She came to enjoy the exciting and busy life. Julia was devastated in 1875 when her husband announced he would not run for a third term.

Even though Grant was a northerner and a Republican, he once owned a slave named William Jones. The thirty-five-year-old man was a gift from Grant's father-in-law. Later, Grant needed money, but he set William Jones free, although the slave was worth at least fifteen hundred dollars.

NO WOMEN'S RIGHTS: Legally, a wife did not exist without her husband. He could not give her property except through a trustee. A ruling in 1872 finally allowed a wife to keep any money she earned herself after marriage, to divorce an abusive husband, and she could be represented in government.

Even then, a woman of the nineteenth century had few rights. Her father was her boss until she married; then at the wedding ceremony, he "gave her away" to her husband. Everything she once owned was now his, including her name. A mother did not have control over her own children.

Children belonged to their father, and he could give them away if he wished. A wife could do no business unless her husband joined her in signing the contracts. All the laws were on the men's side.

BRIGHAM YOUNG DIES: The year 1877 witnessed in Utah the death of Brigham Young, second president of the Mormon church. Under his leadership, the membership grew to more than one hundred fifteen thousand. Most lived in Utah, Idaho, Arizona, Nevada, and Wyoming, in one of the four hundred plus settlements founded under his guidance. Members of the church were called "Latter-day Saints" or "Mormons."

Though he accepted the Methodist faith in 1823, Brigham Young was drawn to Mormonism after reading the Book of Mormon shortly after Smith published it in 1830. Congress outlawed polygamy in 1862, but Young was a dedicated polygamist, marrying a total of fifty-five wives. The policy was burdensome for many in the church.

By the time of his death, Young had fifty-six children by sixteen of his wives. All but ten of his children lived to reach adulthood. At the time of Young's death in 1877, nineteen of his wives had predeceased him, ten divorced him, and twenty-three survived him. The status of four wives is unknown.

LIFE ON THE FARM IN THE '70s: In August 1873, farmers found their crops plagued by drought and grasshoppers. Some farmers were deeply in debt to banks, and they were forced to sell their land. In September a popular brokerage firm, Jay Cooke and Co., failed. Panic followed, taking the nation into a depression caused perhaps by over-production and over-speculation. A worldwide economic depression was felt most severely in Britain and the US.

The free range of the prairie was becoming a private pasture for herdsmen until in 1874 when barbed wire began to fence out herds from lands where homesteaders settled. Cowboys settled down to be ranchers. Fence-cutting wars started between cattlemen and sheep men, between ranchers and cattle thieves, between Indians and cowboys, with farmers against them all. Free-range became fenced in, no longer free, and there were troubles in other places as well.

> *Late one night, when we were all in bed,*
> *Mrs. O'Leary lit a lantern in the shed.*
> *Her cow kicked it over, then winked an eye and said,*
> *"There'll be a hot time in the old town tonight!"*

THE GREAT CHICAGO FIRE 1871: The fire started at about nine p.m. on the eighth of October, in or around a small barn bordering the alley behind the street and belonging to the O'Leary family. The shed next to the barn was the first building to be consumed. City officials never determined the exact cause of the blaze, but the fire spread rapidly due to a prolonged drought, strong winds from the southwest, and the rapid destruction of the water pumping system.

The most famous tale blames Mrs. O'Leary's cow, who allegedly knocked over a kerosene lantern; others accuse a group of men gambling inside the barn who knocked over a lamp. Still, others speculated the blaze was related to other fires on the same day.

Whatever caused the conflagration, the Chicago fire killed up to three hundred people, destroyed more than three square miles, and left more than a hundred thousand residents homeless. After the smoke dispersed, laws were passed requiring all new buildings constructed with fireproof materials such as brick, stone, marble, and limestone.

THE YELLOWSTONE CONFLICT: 1872 saw the first national park, Yellowstone, founded in the territories of Wyoming, Idaho, and Montana in spite of considerable local opposition to the park during its early years. Some of the locals feared the regional economy would become sluggish because of strict federal prohibitions against resource development. Local entrepreneurs wanted to reduce the size of the park to develop mining, hunting, and logging activities. Congressional representatives from Montana introduced numerous bills to remove the federal land-use restrictions.

SHINING A LIGHT: Two Canadians invented and patented the light bulb in 1875. Their patent was picked up by Thomas Edison, who had the financial backing to advance his theory of electricity which was safer than gaslight.

THE STATE OF THE ECONOMY: From the fall of 1873 until the end of Grant's second term the nation was plunged into a full-blown financial panic and a deep depression. It would not recover for five or six years.

WHITE MEN IN BED SHEETS: The Ku Klux Klan, commonly called the KKK, terrorized the South in this decade, using both physical assault and murder against any groups or individuals whom they opposed, but particularly blacks. Members made their unique costumes of white robes, including masks and conical hats, designed not only to be frightening but also to hide their identities. After the election, the American people hoped for an end to the turmoil. However, Grant—who struggled with alcohol throughout his life—provided neither vigor nor reform. Looking to Congress for direction, he appeared bewildered. One visitor to the Capitol noted that Grant always seemed puzzled, like a man with a problem of which he does not understand the terms.

RECONSTRUCTING CONTINUES: Reconstruction in many ways was still a war. The South was under occupation by federal forces. Southern state governments were dominated by Republicans who pressed for granting political rights to the newly freed slaves as key to their becoming full citizens. Yet many radical northerners still wanted to punish the South.

The KKK was born as a way for whites to maintain control. Founded in 1866 by many former CSA veterans as a social club in Pulaski, Tennessee, only four years later the Ku Klux Klan extended into almost every southern state. Former Confederate General Nathan Bedford Forrest served as the first leader, or "Grand Wizard," of the Klan; presiding over a hierarchy of Grand Dragons, Grand Titans, and Grand Cyclops. The KKK members, both male and female, terrorized blacks with senseless beatings, whippings, burning of homes and lynching.

THE REDEEMERS AND THE RADICALS: Redeemers formed the southern wing of the conservative, pro-business faction in the Democratic party. They wanted to kick out the Radicals, a Republican coalition generally led by wealthy landowners, businesspeople, and professionals who domi-nated southern politics in most areas from the 1870s to 1910.

Just after the war came the rise of black codes, restricting the basic human rights of freed slaves. The term "black codes" is used most often to refer to legislation passed by Southern states at the end of the Civil War to control the labor, migration and other activities of newly freed slaves. State and local laws, called Jim Crow law, enforced racial segregation in the southern United States.

Blood determined race, which meant if you had even one drop of black blood in your body, you were considered black. Freedmen could not get together unless they were accompanied by a white person. Even public restrooms, drinking fountains, and other facilities were segregated and not equal.

Many racially motivated riots broke out all over the country. Symbols of black autonomy such as schools and churches became targets for Klan attacks. The KKK organization membership crossed class lines. From small farmers and laborers to planters, lawyers, merchants, physicians, and min-isters; all were involved. In the areas where most Klan activity took place, local law enforcement officials either belonged to the Klan or declined to take any action against it.

Congress finally passed three enforcement acts, the strongest of which was the Ku Klux Klan Act of 1871. Congress authorized President Grant to declare martial law, impose heavy penalties against terrorist organizations, and use military force to suppress the Klan. Grant cited this Act when he needed to suppress KKK activity in South Carolina and other areas of the deep South.

CARPETBAGGERS AND SCALAWAGS: At least ten percent of the black legislators elected during the 1867 and 1868 constitutional conventions became victims of violence during Reconstruction, including seven who were killed. Many northerners moved to the south to start new lives, some-times carrying their belongings in briefcases made of carpet. Southerners called them "carpetbaggers." Southern whites who sided with them were known as "scalawags."

THE SPOILS SYSTEM: Grant's presidency occurred during an era domi-nated by machine politics and the patronage system of political appoint-ments, known as the Spoils System, in which politicians rewarded their supporters with government jobs. The employees, in turn, kicked back part of their salaries to the political party. The standards in many of Grant's appointments were low, and charges of corruption were widespread. Nepotism was prevalent with more than forty family members benefiting from government appointments.

To combat corruption and inefficiency resulting from this system, Grant established a civil service commission with more equitable methods for hiring and promoting government workers. However, public service reform faced opposition from Congress as well as from members of Grant's own administration. By 1876 the commission's funding was cut off and standardized exams discontinued. Lasting reform still did not happen for several more years until President Chester Arthur signed the Pendleton Civil Service Act in 1883.

The unprecedented way that Grant ran his cabinet, in military-style rather than civilian, contributed to the scandals. For instance, Grant never even consulted with cabinet members on the treaty annexation with Santo Domingo. He just sent his private secretary, rather than an official, to negotiate the treaty.

CUSTER'S DEFEAT AND CRAZY HORSE'S WAR: The Black Hills of Dakota have long been sacred to the Sioux Indians. The 1868 treaty, signed at Fort Laramie and other military posts in Sioux country, recognized the Black Hills as part of the Great Sioux Reservation, set aside for exclusive use by the Sioux people. However, after the discovery of gold in the year 1874, everything changed. The US disregarded the treaty and confiscated the land. One year after Gen. George Armstrong Custer's infamous defeat at the hands of Crazy Horse at Little Bighorn and without the consent of *"three-fourths of all adult male Indians"* stipulated by the treaty, the government seized the Black Hills, along with their gold, and began profiting from the protected land.

They forced the Sioux to give up the Black Hills for a fraction of value and opened the area to the gold miners. The War for the Black Hills is sometimes called Sitting Bull and Crazy Horse's War. The Black Hills had long been hunting grounds and sacred territory for the western bands of the Sioux or Dakota Indians.

Red Cloud and Spotted Tail settled on reservations while Sitting Bull and Crazy Horse still led the allied hunting bands, refusing to give up their traditional nomadic way of life.

Figure 53: Sitting Bull and family 1881

His mother, sister, two daughters and grandson at Fort Randall. Standing: Good Feather Woman (sister), Walks Looking (daughter).

Front: Her Holy Door (mother), Sitting Bull, Many Horses (daughter) with her son, Courting a Woman.

Opposing both groups were two generals who had become famous as Union commanders in the Civil War, General William Tecumseh Sherman, now overall commander of the army, and General Philip Henry Sheridan, commander of the Division of the Missouri.

In the field, the generals had various officers, including General George Crook, who previously fought Apache and Paiute, and Lieutenant Colonel George Armstrong Custer, who earlier campaigned against the Cheyenne.

BATTLE OF GREASY GRASS: War broke out when the military ordered the hunting bands led by Sitting Bull and Crazy Horse onto the reservation. When the groups failed to report, the army went after them in the winter of 1876. The Battle of Little Bighorn is the most famous battle in all the Indian wars. It is also called Custer's Last Stand or the Battle of Greasy Grass. The Indians were the victors on this day in 1876. However, it was also the Indians' last stand.

LOOKING BACK: When he accepted the surrender of Robert E. Lee's Army of Northern Virginia in April 1865, Grant offered generous terms and allowed Confederate soldiers and officers to "save face." In addition to focusing on Reconstruction, Grant signed legislation establishing the Department of Justice, the Weather Bureau (now known as the National Weather Service) and Yellowstone, the country's first national park. He also tried, with little success, to improve conditions for Native Americans.

Grant did make strides in foreign policy with the Treaty of Washington in 1871, settling US claims against England stemming from alleged "British-built Confederate warships disrupting northern shipping" during the war. The treaty resulted in improved relations between the United Kingdom and the United States. Grant was not successful in his attempt to annex the Caribbean nation of Santo Domingo (present-day Dominican Republic).

GRANT'S END: At the beginning of Grant's second term, the nation was prosperous. The national debt, government spending, tariffs, and the federal workforce trimmed down, and tax revenues increased. However, a long severe economic depression struck in 1873, and various scandals plagued his administration. He also continued to struggle with Reconstruction issues. Although Grant was never proven to be directly involved with or to have personally profited from the scandals or frauds, his acceptance of personal gifts and his associations with men of questionable character severely damaged his own presidential legacy and reputation. Grant declined to run for a third term.

THE MOST DISPUTED ELECTION IN HISTORY: The presidential election of 1876 between Rutherford B. Hayes (R-Ohio) and Samuel J. Tilden (D-NY) became one of the most disputed presidential elections in American history. They declared Hayes the victor, although Tilden won the popular vote. Confusion reigned in the electoral college, and some of their votes were disputed.

An informal deal known as the Compromise of 1877 resolved the dispute by which all twenty electoral votes were awarded to Hayes. In return for the Democrats' agreement to Hayes' election, the Republicans

Figure 54:
Rutherford B. Hayes

The nineteenth president served one term from 1877 to 1881.

Vice President: William Wheeler

agreed to withdraw federal troops from the South and to end Reconstruction. The Compromise effectively gave more power in the southern states to the Democratic "Redeemers," who continued to disenfranchise black voters.

THE END OF RECONSTRUCTION: For the nineteenth president, Rutherford B. Hayes, this was a time of great pain and endless questions. What should they do with the Confederate leaders who were seen as traitors by many in the North? Hayes knew that whatever he decided was going to be condemned by one side or the other.

Hayes was a Civil War hero and former Ohio governor selected as a dark horse candidate by the Republicans. Southerners desperately wanted to find a way to preserve their way of life. Many were unable to accept the idea former slaves could not only vote but also could hold office. He took office amid a constitutional crisis and left office defending his reputation.

Hayes kept his promise to be a one-term president, and he attacked patronage in the nation's civil service system. He succeeded in firing the suspicious influential Collector of the Port of New York, Chester Arthur, in an epic battle with New York power broker Roscoe Conkling in 1878. Surprisingly, Arthur was destined to become the next president in 1881.

The American economy recovered under Hayes from the disastrous Panic of 1873.

LEMONADE LUCY: Lucy Webb first met Rutherford "Rud" Hayes at Ohio Wesleyan University. At the time, Lucy was fourteen years old, and Rutherford was twenty-three. Rutherford's mother was hopeful the two would find a connection, but at this point, he considered Lucy *"not quite old enough to fall in love with."* Later, he thought differently.

At age eighteen, Lucy graduated from the Wesleyan Female College in Cincinnati. She was unusually well-educated for a young lady of her day. The summer Lucy turned nineteen, she and Rutherford were members of the same wedding party. Lucy so impressed Rutherford he gave her the prize (a gold ring) he had found in the wedding cake. After the couple became engaged, Lucy returned the wedding cake ring to Rutherford. He wore the ring for the rest of his life.

Married in 1852, they lived in Cincinnati, and he soon came to share her profoundly religious opposition to slavery. During the War, she earned the nickname "Mother Lucy" from the troops serving under her husband in Ohio's 23rd Volunteer Infantry.

After the war when they moved into the presidential mansion, a cat, a bird, two dogs, and a goat joined the Hayes family in residence. The Hayes' had eight children, five of whom lived to adulthood.

In the late 1800s, President Rutherford Hayes rode trains to visit thirty states and six territories, earning him the nickname "The Rover." He began the efforts leading to civil service reform and attempted to reconcile divisions left over from the war.

The treasury secretary worked with Hayes to return the country to the gold standard. Lucy Hayes carried out her husband's orders to banish wines and liquors from the mansion dining room to the delight of the Woman's Christian Temperance Union (WCTU). The times were changing.

The most significant change made during Hayes' term was the installation of bathrooms with running water and the addition of a crude wall telephone. Installed in May of 1879, the president embraced the new technology, though he rarely received phone calls because phone service was in its infancy.

There was no one for him to call.

THINKING OF THE VETERANS: The Arrears of Pension Act of 1879 allowed all Union veterans to reapply for pension and receive back payments to the date of their discharge, regardless of when they may have previously applied. This legislation did not change the requirement for pension-qualifying disabilities to be service-related, but it was nevertheless a costly bill setting the stage for a broader fight to come. Veterans could now receive large sums of money for several years of "missed" pension payments. This resulted in a flood of applications and a substantial increase in pension expenditures for the federal government.

MAIL ORDER CATALOGS: In 1872, Aaron Montgomery Ward opened the first mail-order retail business and issued a one-page catalog featuring nearly a hundred fifty items; by 1884 the directory contained more than two hundred pages and listed more than ten thousand items.

Montgomery Ward and the Sears, Roebuck and Company brought the benefits of mass production to farms and small towns by selling everything from clothes to agricultural implements, and even housing. Soon rural free delivery (RFD) service made mail-orders even more accessible in 1896.

Children loved spending hours admiring items in the "wish book" or cutting out the figures for paper dolls. Interestingly, the catalogs also became a source of toilet paper for many outhouses in rural areas, with softer index pages the most prized. Mass manufacturing of modern toilet paper did not begin until the late 19th century.

ROCKEFELLER AND STANDARD OIL CO: The discovery of large quantities of crude oil in northwest Pennsylvania soon changed the lives of millions of Americans. The discovery of oil was not a surprise. People had known of the existence of the product around the world for centuries. They just didn't know what to do with it. Farmers tried to plow around it; others sold it as medicine.

John D. Rockefeller may have changed the oil industry forever with his company, Standard Oil, but there were more intriguing things about him. Rockefeller's early life hardly seemed the way to make a billionaire. He was a self-made man. The family moved often and struggled to make ends meet. His father was a salesman, his mother a stay-at-home mom raising their six children.

John D. was the oldest son. Although he didn't own new suits or an elegant home, his family life was happy. His father taught him how to earn money and hold on to it; his mother instilled honesty, Godliness, and kindness.

Rockefeller always remembered the "momentous day" in 1855, when he began work at age sixteen as an assistant bookkeeper for fifty cents a day. In 1870, he established Standard Oil, which by the early 1880s controlled ninety percent of US refineries and pipelines.

Chapter 9 in Summary from 1870 to 1880:

- ✓ 1870—first census after war and the end of slavery
- ✓ This ninth census listed 37 states
- ✓ Yellowstone National Park was established
- ✓ Many young men /soldiers are missing from this census, particularly in the South
- ✓ Surviving Confederate soldiers and civil servants of rebellious states could not vote
- ✓ The Ku Klux Klan, called the KKK, terrorized the South, especially blacks
- ✓ Former Confederate Gen. Nathan Bedford Forrest, was the first "grand wizard" of the Klan
- ✓ President Grant served two terms
- ✓ Grant used the Act of 1871 to suppress Klan activity
- ✓ The Redeemers and the Radicals battled over Reconstruction
- ✓ The Compromise of 1877 declared Rutherford Hayes the 19th President
- ✓ Hayes oversaw the end of Reconstruction
- ✓ 1879 additional Pension funds became available for Union vets
- ✓ Mail order catalogs were sent through rural free delivery
- ✓ John D. Rockefeller incorporated the Standard Oil Company
- ✓ Mormon leader Brigham Young died
- ✓ "The Great Chicago Fire" happened October 8, 1871
- ✓ Kerosene replaced whale oil for lamps
- ✓ Barbed wire brought the end of free range for cattlemen
- ✓ Danger from germs or dirt was not understood

TEN—1880

Eliminating the Spoils System

A GILDED AGE

The 1880s were part of the Gilded Age in the United States which lasted from 1874 to 1907. This time is often portrayed as one of those dark periods in American history—a period of greed and corruption, of brutal industrial competition, and harsh exploitation of labor.

ROADS AND RAILROADS: From Thomas Edison to Alexander Graham Bell, the nation became aware of light and sound transmitted across the country. Roads improved and expanded, strong bridges replaced ferries and low water crossings. Rails carried people cross country during the era of cowboys and outlaws. Indians moved toward more civility and, unfortunately for the Indians, to life on a reservation.

The Second Industrial Revolution was on the way. Most western states experienced a sizeable economic boom due to the transportation of mass-produced items by improved highways, railroads, and other more convenient methods of travel. The modern city, along with the sky-scraper, arrived in this decade as well, contributing to economic prosperity.

PRESIDENT NUMBER 20 - GARFIELD: Hayes declined to seek re-election in 1880, keeping his pledge not to run for a second term. James A. Garfield, Republican, became the twentieth president—but not for long.

Figure 55: James A. Garfield

Our twentieth president for two hundred days in 1881 before he was assassinated.

Vice President: Chester Arthur would move into the office.

Garfield was:

Inaugurated in March.

Shot in July.

He spent the next eighty days suffering, and died in September.

LUCRETIA GARFIELD: Garfield met his wife Lucretia "Crete" Rudolph while attending Geauga Seminary in Ohio, where Garfield taught Greek at the Eclectic Institute, and Crete was a student. They began a long correspondence. The conversations created a mutual understanding, and Crete left her teaching job prepared to become a full-time wife and mother. But then, when it seemed the marriage would never happen, Crete returned to her work.

She took a job teaching in Cleveland rather than go back to her hometown, but she was not mourning the broken engagement. She found a rented room at a boardinghouse, and in addition to teaching school, she also took drawing lessons, attended lectures, theater, musical concerts, and art shows. She also began teaching art classes.

When Garfield proposed again, she accepted, although she had some doubts. They married and in time became parents of two daughters and five sons. They continued a lengthy correspondence during the early years of their marriage, which they mostly spent apart.

Crete expressed her frustration and anger for his lack of passion towards her and his frequent absences from home. She resented him leaving her with the responsibility of his demanding mother, as well as the presence of a houseguest, Garfield's admiring woman friend, Alameda Booth. Garfield frankly expressed regret at having married. He also pursued a love affair with Lucia Calhoun, a woman in New York. Later, he confessed the sin to his wife, and made the decision to commit to his marriage.

Garfield, a brigadier general in the Civil War at the age of thirty-one, had served nine terms in the US House of Representatives before being elected to the top office. He may have been the first president to talk on a phone when he spoke with Alexander Graham Bell, thirteen miles away.

THE ASSASSINATION: Garfield's death by a deranged office-seeker increased public demand for civil service reform. Charles J. Guiteau, a lawyer, shot President James A. Garfield, age forty-nine, in the Baltimore and Potomac Railroad station in Washington, DC. One of President Garfield's more wearying duties was meeting those citizens seeking jobs in government, and he saw Guiteau at least once. The shooter had followed various professions in his life. In 1880 he decided to get a federal job under the spoils system by supporting the winning Republican ticket. After the election, when Guiteau pressed his claim, he learned he would not receive the position he wanted. Guiteau started planning an assassination, even though he had nothing personal against the president.

Doctors were unable to locate the bullet in Garfield's back. The gunshot didn't kill Garfield, but his doctors did. The ball in Garfield's back lodged in his pancreas. The President died from blood poisoning and complications after surgeons searched endlessly to find the lost bullet, using unwashed fingers and unsterilized tools. Garfield's tenure in office was the second-shortest in presidential history.

Garfield died two months after the shooting on the nineteenth of September 1881. With his term cut short after only two hundred days, and that time spent in ill health trying to recover from the attack, Garfield is little-remembered other than for his assassination. Vice President Chester Arthur was sworn into office the next day.

The assassin, Guiteau, has since been described as possibly a narcissistic schizophrenic; others assessed him as a clinical psychopath and, in fact, Guiteau's counsel claimed insanity. The jury found him guilty and sentenced him to death by hanging.

CENSUS OF 1880: The tenth census included thirty-eight states, and the nation's population reached more than fifty million. A few localities in this US census are either missing or absorbed into other areas.

For the first time, the government allowed women to work as enumerators. This was also the first time to connect the relationship of household members to the head of the household. Simply adding "wife" or "daughter" beside a person's name provides valuable insight about the relationships within the families and could help to identify unmarried daughters. It may even list mothers-in-law, cousins, and other extended family members.

The only new state in the 1880 census was Colorado.

There are several territories including Kansas, Nebraska, New Mexico, Idaho, Arizona, Utah, Wyoming, Montana, Washington, Alaska, Dakota, and Indian Territory.

Every person is listed by name, whether white, black, mulatto, Indian or Chinese. The record states sex, age, and month if born within the year, occupation and months unemployed, the name of state, territory, or country of birth, father's birthplace, and mother's birthplace. Also, school attendance within the year, inability to read or write if aged ten or older, whether sick or temporarily disabled on the day of enumeration, and the reason for the disability. Illnesses and physical and mental disabilities are also given. The census reported whether an individual was blind, deaf, dumb, idiotic, insane, maimed, or crippled.

They recorded urban households more accurately, with both street names and house numbers.

The census act provided for collecting detailed data on the condition and operation of railroad corporations, incorporated express companies, telegraph companies, and of life, fire, and marine insurance companies. Fines were imposed on officials of "every corporation...who shall...willfully neglect or refuse to give true and complete answers to any inquiries authorized by this act."

The superintendent of census collected and published statistics of the population, industries, and resources of Alaska, with as much detail as possible. They also enumerated all untaxed Indians within the jurisdiction of the United States. This census has a free online index. Look for it at FamilySearch.org. They made a copy of every census schedule. The original was to be bound by county and located in the county courthouse. The copy went to Bureau of Census in Washington, DC.

Five schedules made up the 1880 census. They included:

- Schedule 1 — Population: similar to that used for the previous census, with a few exceptions.
- Schedule 2 — Mortality: used the same inquiries as 1870, with additional questions on marital status, birthplace of parents, length of residence in the United States or territory, and name of the place where the disease was contracted, if other than the place of death.
- Schedule 3 — Agriculture: greatly expanded inquiries concerning various crops (including acreage for their principal crop), questions on farm tenure, weeks of hired labor, annual cost for fence building or repair, fertilizer purchases, and the number of livestock.
- Schedule 4 — Social Statistics: these answers became the responsibility of experts and special agents, rather than the enumerators. The majority of the data came from correspondence with officials of institutions providing care and treatment of certain members of the population.
- Schedule 5 — Manufacturing: included information on the greatest number of helpers employed at any time during the year, the number of hours in the ordinary work day from May to November and November to May, the average daily wages paid to skilled mechanics and laborers, months of full- and part-time operation, and machinery used.

SPECIAL CENSUS OF INDIANS: A complete list of the tribes included in this census can be found at the beginning of microfilm roll number one and is available on Ancestry.com. The Bureau used a particular Indian population schedule containing forty-eight questions. Each record includes two images where the census taker was to record details about the residents of the dwelling. Multiple households were sometimes recorded on one sheet. The cover page gives the names of the tribe, reservation, agency, and post office.

The dwelling number in order of visitation is given, as well as the type of structure. Abbreviations used were "H"—house, sometimes with a description of what it was made of, "P"—pueblo, or "L"—lodge, sometimes including how it was constructed.

- The Indian name of each person in the family, with an English translation
- Relationship to the head of the family
- Marital and tribal status
- The degree of tribal ancestry
- Length of time on the reservation
- Whether individual wore "citizen's dress" (white man's clothing)
- What languages spoken
- Gender
- Age (as of census date of 1 October 1880), and the month they were born
- Occupation
- Whether sick or disabled, type of infirmities, and whether vaccinated
- Literacy and whether attended school within the year
- Number of horses, cattle, sheep, swine, and dogs owned
- Number and types of firearms owned
- Amount of property owned and cultivated, whether by patent, allotment, or tribal regulation
- Whether self-supporting or supported by family, government, civilized industries, hunting, fishing, or gathering
- Sometimes, information about the tribe's customs or manner of living.

There is no name index for this census of all Indians not taxed, whether on reservations or in unsettled areas. With the budget provided, the Census Bureau also undertook Native American enumerations in Washington Territory, Dakota Territory, and California.

BETTER LUCK HERE: You might have better luck with another special Indian census on Ancestry.com. The Indian Census Rolls, 1885-1940 contains an index. The information provided in this database is digital and includes:

- Name (Indian and/or English)
- Gender

- Age
- Birth date
- Relationship to head of family
- Marital status
- Tribe name
- Agency and reservation name

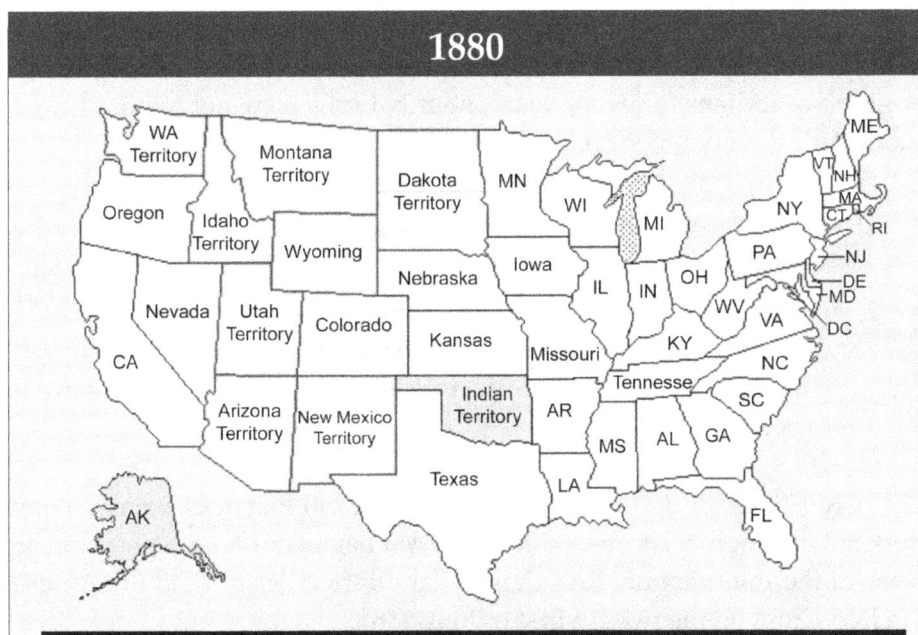

Figure 56: The 1880 census under Rutherford Hayes

The USA includes thirty-eight states, and Colorado was the only new state in this census. Twelve new territories were included: Kansas, Nebraska, New Mexico, Idaho, Arizona, Utah, Wyoming, Montana, Washington, Alaska, Dakota, and Indian Territory.

This census was the first to document the relationship between each person and the head of household, as well as the first census to list marital status, street name and house number, and the birthplace of each individual's parents. Census schedules exist for all the white colored areas. No census for Alaska or Indian Territory.

Other information about an individual, such as the degree of Indian blood, may be available on the original record. View the image to be certain you collect all information available about an individual.

The Indian Census schedules are usually submitted each year by agents or superintendents in charge of the Indian reservation. The data on the rolls varies. For 1935, 1936, 1938, and 1939, only supplemental rolls of additions and deletions were compiled. Most of the rolls for the year 1940 were retained by the Bureau and are not included in this database.

Only persons who maintained a formal affiliation with a tribe under federal supervision are listed. There is not a census for every reservation or group of Indians for every year. The tribal rolls were not required to be submitted, so very few records are available.

When browsing this extensive collection, remember:

1) Family groups might be listed together, listed alphabetically by surname of the head of the family, or sometimes not in any order.

2) In the census rolls themselves, phonetic spellings are commonly used, and the name of a tribe may be spelled several ways in different tribal rolls. Sometimes the tribe's name even differed from year to year.

RED CROSS: Clara Barton was working in the US Patent Office as a copy clerk in Washington, DC, when the Civil War began in 1861. Inspired by the work of the International Red Cross, Clara Barton established the American Red Cross on the twenty-first of May 1881.

Like many women around the nation, Barton helped collect bandages and other much-needed supplies, but she soon realized she could best support the troops by going in person to the battlefields. Barton never married and strongly disliked the restrictions placed on women in her day. As a way to treat soldiers without a formal nursing education, Barton began aiding the wounded in Washington City. She refused to join the "women nurses" because nurses were not allowed on the battlefield. She risked her life to bring supplies and support to soldiers in the field. Through many major battles of the war, Barton nursed, comforted, and cooked for the wounded, earning the nickname the "Angel of the Battlefield."

CONSUMPTION: The bacterial infection of tuberculosis (TB), also known as consumption, was rampant among Europeans, including those who immigrated to the USA in the seventeenth, eighteenth, and nineteenth centuries.

The victims had no idea every time they coughed they exposed their family members to the disease. In the absence of effective treatment, roughly two out of three people died within five years of diagnosis. The exact nature of TB was unknown until 1882 when they discovered the tubercle bacilli.

Dr. Benjamin Rush, one of the leading physicians in the early years of the nineteenth century, advocated horseback riding as a remedy for consumption, and another quack remedy called Tuscarora Rice. A new theory emerged in the late 1800s, recommending fresh mountain air and sunshine to control the disease. When the sanatorium movement gravitated to the Rocky Mountains, more people came to Denver to seek "the cure" than for the gold rush.

DON'T SPIT ON THE SIDEWALK: Gradually doctors learned TB is spread through the air. When infected people cough, sneeze or spit, they propel the germs into the atmosphere. A person needs to inhale only a few of these germs to become infected. In the 1880s, Dr. Samuel Crumbine of Dodge City campaigned for prevention of tuberculosis.

He watched tuberculosis patients spitting on the floor of a train. He became truly alarmed when one of these patients took a drink from a public drinking cup and then saw a mother giving her child a sip from the same mug without first rinsing it. His health campaigns included getting a brick maker to stamp bricks admonishing, "Don't Spit on the Sidewalk." In the twentieth century, researchers discovered new antibiotics to either cure the disease or put it in remission.

LONGEST SUSPENSION BRIDGE IN THE WORLD: Meanwhile, in New York, after fourteen years the Brooklyn Bridge over the East River is opened, connecting the great cities of New York and Brooklyn for the first time in history. Previously the two cities were linked only by ferry boats. The span, originally named the East River Bridge, featured two carriageways and two railway lines.

The raised middle platform allowed pedestrians to cross the bridge on foot for the price of one cent. The toll was five cents for a horse and rider and ten cents for a horse and wagon. Farm animals were allowed at a price of five cents per cow and two cents per sheep or hog.

The famous bridge had a dark side. At least twenty workers died during the bridge's construction, and the main engineer who worked with laborers in underwater chambers became seriously ill with decompression sickness (the bends).

Less than a week after the bridge's opening, a stampede caused at least twelve people to die when pedestrians panicked. On a holiday in perfect weather an estimated twenty thousand citizens got out to walk the new bridge a hundred thirty-five feet above the water.

Two flights of steps leading down from the planked footway to the asphalt pavement became a death trap when a woman fainted, another screamed, and the crowd in the rear, not knowing the cause but fearing a bridge collapse, panicked and pushed ahead trampling to death those who were in front and seriously injuring many others. Within minutes men, women and children piled on top of each another and became trapped against the iron fences lining the narrow promenade.

In true old-time New York fashion, pick-pockets came to rob the helpless victims.

The dead and injured were taken to Chambers Street Hospital where their families could find and identify them.

The matron of the hospital said: *"I have been engaged in this hospital for several years, but I never saw such heartbreaking incidents as I have today. You see quite a number of the injured and dead are children, and their parents have wrung my heart with their appeals and grief."*

A year later, people were still unsure the bridge would not collapse so circus promoter P.T. Barnum displayed the strength of the bridge by leading twenty-one elephants across it. Jumbo, his famous thirteen-foot and seven-ton African elephant, did indeed cross the bridge in 1884, along with twenty other elephants, seven camels and ten dromedaries in what was known as Barnum's legendary "elephant walk."

THE RICH AND SUPER RICH: The super-rich were living in grand homes, entertaining lavishly and taking pleasure trips abroad. They left money so their children could live in idleness or devote themselves to "service" if they wished. There was little philanthropy by the wealthy in the early 1880s, but John D. Rockefeller and Andrew Carnegie, two leading owners of industries concerned with opportunities for others, invested outside their business interests.

THE LADIES BLESS 'EM: Tight corsets were fashionable in the 1880s. Some were laced so tightly it seemed hardly possible for the woman wearing one to live and breathe.

The girls who worked in factories did not wear these straitjackets on weekdays or they would not have been able to work at the machines, but they tried to make up for their transgressions on Sundays. Girls bound up in this fashion could eat and drink very little, for their compressed bodies left little or no room for food.

Once reaching home on Sunday afternoon, the corset wearers would hasten out of their girdles in the quickest possible time, when they might lie on a bed or sofa and pant with relief.

VICE PRESIDENT CHESTER ARTHUR: The son of a Baptist preacher, "Chet" Arthur was born in Fairfield, Vermont, in 1829. Arthur's father, an immigrant from Northern Ireland, was an abolitionist. Arthur graduated from Union College in 1848, taught school, was admitted to the bar, and practiced law in New York City. Early in the Civil War, he served as quartermaster general of New York where he became active in Republican politics.

Figure 57: Chester Arthur

The twenty-first president, Arthur, completed the unexpired term of James Garfield frm 1881 to 1885.

Vice President: None

Arthur took office after the assassination of President James Garfield. To be kind, President Garfield was less than a good housekeeper. He and earlier presidents had been rough on the mansion. The carpets were soiled, the furniture worn and stained, and the inside walls covered with smoke stains and mold. Twenty-four wagonloads of boxes, furniture, and old clothing were cleared out and hauled away.

Everything was offered at an open auction. Prices were high and bidding strong.

ARTHUR CLEANS HOUSE: President Arthur was a conscientious man with high standards of cleanliness. He stayed in his own home until the mansion could be cleaned and new furniture provided. Before he moved in, Arthur hired designer and stained-glass artist Louis Comfort Tiffany to redecorate the staterooms.

As president, Arthur advocated civil service reform and eliminating the Spoils System. While in office, Arthur rose above partisanship and in 1883 signed the Pendleton Act, which required government jobs to be distributed based on merit.

He also called for three measures to help assimilate the Indians: robust education funding, individual land ownership, and state laws applicable to Indian reservations. The goal was to convince the natives to "sever their tribal relations," leaving the "blanket society," so they could be absorbed into American social groups and become citizens.

IMMIGRATION AGAIN: Arthur viewed cultural diversity as a threat to America. His administration enacted the first general Federal immigration law in 1882, which established categories of foreigners deemed "undesirable" for entry and gave the Secretary of the Treasury authority over immigration enforcement. The measure excluded paupers, criminals, and lunatics. Congress even suspended Chinese immigration for ten years, later making the restriction permanent. He also outlawed the practice of polygamy by legislation.

ELEGANT ARTHUR: Nicknamed the "Gentleman Boss" and "Elegant Arthur," the president reportedly owned eighty pair of pants. He married Ellen Lewis "Nell" Herndon, and they became parents of two sons and a daughter. His wife died suddenly of pneumonia a year before his term began.

The president's sister Mary Arthur McElroy served as hostess and unofficial first lady for Arthur's social activities, and also cared for the Arthur children. After taking office, Arthur, who could see St. John's Episcopal Church in Lafayette Square from his office, commissioned a stained-glass window dedicated to his wife at the church. He had it installed where he could view it at night, as the lights were kept on within the church. Additionally, he ordered fresh flowers placed daily before her portrait in the mansion.

Arthur became the most eligible bachelor in DC. His social life became the subject of wild romantic rumors, though actually he remained singularly devoted to the memory of his late wife.

MEANWHILE OUT WEST: Throughout the 1800s, America's frontier moved steadily westward. Yet for several years, immigrants to the West saw most of the region as an obstacle, not a destination. Immigrants to the West had to adapt and find new ways of doing things to survive.

Early pioneering families had to be self-sufficient. They made their own clothing, food, shelter, and fuel. Men and boys wore overalls made from denim or recycled grain sacks and a short jacket. Women wore a calico or gingham dress and a sunbonnet.

TABERNACLES ON THE PLAINS: As far as religion, the established Eastern churches were slow to meet the needs of the frontier. The Presbyterians and Congregationalists, since they depended on well-educated ministers, were shorthanded in evangelizing the frontier. The Baptists set up small independent churches where they founded each local church on the principle of independence of the local congregation. On the other hand, bishops of the well-organized, centralized Methodists assigned circuit riders to specific areas for several years at a time, then moved them to fresh territory.

A Low Dutch colony from back east begged the Dutch Reformed classes in New Jersey to send a Dutch speaking Domine (pastor) to the Kentucky frontier. They started building their Meetinghouse of mud and wattle in 1800 at Harrod's Fort, and a religious head finally came. The newly ordained Domine, Peter Labagh, stayed a couple months and then went home. Unable to get the Dutch Reformed leader they wanted, the group eventually defaulted to Presbyterian faith, which was most like the strict Calvinist worship they were used to. Some Low Dutch families were the first converts to the Shaker religion. They called themselves Low Dutch because they were from the lowlands of Europe (now The Netherlands), to distinguish from the high Deutch from Germany who spoke a similar but different language,

Pleasant Hill, Kentucky became the site of a Shaker religious community active from 1805 to 1910. The site, now a National Historic Landmark, has become a popular tourist destination. Eleven Shaker communities were already established in New York and New England under the doctrine of Mother Ann Lee who believed in celibacy, and a member of the Quaker sect called the Shaking Quakers. Shakers believed they were living in the last millennium and since all people shared a brother / sister relationship, they should not marry as there was no longer a need to procreate. Instead they believed people should live communally as a family of brothers and sisters. Several other new denominations formed, of which the largest was the Disciples of Christ, which grew out of a camp meeting at Cane Ridge, Kentucky, in the early 1800s.

THOSE LONESOME DOVES: It was not uncommon for bordellos in western towns to operate openly, without the stigma from East Coast cities. Gambling and prostitution were central to life. Later, when the female population increased, reformers moved in and other civilizing influences arrived. Only then did prostitution become less blatant and more uncommon. Reformers moved in, and other civilizing influences arrived, only then did prostitution become less blatant and more uncommon.

GET ALONG LITTLE DOGIES: Ranchers and their cowboys drove Texas herds north along the Western, Chisholm, and Shawnee trails some eight hundred miles to the railhead at Abilene, Kansas. A typical drive might take three to four months and contained two miles of cattle six abreast. The cattle were shipped to Chicago, St. Louis, and points east for slaughter and consumption in the fast-growing cities. Despite the risks, a successful drive proved very profitable to everyone involved, as the price of one steer was four dollars in Texas, and ten times that money back East.

While camping every night, the cowboys on watch would often sing to their herd (dogies) to keep them calm.

> *Whoopee ti yi yo, get along little dogies*
> *It's your misfortune, ain't none of my own*
> *Whoopee ti yi yo, get along little dogies*
> *You know that Wyoming will be your new home.*

END OF THE TRAIL: Bad weather, greed, and technology combined to end the great cattle drives. Especially harsh winters in the mid-1880s killed tens of thousands of cattle trying to forage on the open range. Too many ranchers had overstocked the grass, leading to lower prices and leaving animals unable to feed themselves on lands that did not produce enough grass in dry weather. Further expansion of western railroads made it cheaper and quicker to haul cattle by train rather than drive them.

DRIFT FENCES: To control the number of cattle drifting south onto Texas ranges the Panhandle Cattlemen's Association, working with large cattle companies in northern Texas, erected the region's first drift fence in 1882. The longest line of fencing in the world is the wire fence extended from Indian Territory west across the Texas Panhandle and thirty-five miles into New Mexico, a total of two hundred miles along the Canadian River. That stopped the drift of northern cattle.

KILLING THE BISON: The rise of the cattle industry and the cowboy came because of the demise of the huge herds of bison, usually called buffalo. Once, more than twenty-five million of the huge furry animals thundered across the Great Plains. Those grass-eating herds were a vital resource animal for the Plains Indians, providing food, hides for clothing and shelter, and bones for implements. Loss of habitat, disease, and over-hunting steadily reduced the herds through the nineteenth century to the point of near extinction. The tribes who had depended on the buffalo had to accept a government offer of reservations, where the government would feed and supply them on condition they would not go on the warpath. If only that promise and others had not been broken, many lives would have been saved.

GUNFIGHT AT THE OK CORRAL: The Gunfight at the OK Corral was a thirty-second shootout between lawmen (the Earp brothers) and members of a loosely organized group of outlaws and rustlers called the Cowboys (the McLaurys and Clantons). This most famous shootout in the history of the American West took place around 3:00 p.m. on Wednesday, the twenty-sixth of October 1881, in Tombstone, Arizona Territory. Here is the rest of the story.

James, Virgil, and Wyatt Earp, together with their wives, arrived in Tombstone in 1879 during the period of rapid growth associated with mining when there were only a few hundred residents. Virgil was appointed Deputy US Marshal. In the summer of 1880, Morgan and Warren Earp also moved there. Wyatt bought a stagecoach, only to find the business very competitive. The Earp boys were Republicans from Illinois and had never worked as cowmen or ranchers.

Their work as lawmen was not welcomed by the McLaury Cowboys, who viewed the Earp brothers as badge-toting tyrants. They were known to bend the law in their favor when it affected their gambling and saloon interests.

Tensions between the Earp family lawmen and the Cowboy clan grew lethal. Billy Clanton was one of the first cowboys killed at the shoot-out. The lawmen, Virgil, Doc, and Morgan, were all injured, leaving only Wyatt stepping away clean. Over time the fight came to symbolize the spirit of the western territory as, "you don't have to obey the law."

The gunfight was not the end of the conflict. At the end of December 1881, Virgil Earp was ambushed and maimed in a murder attempt by the Cowboys. Three months later, a Cowboy fired through the glass door of a saloon, killing Morgan Earp. In both incidents, other members of the Cowboys provided alibis for the suspects.

Wyatt Earp, the newly appointed Deputy US Marshal for Cochise County, then took matters into his own hands. The interpersonal conflicts and feuds leading to the gunfight were complex. Each side carried strong family ties.

In spite of wild west tales, hay and feed for horses remained a big part of the economy. Also, the industries of blacksmithing, saddle-making, harness-making, and the construction of horse-drawn wagons, carriages, buggies, and sleighs contributed to the legacy.

THE JAMES GANG IN MISSOURI: Further east in 1881, Robert Ford shot the outlaw, Jesse James. The James brothers, Frank and Jesse, were followers of William Quantrill (Quantrill's Raiders) and "Bloody Bill" Anderson. They joined some pro-Confederate "bushwhackers" operating in Missouri and Kansas during the Civil War. After the war, they robbed banks, stagecoaches, and trains across the Midwest, gaining national fame and often popular sympathy despite the brutality of their crimes.

Another member of the James Gang wanted the five-thousand-dollar reward offered for Jesse James. The Ford brothers, Charles and Robert, had been planning to rob the Platte City Bank, but instead opted to collect the prize for their infamous leader, who used the alias Thomas Howard. The Missouri governor promised the Ford boys a large reward, but they only received a small amount. The brothers were surprised by the hostility toward them for killing James.

Both men were immortalized in an American folk song, with the well-known lyrics beginning, *"That dirty little coward who shot Mr. Howard, he laid Jesse James in his grave."*

JUST IN TIME: Five standard time zones, established by the contiguous United States and Canadian railroad companies in 1883, ended confusion over thousands of local time zones. Before the adoption of four standard time zones for the continental United States, many towns and cities set their clocks to noon when the sun passed their local meridian. Noon occurred at different times, but time differences between distant locations were barely noticeable before the nineteenth century because of long travel times and the lack of instant long-distance communications before the invention of the telegraph.

DEATH OF A FORMER PRESIDENT: Throughout Chester Arthur's presidency, he suffered from Bright's Disease, a fatal illness of the kidney. He kept his poor health a secret and died less than two years after leaving office.

GROVER CLEVELAND ELECTED: Unlike most of his peers, Grover Cleveland did not enlist in the Civil War. When the Conscription Act passed in 1863, Cleveland paid a Polish immigrant to serve in his place, an acceptable option at the time. Up until three years before his Democratic nomination, Cleveland had been a lawyer with an excellent reputation in Buffalo, New York.

GROVER-NOT-SO-GOOD: The Republican Party nominated the scandal-tainted James Blaine for president in 1884, so Democrats decided to show a contrast by nominating Grover the Good. The problem was Cleveland was not so perfect; his secret past soon came to light. Ten years earlier, they said he had fathered an illegitimate child and sent the child to live in an orphanage. Cleveland admitted he'd had a brief affair with the child's mother, Maria Halpin, and he agreed to provide financial support when she named him as the father, though he was uncertain whether the child was really his. Many people believed the child's father to be Cleveland's law partner, Oscar Folsom. Cleveland won the people's confidence, and the election.

CLEVELAND'S YOUNG BRIDE: Upon the death of his law partner, Cleveland became the legal executor of his friend's estate and was looking after his friend's nine-year-old daughter, Frances "Frankie" Folsom. A dozen years later, Frances was a striking young woman five foot seven with black hair and blue eyes.

The president proposed, she accepted, and reporters stalked every move of the bride as she made her way from New York to Washington, DC. They were married at the presidential palace in June 1886, making her at the age of twenty-one the youngest first lady ever. Her new husband was almost three decades older. In time they became parents of five children—three daughters and two sons. Their first baby, Ruth, was the first child ever born in the white house.

Frances Cleveland did not help her husband campaign in the 1884 election, and she was not in attendance at the 1885 inauguration because of her youth. She was still in school and couldn't get permission to miss class in her last year at Wells College.

Figure 58: Grover Cleveland

Cleveland was the twenty-second and the twenty-fourth president. His two terms, (1885 to 1889) and (1892 to 1896), were not consecutive.

Vice President: Thomas Hendricks

Cleveland, an exceptionally hard-working president, often took time off to play poker on Sunday afternoons. *"My father used to say it was wicked to go fishing on Sunday," he once explained, "but he never said anything about draw-poker."*

A SECRET SURGERY AT SEA: A workaholic micromanager, Grover Cleveland wrote his own letters in longhand and answered the phone himself. During the economic depression, while he and his family were at their summer home, Cleveland was diagnosed with jaw cancer requiring immediate surgery.

The president and Mrs. Cleveland believed a public disclosure of the president's condition would unnecessarily alarm the nation, so the president had the surgery secretly performed at sea, aboard his friend's yacht, *"Oneida."* A team of six surgeons removed the tumor along with five teeth and much of Cleve- land's upper left palate and jawbone, on a moving boat using ether for anesthesia.

Part of Cleveland's jaw was reconstructed of vulcanized rubber, but the public remained in the dark because the president's trademark mustache was left untouched.

The reason for his four-day absence from public life was said to be "a fishing trip." Mrs. Cleveland played a large part in the successful deception of the press, explicitly misleading those who questioned his whereabouts.

LADY LIBERTY: President Cleveland dedicated the Statue of Liberty on Liberty Island in New York Harbor in 1886. Known during its construction and erection as "Bartholdi's Light" or "Liberty Enlightening the World," the status symbol was first shown at the Centennial Exhibition in Philadelphia ten years earlier. The huge copper sculpture by French artist Auguste Bartholdi provided the beacon to millions of immigrants and citizens who would pass its position in the decades to come.

GIVE ME YOUR TIRED: A tablet at the base declares the statue as a "gift from the people of the Republic of France honoring the alliance of the two nations in achieving independence," and attests their abiding friendship. The original agreement said France would finance the monument if Americans paid for the pedestal. Several fund-raising campaigns were held to make the statue possible. Emma Lazarus wrote her famous sonnet for a fundraiser auction, *"Give me your tired, your poor, your huddled masses yearning to breathe free ... ."*

But the fund-raising was not working until the early 1880s when newspaper publisher Joseph Pulitzer took up the cause of the statue's pedestal. He mounted an energetic fund drive, promising to print the name of each donor, no matter how small the donation. Pulitzer's audacious plan worked, and millions of people around the country began donating whatever they could.

PENNIES FOR THE PEDESTAL: Schoolchildren across America collected pennies. For instance, a kindergarten class in Iowa sent $1.35 to Pulitzer's fund drive. Pulitzer and the New York newspaper announced they received the final one hundred thousand dollars for the statue in August 1885.

HAYMARKET RIOTS: The Haymarket riot and bombing in Chicago, Illinois, began three days after the start of a general strike pushing for shorter working hours. The uprising happened in reaction to the killing of several workers by the police the previous day during a peaceful rally in support of the striking workers. Suddenly someone threw a dynamite bomb at police as they tried to disperse the public meeting in Chicago's Haymarket Square. The blast and ensuing gunfire resulted in the deaths of seven police officers and at least four civilians. Dozens of others were wounded.

A harsh anti-union clampdown followed the incident. Community and business support for the police came pouring in. Many thousands of dollars were donated for their medical care. The entire labor community and immigrant population, mainly Germans and Bohemians, came under suspicion. Police carried out raids on homes and offices of suspected anarchists. Dozens of suspects were arrested, many only remotely related to the Haymarket affair.

CLEVELAND THE WATCHDOG: Not regarded as an original thinker, Grover Cleveland seemed to consider himself a watchdog over Congress rather than an initiator. His plan appeared to be to keep them from doing anything. He vetoed twice as many congressional bills as all twenty-one of the preceding presidents combined, delivering four hundred fourteen vetoes in his first term.

LIFE FOR THE INDIANS: In 1887, Congress passed the General Allotment or Dawes Act, an attempt at assimilating the Indians. Reservations were divided into tracts of land, one hundred sixty acres per family named on the Dawes list. Those who accepted allotments and lived separately from the tribe would be granted United States citizenship. Many of these Indians did not see themselves as farmers and quickly sold out.

WHAT ABOUT THE DAWES ACT? The objectives of the Dawes Act were to abolish tribal and communal land ownership of the tribes into individual land ownership. Actually, the act authorized the president to confiscate and redistribute tribal lands in the American West.

By the end of the 1880s, a general consensus seemed to be the assimilation of Native Americans into American culture was a top priority, believing they should leave behind their tribal landholding, reservations, traditions, and ultimately their biological identities.

These Dawes Act lists are quite beneficial for genealogists in proving Indian heritage. The rolls contain each person's name, blood degree, sex, and census number. Before you start searching the Dawes Rolls' online index for potential information on your genealogy, you need to know your specific ancestor's name and tribal affiliation.

If you want to become a member of one of the Five Civilized Tribes, you will have to prove your affiliation to a member with a tribal number. Of course, you first must verify that the individual—your ancestor—actually can be found listed in one of the tribal rolls. Many citizens have a family legend of being Indian.

WASHINGTON'S MONUMENT: Plans for a memorial had been in place even before George Washington died in 1799, but the ideas never became concrete until the 1830s when a group began collecting donations and searching for a suitable design.

Construction on the obelisk started in 1848, and the work progressed slowly for six years until funding dried up eight years later. The Civil War caused further delays. The monument was finally completed in December of 1884.

The Corps of Engineers positioned the capstone, weighing more than three thousand pounds, atop the Washington Monument. The monument stood close to six hundred feet tall when completed.

After nearly thirty-seven years of work, the masterpiece

Figure 59: Washington's Monument under construction.

opened to the public in 1888 as the world's tallest construction, until completion of the Eiffel Tower three years later. Laus Deo (Latin for "praise be to God") is inscribed on the East face of the aluminum apex of the pyramid capstone on top of the finished stone obelisk.

GHOST DANCE SHIRTS: In 1889, during a solar eclipse, a Northern Paiute Indian named Wovoka claimed he had traveled to heaven during a vision. Just as troubled Jews looked for a messiah to rescue them, Wovoka's idea of a coming savior spread among the Plains Indians. They believed death of all whites and the resurrection of Indians would happen on his arrival. A "ghost dance" was part of Wovoka's prediction, and the event became a national spiritual movement. Special clothing items created by the ghost dancers were believed to have mysterious spiritual powers. Several factions of the Lakota people believed the sacred ghost dance shirts to be bulletproof.

The words and practices of Wovoka reached across the Cheyenne, Arapaho, Kiowa, Wichita, Caddo, and Apache tribes. The message the ghost dance brought was not about hatred or rebellion, but of returning their people to the culture and life they enjoyed before the white settlers came.

The ghost dance gave them hope such times could return. These tribes were all suffering from dreadful conditions. Handouts of rations and supplies guaranteed by the treaties were of poor quality if they arrived at all. Indian life was just as desperate in 1890 as it had been in 1870. The ghost dance craze continued into the next decade.

GOODBYE GROVER: Grover Cleveland was the only president to leave the president's house and return for a second term four years later. As Frances Folsom Cleveland departed the mansion in 1889, she told a staff member, "Now, Jerry, I want you to take good care of all the furniture and ornaments in the house, for I want to find everything just as it is now, when we come back again."

When asked when she would return, she responded, "We are coming back four years from today." And so they did, when Grover Cleveland was re-elected to serve a second term.

PRESIDENTIAL ELECTION OF 1888: A Civil War hero, Benjamin Harrison, or "Ben" as he was known, was elected as the twenty-third president to serve from 1889 to 1893. His only apparent qualification for the office was he happened to be the grandson of the ninth president, William Henry Harrison, a soldier who died after a month in office. Benjamin and William Henry Harrison are the only grandfather-grandson duo to hold the top office. Ben also was a great-grandson of a founding father, who was also named Benjamin Harrison.

SWEET CAROLINE: Caroline Lavinia Scott, daughter of John Witherspoon Scott, a Presbyterian minister and professor, met Ben Harrison, when he was one of her father's freshman students at Farmer's College near Cincinnati. They fell in love.

Caroline often took Ben dancing against the wishes of his father, who frowned on such activities. The first few years of marriage were a struggle. The couple rarely spent time together as Ben worked to establish his law practice and was active in fraternal organizations to build up his business network. When Caroline became pregnant, she returned to Oxford to stay with her parents.

Ben and Caroline became parents of two children. During the Harrison administration, many family members joined them in Washington. Their daughter, Mary Harrison McKee with her two children, Caroline's father, and other relatives lived at the presidential home. The first lady tried to have the overcrowded mansion enlarged but was unsuccessful.

In 1889, Caroline Harrison raised the first Christmas tree in the white house, as the custom was becoming popular. She introduced the use of orchids as the official floral decoration at state receptions. A talented artist, Caroline conducted china-painting classes for other women. In late 1891, she began to battle tuberculosis, which at the time had no known treatment other than rest and proper nutrition. As her condition worsened, Caroline went to spend the summer in the Adirondack Mountains where the air was considered healthful for TB patients. After her illness became terminal, Caroline returned to the mansion where she died at the age of sixty in 1892.

A SECOND WIFE: Four years later, Benjamin Harrison married his late wife's niece and former secretary, the widow Mary Scott Dimmick, and they became parents of a daughter, Elizabeth. Harrison was called by some people the "human iceberg" for how stiff he appeared with people. Many may have misread his anxiety for aloofness.

Figure 60:
Benjamin Harrison

Harrison was our twenty-third president, serving one term from 1889 to 1893.

Vice President: Levi Morton

Thomas Edison filed a patent for his electric incandescent lamp and supplied the first power to customers in 1882, so Harrison was the first president to have electricity in the executive mansion. However, he received an electric shock and was so scared of being electrocuted he refused to touch the light switches. He often went to bed leaving the lights on.

RUNNING FOR LAND: During Harrison's administration, six western states were admitted to the Union. Harrison opened up Oklahoma lands to white settlement, beginning the twenty-second of April 1889, when the first of five land runs in the former Indian territory started at high noon. More than fifty thousand people waited at the starting line to race for one-hundred-sixty-acre parcels in central Oklahoma. Provided he or she lived on the land and improved it, the settler could then receive title under the Homestead Act of 1862. The Indian Appropriations Act allocated funds to move Western tribes onto reservations. This bill made it significantly easier for the federal government to secure lands that were previously owned by Native Americans.

Chapter 10 in Summary from 1880 to 1890:

- ✓ Census of 1880 shows name of the street and house
- ✓ Genealogists love the census of 1880
- ✓ Gunfight breaks out at the OK corral in Tombstone, AZ, on October 26, 1881
- ✓ James A. Garfield, elected 1881, became the 20th president.
- ✓ Garfield, a Civil War brigadier general, served as president only two hundred days
- ✓ Garfield is shot, dying two months later Chester "Chet" Arthur is the 21st president in 1881
- ✓ President Arthur eliminated the spoils system
- ✓ Grover Cleveland, a NY lawyer, called Grover the Good
- ✓ Cleveland's secret revealed fathering a bastard child
- ✓ Cleveland weds a young wife in the presidential mansion
- ✓ 1889 Ben Harrison, grandson of Old Tippecanoe, elected
- ✓ Haymarket massacre in Chicago
- ✓ Dawes Act lists the Indians and allots land
- ✓ The Ghost Dance craze continues into the next decade
- ✓ Refrigerated transports allowed for more variety in food
- ✓ Thomas Edison patents electric incandescent lamp 1880
- ✓ Clara Barton establishes American Red Cross, 1881
- ✓ Cause of TB (Bacilli) discovered
- ✓ Federal immigration law of 1882 excluded Chinese
- ✓ Five standard US time zones established
- ✓ Statue of Liberty dedicated on Liberty Island, NYC

ELEVEN—1890

Battle of Wounded Knee

THE CENSUS IS MISSING

The 1890 census is gone. Only a shred remains, so you probably won't be able to find your ancestors listed that year. Of all the 1890 census records, more than ninety-nine percent burned up in a fire in Washington, DC, in 1921. The census had included six new states, forty-two total. Fragments exist only for the states of Alabama, Georgia, Illinois, Minnesota, New Jersey, New York, North Carolina, Ohio, South Dakota, and Texas, and the District of Columbia.

Surprisingly, the Oklahoma Territory census survived because they had not sent it to Washington city. The Oklahoma Historical Society (OHS) Research Center created an index to the 1890 Oklahoma Territorial Census. The OHS archives house the original pages, and you can search them online at http://www.okhistory.org/research/1890.

This census lists individuals residing in Oklahoma Territory, which then consisted of just seven counties. The counties are often listed only by a number on the record. This was the first census to be compiled on a tabulating machine. The new technology reduced the time taken to tabulate from seven years for the 1880 census to two and a half years for the 1890. This special census includes almost seventy-five thousand schedules enumerating veterans and widows of veterans even without the missing records.

SUBSTITUTE FOR 1890: Data used includes not only fragments of the original files, but also special veteran's schedules, several Native American tribal census counts for years surrounding 1890, some state censuses (1885 or 1895), city and county directories, alumni directories, and voter registration documents. Perhaps eventually more of the missing genealogical information will be found. Ancestry.com has been acquiring assorted records to help find ancestors around the time of the 1890 census.

PENSIONS FOR VETERANS: In addition to previous pension bills, the Dependent and Disability Pension Act of 1890 passed by Congress was signed into law by President Harrison. This bill provided pensions for all veterans who served at least ninety days in the military or naval forces, were honorably discharged, and were unable to perform manual labor. They got a pension regardless of their financial situation or when the disability happened. The bill became a source of contentious debate. The Act did provide pensions to disabled Civil War veterans regardless of the cause of their disability; however, it also depleted the federal budget surplus. Pension expenditures reached a hundred thirty-five million dollars under President Harrison, the most massive budget in American history. Pension Bureau commissioner James R. Tanner's expansive interpretation of the law exacerbated the problem.

A VETERAN'S CENSUS: The bureau called for a special 1890 count of Civil War Union veterans and widows of veterans, even if they lived in the South. The US Pension Office requested this particular enumeration to help Union veterans locate comrades to testify in pension claims, and also to determine the number of survivors and widows for pension legislation.

Even here, records for some states are missing. If your ancestor was at the right place at the right time, you might learn about a man's service, his wounds, death or disability, an address, or a widow's remarriage. Confederate veterans also got pensions in some cases.

This special veteran listing is available on microfilm or online at Ancestry.com. However, if your ancestor lived in a state alphabetically listed before Kentucky (A to Ken.), you are still out of luck. Nobody seems to know what happened to those records, but Kentucky lost or destroyed about half of the records before transfer to the National Archives in 1943. Even without the missing records, this special census includes almost seventy-five thousand schedules enumerating Union veterans and widows of veterans.

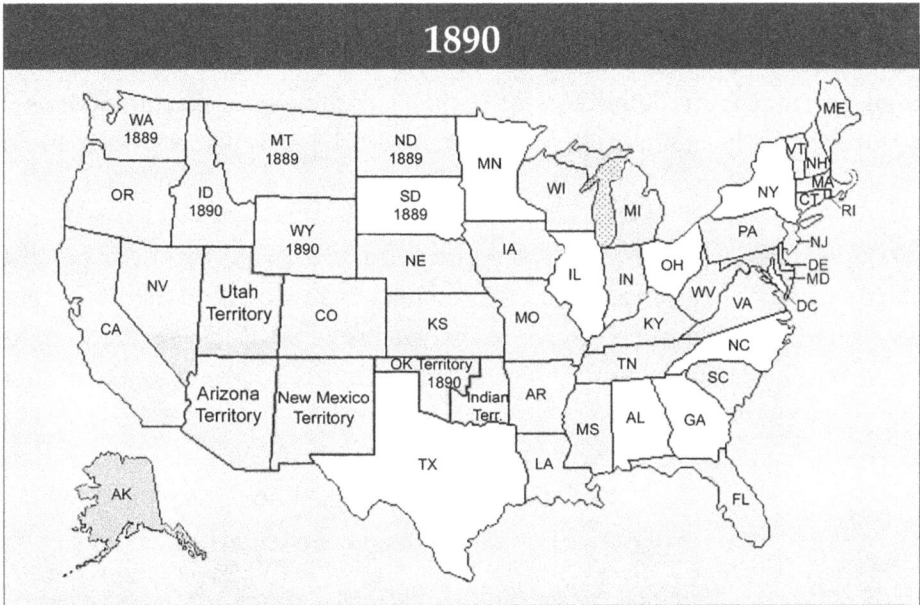

Figure 61: The 1890 census, Benjamin Harrison, president.

Six new states are added this decade: North Dakota, South Dakota, Montana, Idaho, Wyoming, and Washington for forty-two states total. Territories include Arizona, Utah, New Mexico, Montana, Alaska, Oklahoma Territory, and Indian Territory. Most of the 1890 population schedules were badly damaged by fire in the commerce department building in January 1921. The white colored states have only a few remaining schedules.

PRESIDENT NUMBER 23, BEN HARRISON: Republican Benjamin Harrison became president number twenty-three, to serve through 1893. He had conducted one of the first "front-porch" campaigns, delivering short speeches to delegations visiting him in Indianapolis.

Harrison was a colonel in the Union Army and was confirmed by the Senate as a brevet brigadier general of volunteers in 1865.

As he was only five feet, six inches tall, Democrats referred to him as "Little Ben." Harrison substantially strengthened and modernized the US Navy and conducted an active foreign policy. However, he was unsuccessful in securing federal education funding as well as voting rights for African Americans.

Long before the Harrison Administration ended, the Treasury surplus had evaporated. Happiness and prosperity seemed about to disappear as well. Citizens were definitely not happy. Congressional elections in 1890 went stingingly against the Republicans, and party leaders decided to abandon Harrison.

THE GAR FOR UNION VETS: After the end of the war, various state and local organizations were formed for veterans to network and maintain connections with each other. Many of the veterans used their shared experiences as a basis for fellowship. Groups of men began joining together, first for camaraderie and later for governmental power. The most well-known of these groups is the Grand Army of the Republic (GAR), an organization for Union veterans only. With the assistance of the Republican party, which

1890 Veterans and Widows

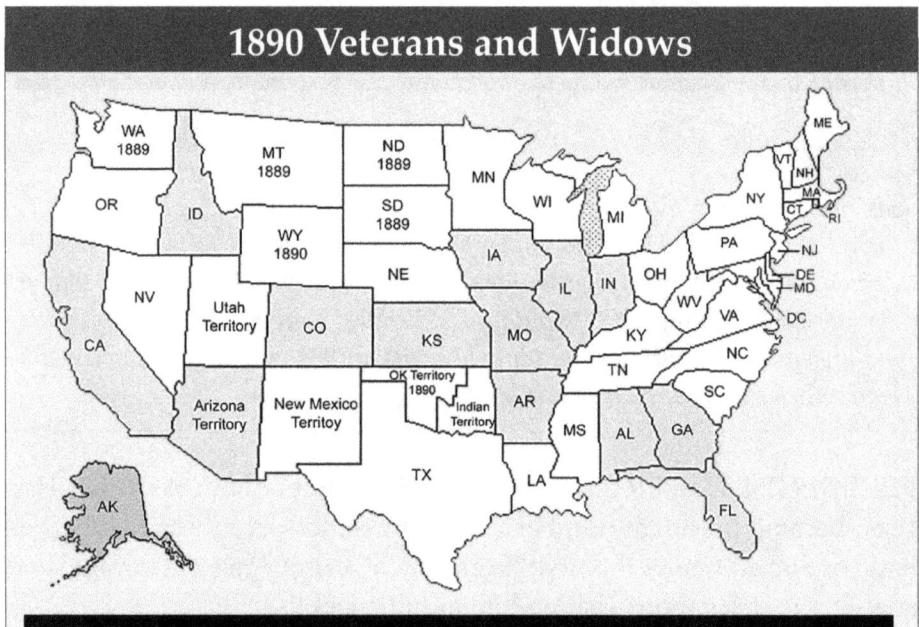

Figure 62: A special census of Union veterans and widows.

The records give name, rank, company, regiment or vessel, dates of enlistment and discharge, length of service, residence, disability, and remarks—if your ancestor was in one of the lucky states. Census schedules exist only for the unshaded states and even then, some counties are missing.

opposed the Democratic party on the issue of pensions, the GAR became much more active in the call for liberal pension legislation following passage of the Arrears Act of 1879.

Proposals favored by the GAR were generally either service pension plans or disability pension plans. Service plans included pensions for any veteran if he served some minimum term in the armed forces. Disability plans more closely represented the final bill passed in 1890 and included pensions for any veteran incapacitated by a disability, regardless of how it happened. The GAR held an annual "National Encampment" every year from 1866 to 1949. Every state, even those of the former Confederacy, fell within a GAR "Department," and within these Departments were the Posts, forerunners of later American Legion Halls and Veterans of Foreign Wars (VFW) Halls. Records of attendance at those encampments are hard to find, but many remain in existence.

WOUNDED KNEE MASSACRE: Kicking Bear, a Sioux Miniconjou Indian, visited the respected leader Sitting Bull in 1890 at Standing Rock.

BULLETPROOF SHIRTS: Kicking Bear told his friend Sitting Bull of the many Indian tribes referring to Wovoka as the Christ. He also told Sitting Bull of the prophecy the next spring when the grass was high, the earth would be covered with new soil burying all white men. Sweetgrass would grow and spread over the new soil. Running water, trees, and vast herds of buffalo and wild horses would return. They believed all Indians who danced the Ghost Dance would be taken up into the air and suspended there while the new earth was laid down. Then they would return to earth along with the ghosts of their ancestors.

The Indians began making "ghost dance shirts" they believed would protect them from bullets.

White settlers on the plains became alarmed. President Harrison responded to their fears by sending the US Army to these reservations to stop the threat, hoping to end the potential conflict believed rising between the Indians and whites.

The Sioux tribe had been cornered and agreed to turn themselves in at the Pine Ridge Agency in South Dakota. The Army had orders to escort the Sioux to the railroad for transport to Omaha, Nebraska. They were the very last Sioux tribal members to go.

TRIBAL POLICE ARREST SITTING BULL: The next day, the Bureau of Indian Affairs (BIA) government agent in charge of the Lakota sent tribal police to arrest Sitting Bull to force him to stop the Ghost Dance. He was camped with other Sioux Indians near Wounded Knee Creek on the Pine Ridge Indian Reservation in South Dakota.

There was some confusion and in the struggle Sitting Bull was killed, along with many tribal policemen in an incident known as the Wounded Knee Massacre.

The soldiers of the Seventh Cavalry ordered the Indians to surrender all firearms. Black Coyote, who was deaf, refused to hand over his gun to a soldier. During the tug of war and scramble to get the gun, it accidentally fired. Then, nervous troops opened fire because they thought they were under attack and needed to regain order. The Lakota, who had no weapons, tried to flee. The military chased down all those who attempted to escape, constantly firing all the way. The gunfire continued for hours as the soldiers pursued the Lakota people.

A MASSACRE AT WOUNDED KNEE: At least two hundred Sioux were killed, many of them women and children. More than a hundred Lakota are believed to have fled the chaos, with an unknown number later dying from hypothermia in the following three-day blizzard. When it became apparent the ghost shirts were not "bulletproof," and the expected resurrection did not happen, most believers quit the movement. After Wounded Knee, the remaining Indian tribes were either subdued or forcibly assimilated into mainstream white society. The Battle of Wounded Knee in South Dakota (29 December 1890) was the last major battle between United States troops and Native Americans.

PAYING OFF THE NATIONAL DEBT: Congress passed the McKinley Tariff, a dramatic increase in import fee, in 1890. The tariff angered Americans because of the escalation in prices of consumer goods. In reaction, they gave Democrats control of both houses of Congress, and in the next election of 1892 returned Grover Cleveland to the top office.

ELLIS ISLAND IMMIGRATION: Ellis Island Immigration Station first opened for processing immigrants to the United States on the first day of January 1892.

Previously, individual states regulated immigration rather than the federal government. "New immigration" was a term from the late 1880s about the influx of Catholic and Jewish immigrants from Italy and Russia (areas previously providing few immigrants). The majority of immigrants came through overcrowded New York, thus making the northeast a principal target of settlement. There were various efforts, such as the Galveston Movement, to redirect immigrants to other ports and disperse some of the settlers to other areas of the country.

Nativists feared the new arrivals lacked the political, social, and occupational skills needed to assimilate into American culture successfully. This raised the issue of whether the USA was still a "melting pot" or if it had just become a "dumping ground." Many old-stock Americans worried about adverse effects on the economy, politics, and culture. They proposed requiring a literacy test, whereby applicants had to be able to read and write in their own language.

SEPARATE AND NOT EQUAL: In the South, segregation was increasing. Blacks had been getting together for education and in their churches by choice. Beginning in 1890 Louisiana passed a law demanding separate accommodations and separate railway cars for blacks.

Homer Plessy, seven-eighths white and one-eighth black, purchased a first-class ticket and was arrested for violating this law. His case made it to the US Supreme Court in 1896 as Plessy v. Ferguson. The court decided against Plessy, standing on the "one-drop rule," asserting "any person with even one ancestor of African ancestry is classified Negro."

Southern custom required separate (at the back) seating on buses and trains, different waiting rooms, separate lavatories, separate entrances to circuses and factories, separate parks, even separate water fountains, and denial of service to blacks at restaurants and lunch counters.

The whites who favored this segregation believed the fictional "separate but equal." It was not equal at all. Instead of equality, southern whites continued to apply pressure on blacks to show deference to whites. No matter how accomplished the Negro or how low-standing the white, the black male was called boy, and the white called sir or ma'am. Devices to deny the vote to Africans were always in process.

GROVER AGAIN IN 1892: The presidential election was the first and only one where an incumbent US president and an ex-US president both ran as

Figure 63: Grover Cleveland

Cleveland was our twenty-fourth president, and his second term ran from 1892 to 1897.

Vice President: Adlai Stevenson

major-party nominees. Democrat Grover Cleveland won the general election competition with Republican Ben Harrison by three percent, the largest popular vote margin in twenty years.

THE PRESIDENT'S YOUNG FAMILY: Frances Cleveland was a different woman in 1893 from the bride who assumed the first lady role eight years before. Her most immediate priority proved to be her three small daughters, two born during her husband's second term. Without planning to, Frances Cleveland helped change the public image of her husband from the coarse Buffalo NY politician who fathered an illegitimate son and enjoyed drinking beer, into a devoted husband and doting father of his toddler daughters.

THE JOHNSON COUNTY WAR: A range conflict, the Johnson County War, occurred in Wyoming from 1889 to 1893. Cattle companies began ruthlessly persecuting alleged rustlers in the area. Many innocent settlers competed with the cattle companies for land, livestock and water rights. As tensions swelled between the extensive established ranch owners and the smaller farmers, violence culminated near the Powder River. The ranchers hired armed men to invade the county. The events became a highly mythologized and legendary story of the Wild West.

Over the years variations of the storyline included some of its most famous historical figures like Cattle Kate, James Averell, Nate Champion of the KC Ranch, Tom Horn, and the Sheriff, Red Angus.

An alleged cattle rustler and saloon owner, Averell was hanged along with Cattle Kate by a faction in 1889. Later investigations into the whole incident found that most likely neither James Averell nor his girlfriend,

Ellen "Cattle Kate" Watson, were guilty of any crime. This is just one of the many incidents that led to the Johnson County War.

In the early days of Wyoming, most of the land was in the public domain, which was open range for cattle and homesteading farmlands. Large numbers of bovines belonging to large ranches grazed on the free range. The fencing of public land and water sources led to widespread fence cutting in many areas of the West. Each spring, round-ups were held to separate the herds. Before a roundup, an unbranded orphan or stray calf was sometimes surreptitiously branded, which was the standard way to identify the cow's owners. The round-up foreman would settle disputed brand markings. As a last resort, they would kill the bovine and examine the hide from the flesh side to reveal if someone had altered the original brand.

Cattle barons generally ran their ranches with a "hands-off" approach, hiring cowboys and foremen to do the work. They usually forbade their employees from owning cattle so there was no temptation to take a few strays. Land and water rights were typically distributed to whoever settled the property first. Farmers and ranchers had to respect these boundaries.

Actually, this Johnson County range war took place in three Wyoming counties: Johnson, Natrona, and Converse. The Wyoming Stock Growers Association (the WSGA) and the Northern Wyoming Farmers and Stock Growers' Association (NWFSGA) comprised the combatants.

WSGA was an older organization, including some of the state's wealthiest and most well-known residents who held political sway in the state and region. A primary function of the WSGA was to organize the cattle industry by scheduling roundups and cattle shipments. Time after time the WSGA ranchers had to hire gunmen to invade the county with the intent to eliminate alleged rustlers in Johnson County and break up the NWFSGA. The siege ended when President Harrison ordered the US Cavalry to control the range war. Only scattered fighting persisted in the months following.

MURDER AT THE FAIR: The Chicago World's Fair, also known as the World's Columbian Exposition, was held to celebrate the four hundredth anniversary of Christopher Columbus's discovery of the New World. The Exposition was an influential social and cultural event and had a profound effect on architecture, sanitation, the arts, Chicago's self-image, and American industrial optimism. Many of today's brand names—Campbell's soup, Nabisco crackers, and Coca-Cola—were introduced there.

However, the Chicago World's Fair became better known for a gruesome exhibit, the so-called "Murder Castle" of H. H. Holmes, America's first documented serial killer. His real name was Herman Webster Mudgett, who was also a con artist, a bigamist, and the subject of more than fifty lawsuits in Chicago alone. As a medical student, he stole corpses and then planted the bodies, making it look as if they had been killed in an accident. He held insurance policies and once the bodies were discovered Mudgett collected the money.

A DEVIL IN THE WHITE CITY: When the Exposition opened, Holmes listed his home as a hotel for visitors, labeling it as the "World's Fair Castle" hotel. Many who went in, never came out. Holmes lured many Exposition visitors to his sinister lair, with the promise of cheap lodgings. Historians still debate the exact number of his victims. More than fifty were reported to the police as "missing" when the Fair closed. His victims ranged from his female employees, to lovers, and hotel guests.

When the police searched the "Castle," they were horrified. They found trap doors, a gas chamber, and a crematorium in the basement. Some bedrooms were soundproofed and fitted with gas lines the murderer could use to suffocate his victims. Another on the second floor was dubbed "the secret hanging chamber."

A blood-spattered dissection table held vats of acid, surgical implements, various jars of poison, and pots of quicklime. Torture devices hung on the walls. Holmes is thought to have stripped many of the bodies down to their skeletons to sell for medical study, others he chopped up.

Mudgett, alias Holmes, was hanged in Philadelphia in 1896. Fire mysteriously gutted the Castle without destroying it. The building remained in use until officials demolished the structure in 1938.

THE PANIC OF 1893: In his second term, President Grover Cleveland angered many of his original supporters. Cleveland seemed overwhelmed by the severe national depression. Thirteen days before his inauguration, the Philadelphia and Reading Railroad (P&R) went into receivership, and that started the worst financial frenzy in the country's history.

Like dominoes falling, the panic set off a widespread economic depression in the United States lasting for three years. It began with the P&R

bankruptcy, followed rapidly by numerous bank failures, a stock market crash, a nationwide credit crisis, and the failures of three more railroads: The Northern Pacific, the Union Pacific, and the famous Atchison, Topeka & Santa Fe (AT&SF).

Next, a series of strikes crippled the coal and transportation industries. As a result, stock prices continued to decline. The Democrats and the President took the blame.

The decline of gold reserves in the Treasury fell to a dangerously low level. People rushed to withdraw their money from banks and caused disastrous bank runs. The 1890 wheat crop failed, and three years later wheat prices crashed. More than five hundred banks closed, fifteen thousand businesses failed, and numerous farms ceased operation.

Unemployment was estimated as high as nineteen percent. The massive spike in joblessness, combined with a loss of life savings by failed banks, meant a once-secure middle-class could not meet their mortgage obligations. As a result, many walked away from recently built homes. Facing starvation, people chopped wood, broke rocks, and sewed by hand with needle and thread in exchange for food. In some cases, women resorted to prostitution to feed their families. The president got the blame. The American economy did not recover until late 1896 when the Klondike gold rush in the Yukon touched off a new decade of rapid growth.

Widespread unemployment and dissatisfaction with Cleveland's lack of response led to tense and fearful clashes between unemployed citizens and local authorities throughout the country. Death threats to the president sharply increased. Frances Cleveland, without knowledge or permission of her husband, requested more Secret Service protection for him and the presidential mansion.

COXEY'S ARMY 1894: Unemployed workers, led by labor leader Jacob Coxey, marched to protest unemployment. The protest march, caused by the Panic of 1893, inspired a lobby for the government to create jobs building roads and other public work improvements. Originating with one hundred men in Massillon, Ohio, on Easter Sunday, the group began moving eastward along the route of the old National Road, the original federal highway built from Washington, DC, to Ohio in the early nineteenth century.

As "Coxey's Army" marched, many more workers joined along the way. Newspaper accounts of the five-week march mention hundreds and even thousands of residents welcoming marchers as they camped near their towns. This indicated widespread public support for the protest.

When Washington police blocked the marchers, Coxey and others climbed a fence and got arrested for trespassing on the Capitol lawn. Coxey's supporters demanded the government immediately assist workers by hiring them to work on public projects. The Congress and the President refused, and law enforcement officials arrested Coxey for trespassing on public property. The "Army" quickly dispersed upon their leader's arrest.

Perhaps Coxey's Army did not produce tangible results in 1894, but it did serve as the precursor for the massive protest marches of the twentieth century.

CARS HIT THE ROAD: Commercial production of automobiles was reaching an early stage. The Duryea Motor Wagon Company, founded by siblings Charles and Frank Duryea, arguably became the first American automobile firm. In 1893, the Duryea brothers tested their first gas-powered automobile model, and three years later established their company to build the Duryea model.

The Mormons, or members of The Church of Jesus Christ of Latter-day Saints, considered Utah Territory their promised land. They petitioned for statehood as the state of Deseret which was promptly denied by Congress. The lawmakers' hostility was mostly toward the church's practice of polygamy. After five unsuccessful petitions from the Mormons beginning in 1856, church president Wilford Woodruff finally issued a statement officially disavowing the practice of plural marriage by church members in 1890. Congress then passed an Enabling Act, permitting Utah to apply for statehood, but requiring the state constitution ban polygamy. Utah joined as the forty-fifth state on the fourth of January 1896.

After Grover Cleveland left office in 1897, he still made his views known in political matters, right or wrong. This one was wrong. In a 1905 article in The Ladies Home Journal, Cleveland weighed in on the women's suffrage movement, writing *"sensible and responsible women do not want to vote. The relative positions to be assumed by men and women in the working out of our civilization were assigned long ago by a higher intelligence."* I don't think Cleveland would say that in a campaign speech today.

PRESIDENT NUMBER 25, WILLIAM MCKINLEY: During the campaign, candidate McKinley made himself available to the public every day except

Sunday, receiving delegations from the front porch of his home.

His opponent, William Jennings Bryan, an American orator and Democrat of Nebraska, had been unsuccessful three times as the party's nominee for President in the 1896, 1900, and 1908 elections. Here he is, running again.

McKinley was the first candidate to use campaign buttons. He defeated Bryan and won election as the twenty-fifth president. McKinley served from 1897 through 1901. A war hero, McKinley raised protective tariffs to promote American industry. He hoped to persuade Spain to grant independence to rebellious Cuba without conflict, but when negotiation failed, he led the nation to war in 1898.

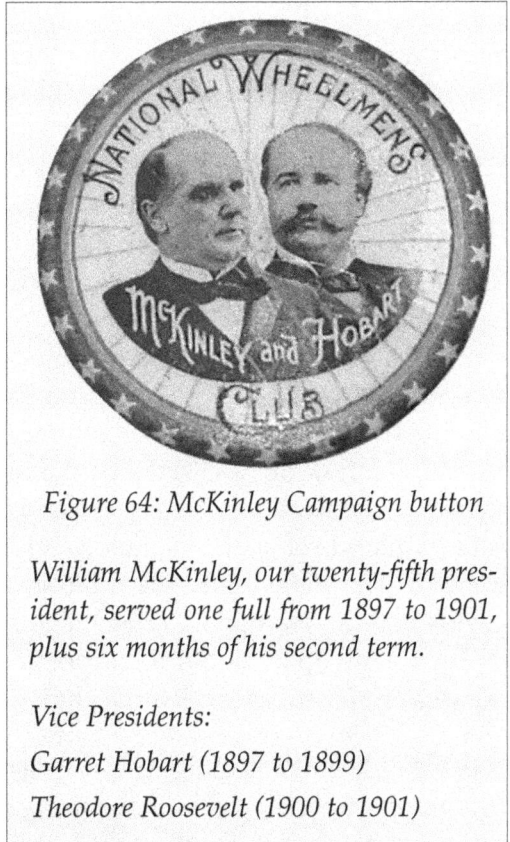

Figure 64: McKinley Campaign button

William McKinley, our twenty-fifth president, served one full from 1897 to 1901, plus six months of his second term.

Vice Presidents:

Garret Hobart (1897 to 1899)

Theodore Roosevelt (1900 to 1901)

SPANISH AMERICAN WAR: For some reason, this war was immensely popular with the American people. The war began with the Cuban struggle for independence from Spain. American sympathy for the rebels grew until America joined the fight in 1898 following the sinking of the battleship USS Maine in Havana harbor killing two hundred sixty American sailors. It remains controversial whether the explosion was caused by a malfunction aboard the ship or by Spanish sabotage. Public opinion and political pressures pushed McKinley into a war that he had wished to avoid.

For the first time, men from the North and the South closed ranks and marched together to another war, with bands playing the marches of John Philip Sousa.

THE ROUGH RIDERS: Theodore "Teddy" Roosevelt resigned his post as assistant secretary of the Navy to organize the first volunteer cavalry. The original plan for this unit called for filling it with men from the Indian Territory, New Mexico, Arizona, and Oklahoma. However, it quickly became a diverse and colorful group of cowboys, miners, law enforcement officials, and Native Americans called the Rough Riders.

Theodore Roosevelt is best known for leading his men on foot in the charge to capture San Juan Hill in Cuba. Some reported the charge would have had little success were it not for the support of seasoned African American soldiers serving in segregated infantry and cavalry units.

The United States scored a triumphant victory over Spain in less than a hundred days, losing fewer than three hundred Americans in battle. This "splendid little war," as Secretary of State John Hay called it, changed the course of American history and secured Cuba's independence from Spain. After hundreds of years, Spain was no longer a power in North or South America. The victory gave the Americans control of the heights overlooking the Spanish stronghold of Santiago and doomed the Spanish to defeat in Cuba. With Spain out of the running, the only power of importance in the Western Hemisphere was the United States.

THE US BECOMES IMPERIALIST: As a result of the war, the United States became an imperialist power acquiring Puerto Rico, Guam, and the Philippines as territories. Fearful that Japan might attempt to take control of Hawaii while the United States was distracted by Spain, President William McKinley also signed a resolution formally annexing Hawaii on the seventh of July 1898. The United States victory was quick and decisive. Returning a war hero, Roosevelt was elected Governor of New York. Having led his Rough Riders in a victorious skirmish with the Spanish in Cuba, Colonel Theodore Roosevelt became a national hero.

THE PHILIPPINE ISLANDS: For Filipinos, who had allied with US forces to oust Spain, the outcome of the war was a cruel joke. Although American leaders were unwilling to allow the Philippines to remain in the hands of the Spanish, they were also unwilling to give Filipinos their freedom. For two years, the United States fought to put down the Filipino insurrection, even resorting to some of the same tactics the Spanish had used. In 1901, the United States defeated the rebels, and the Philippines became an American territory. For Filipinos, it meant neither citizenship nor independence.

A YOUNG HERO: One young lad, a member of the Oklahoma Volunteer Cavalry, was one of the more than two hundred US soldiers killed. He gave his life for the Spanish-American victory.

Roy V. Cashion, a graduate of the Hennessey High School Senior Class of 1897, had a strong passion and belief in the freedom of the Cuban people. He titled his graduation speech, "Liberty for Cuba."

When the territorial governor, Frank Frantz—a member of the Rough Riders—asked for volunteers, Cashion's name was the first one on the list. He rode his horse through the frontier town now named "Cashion" on his way to Guthrie to join Theodore Roosevelt's Rough Riders.

The seventeen-year-old enlisted on the fifth of May 1898 and a few months later he was dead. After his regiment helped in the victory at Las Quasimas in the Cuban struggle for independence from Spain, young Roy Cashion was killed by a gunshot to the head as the group charged over San Juan Hill. He is believed to be the first Oklahoman to die in battle on foreign soil. Cashion is remembered with a statue in the small park of his hometown, sharing space with a memorial for Pat Hennessey, a freighter found massacred on the site twenty years earlier.

Oklahoma was not a state in 1898. The monument was paid for with funds collected from school children, town appropriations, and a warrant drawn on the territorial treasury.

McKINLEY'S TERM: William McKinley was the last president to have served in the Civil War, beginning as a private in the Union

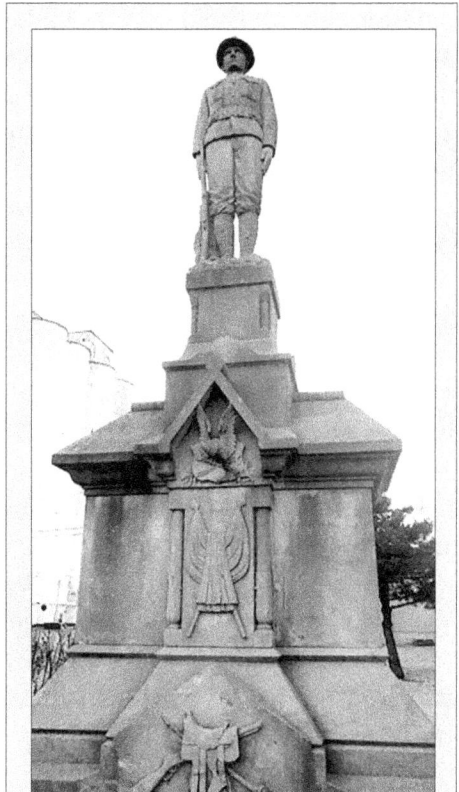

Figure 65: Roy V. Cashion, age 17

Oklahoma teenager Roy Cashion, born 1881, died in 1898 in the charge up San Juan Hill with Roosevelt's Rough Riders.

army and ending as a brevet major. After the war ended in 1865, McKinley decided on a career in law and later went into politics.

IDA SAXTON MCKINLEY: William McKinley's social life blossomed as he wooed Ida Saxton, the daughter of a prominent Canton, Ohio, banking family. William and Ida married in 1871. Just before the wedding, Ida's grandmother Christiana Dewalt died. Just after the wedding she lost her grandfather, John Saxton. William and Ida's first child, Katherine "Katie," was born on Christmas Day that year. Ida's mother died two weeks before Ida gave birth to her second child in March of 1873. The infant then died only four months later. Ida McKinley descended into a deep depression at her baby's death. Her health, never robust, grew worse. Two years after the death of baby Ida, the remaining child "little Katie" died of typhoid fever, a serious disease spread by contaminated food and water. Ida McKinley never recovered from her grief. The McKinleys had no more children, but contrary to persistent misperception Ida McKinley never became a permanent invalid.

William McKinley initially traveled alone to Washington, DC, in January of 1877, following his first election to the US House of Representatives while Ida McKinley was placed in the medical care of neurologist Silas Weir Mitchell in Philadelphia. Mitchell developed the "rest cure," to treat women of both physical and emotional problems which he believed the result of their brains being overworked in coping with issues he deemed only the male brain capable of resolving. His "cure" forced women into sedentary isolation and in the case of Ida McKinley that was what likely led to her developing chronic phlebitis.

In preparation for his anticipated 1896 presidential campaign, the McKinleys rented the same house which they had leased for the first two and a half years of their marriage from Ida's father. They chose the home to further a sense of sentimentality in the press about their marriage, an intention which took hold by the two-day silver wedding anniversary celebration they hosted there, with prominent political figures attending as guests. The event also served the purpose of permitting the press and public to meet Ida McKinley for themselves and reduce speculative gossip about the true nature of her health conditions and the prospect of her being a potential distraction to William McKinley as president.

As his first term drew to a close, McKinley was optimistic about his chances at re-election in 1900. Actually, McKinley's popularity in his first term assured him of being nominated for a second. McKinley did need a new running mate; his vice president, Garret Hobart had died in late 1899.

The 1900 McKinley re-election campaign was again based at the Canton house from which the previous one had been conducted. During this second campaign, neither William nor Ida McKinley were involved in public activities to the degree which had characterized the initial one.

Ida McKinley participated in all of the 1901 inauguration events without incident, much of the press and public focus having shifted to the new Vice President and his wife, Theodore and Edith Roosevelt.

The issues of the campaign had changed. Free silver was still a question animating many voters, but the Republicans focused on victory in war and prosperity at home as the issues they believed favored their party. McKinley would be elected to a second term in 1901 but was assassinated soon after.

After the Spanish-American War, the United States would never be the same.

Chapter 11 in Summary from 1890 to 1900:

- ✓ The 1890 Census was mostly destroyed in a fire in Washington, DC
- ✓ Civil War Union veterans and widows enumerated
- ✓ In 1893 Grover Cleveland defeats Ben Harrison
- ✓ Panic of 1893 began with the bankruptcy of Philadelphia and Reading Railroad (P&R)
- ✓ 500 bank failures, nationwide credit crisis, stock market crash followed for 3 years
- ✓ Unemployment 19% worst financial crisis in US history
- ✓ Strikes crippled the coal and transportation industries
- ✓ 15,000 businesses failed, and many farmers quit
- ✓ People were starving. The economy slowly began to recover in late 1896
- ✓ 1897 William McKinley becomes twenty-fifth president
- ✓ McKinley was a Union veteran war and hero of Spanish-American War
- ✓ Civil War veterans pension act passed
- ✓ America declared war on Spain in April 1898
- ✓ Teddy Roosevelt organized the Rough Riders
- ✓ Rough Riders' charge up San Juan Hill, US was victorious
- ✓ Teenage Rough Rider from Oklahoma was killed on San Juan Hill
- ✓ Theodore Roosevelt vice president takes office
- ✓ Segregation increases in the South
- ✓ McKinley elected to a second term but assassinated soon after. Theodore Roosevelt vice president moves into office.
- ✓ Wyoming range wars raged between major cattle companies
- ✓ The 1893 Chicago World's Fair was a success
- ✓ The Duryea is the first commercial auto produced

CONCLUSION:

Not all US Presidents were courageous, yet this book shows how several of them have, at crucial moments, made courageous decisions for the national interest although they knew they might be jeopardizing their careers.

The First Hundred Years demonstrates the demons we face today we have met before and more often than not, we faced them down. Our country's success is probably credited more to good luck and God's grace than to the leadership.

To be continued in Volume II, *The Second Century.* Coming soon ... .

Carpe Diem
The Author

History of Currency in the United States

- **Article 1, section 8,** the Constitution of the United States authorizes congress "to coin money, and to regulate the value thereof."

- **1690 Colonial Notes:** The Massachusetts Bay Colony, one of the 13 original colonies, issues the first paper money to cover costs of military expeditions. The practice of issuing paper notes spread to the other colonies.

- **1739 Franklin's Unique Counterfeit Deterrent:** Benjamin Franklin's printing firm in Philadelphia prints colonial notes with nature prints—unique raised impressions of patterns cast from actual leaves. This process added an innovative and effective counterfeit deterrent to notes, not completely understood until centuries later.

- **1775 Continental Currency:** The Continental Congress issues paper currency to finance the Revolutionary War. Continental currency was denominated in Spanish milled dollars. Without solid backing and easily counterfeited, the notes quickly lost their value, giving rise to the phrase "not worth a Continental."

- **1792 Monetary System:** The Coinage Act of 1792 creates the US Mint and establishes a federal monetary system, sets denominations for coins, and specifies the value of each coin in gold, silver, or copper.

- **1861 Greenbacks:** The first general circulation of paper money by the federal government occurs. Pressed to finance the Civil War, Congress authorizes the US Treasury to issue non-interest-bearing Demand Notes. All US currency issued since 1861 remains valid and redeemable at full face value.

- **1861 First $10 Bills—Demand Notes:** The first $10 notes are Demand Notes, issued in 1861 by the Treasury Department. A portrait of President Abraham Lincoln is included on the face of the notes.

FIGURE 66: SPANISH DOLLAR ALSO KNOWN AS "PIECES OF EIGHT"

Imagine living in a world without money, like our ancestors did when they were organizing a new country. It was a challenge to find mediums of exchange available and acceptable to both natives and new citizens. At first it was shells and beads. Later as coins and paper money became more available, the varieties of exchange used were numerous and fascinating.

Spanish, Portuguese, and French coins appeared in the colonies as a result of trade with the West Indies. The most famous of these was the Spanish dollar, which served as the unofficial national currency of the colonies for much of the 17th and 18th centuries. With its distinctive design and consistent silver content, the Spanish dollar was the most trustworthy coin the colonists knew. To make change, the dollar was actually cut into eight pieces or "bits." Thus, came the terms "pieces of eight" from these early times and "two bits" from our time.

FIGURE 67: THE $1 BILL FEATURES GEORGE WASHINGTON

The current $1 bill was designed in the 1860s and remains almost unchanged to this day. The greenbacks solved the problem of financing the Civil War and a new system of national banks also brought some stability to the nation's finances. An individual dollar bill is also less formally known as a one, a single, a buck, a greenback, a bone, a bill, and a clam.

The motto "In God We Trust" was added on the bill by law in 1957. Turn the bill over, to see two circles which comprise the Great Seal of the United States. See the pyramid? The face is lighted, and the western side is dark. The pyramid is uncapped, signifying that we were not even close to being finished. The all-seeing eye is an ancient symbol for divinity.

FIGURE 68: THE $2 BILL AND THOMAS JEFFERSON

Jefferson's image has been the only one used since on the $2 bill since its inception as a United States note in 1869. The bill remains in circulation despite its unpopularity.

FIGURE 69: ABRAHAM LINCOLN IS ON THE $5 BILL

To commemorate his legacy and the sacrifices that he made for the United States while serving as president in the 1860s, Lincoln's face is also featured on the United States one-cent coin and on Mount Rushmore.

FIGURE 70: THE $10 BILL AND ALEXANDER HAMILTON

Alexander Hamilton was the first secretary of the Treasury. The 1792 Coinage Act created the US dollar as the country's standard unit of money, established the US mint and regulated the coinage of the country. This combined Alexander Hamilton's idea of a bimetallic standard with Thomas Jefferson's proposal for the dollar to be the standard unit of money.

FIGURE 71: THE $20 BILL FEATURES PRESIDENT ANDREW JACKSON

An image of the polarizing and controversial Jackson (president in the 1830s) replaced Grover Cleveland's image in 1928. A new design with underground railroad crusader Harriet Tubman was anticipated in 2020, but President Trump's administration announced Jackson would remain on the bill. About one in ten notes in circulation are $20-dollar bills.

FIGURE 72: PRESIDENT U. S. GRANT ON THE $50 BILL

The note, created in 1861, has existed in other forms since then. The former general has been seen on this bill since 1913. He also appeared on various gold and silver certificates.

Congress has twice introduced legislation to replace Grant on the $50 bill, but the action was voted down both times.

FIGURE 73: BENJAMIN FRANKLIN ON THE $100 BILL

US Founding Father Franklin has been featured on the $100 bill since 1914. Previously, $100 notes were graced by various American figures, including President James Monroe, and Admiral David Farragut.

FIGURE 74: GROVER CLEVELAND AND THE $1,000 BILL

This bill has been out of print since 1945, and out of circulation since 1969, but is still legal tender.

Grover Cleveland, president in 1893, also graced the $20 bill until he was replaced by Andrew Jackson in 1928.

FIGURE 75: $5,000 BILL AND PRESIDENT JAMES MADISON

NOTE: This bill has not been printed since 1945.

Statehood Dates

#	STATE	DATE (RATIFIED OR ADMITTED)	FORMED FROM
1	Delaware	07 Dec 1787	Crown Colony of Delaware
2	Pennsylvania	12 Dec 1787	Crown Colony of Pennsylvania
3	New Jersey	18 Dec1787	Crown Colony New Jersey
4	Georgia	02 Jan 1788	Crown Colony of Georgia
5	Connecticut	09 Jan 1788	Crown Colony Connecticut
6	Massachusetts	06 Feb 1788	Crown Colony Massachusetts Bay
7	Maryland	28 Apr 1788	Crown Colony of Maryland
8	South Carolina	23 May 1788	Crown Colony South Carolina
9	North Hampshire	21 Jun 1788	Crown Colony New Hampshire
10	Virginia	25 Jun 1788	Crown Colony of Virginia
11	New York	26 Jul 1788	Crown Colony New York
12	North Carolina	21 Nov 1789	Crown Colony North Carolina
13	Rhode Island	29 May 1790	Crown Colonies of Rhode Island & Providence
14	Vermont	30 Mar 1791	Vermont Republic
15	Kentucky	01 Jun 1792	Virginia
16	Tennessee	01 Jun 1796	Southwest Territory
17	Ohio	01 Mar 1803	Northwest Territory (part)
18	Louisiana	30 Apr 1812	Territory of Orleans
19	Indiana	11 Dec 1816	Indiana Territory
20	Mississippi	10 Dec 1817	Mississippi Territory
21	Illinois	03 Dec 1818	Illinois Territory (part)
22	Alabama	14 Dec 1819	Alabama Territory
23	Maine	15 Mar 1820	Massachusetts
24	Missouri	10 Aug 1821	Missouri Territory (part)

#	STATE	DATE (RATIFIED OR ADMITTED)	FORMED FROM
25	Arkansas	15 Jun 1836	Arkansas Territory
26	Michigan	26 Jan 1837	Michigan Territory
27	Florida	03 Mar 1845	Florida Territory
28	Texas	29 Dec 1845	Republic of Texas
29	Iowa	28 Dec 1846	Iowa Territory (part)
30	Wisconsin	29 May 1848	Wisconsin Territory (part)
31	California	09 Sept 1850	unorganized territory (part)
32	Minnesota	11 May 1858	Minnesota Territory (part)
33	Oregon	14 Feb 1859	Oregon Territory (part)
34	Kansas	29 Jan 1861	Kansas Territory (part)
35	West Virginia	20 Jun 1863	Viginia
36	Nevada	31 Oct 1864	Nevada Territory
37	Nebraska	01 Mar 1867	Nebraska Territory
38	Colorado	01 Aug 1876	Colorado Territory
39	North Dakota	02 Nov 1889	Dakota Territory (part)
40	South Dakota	02 Nov 1889	Dakota Territory (part)
41	Montana	08 Nov 1889	Montana Territory
42	Washington	11 Nov 1889	Washington Territory
43	Idaho	03 July 1890	Idaho Territory
44	Wyoming	10 July 1890	Wyoming Territory
45	Utah	04 Jan 1896	Utah Territory
46	Oklahoma	16 Nov 1907	Oklahoma Terr,Indian Terr
47	New Mexico	06 Jan 1912	New Mexico Territory
48	Arizona	14 Feb 1912	Arizona Territory
49	Alaska	03 Jan 1959	Territory of Alaska
50	Hawaii	21 Aug 1959	Territory of Hawaii

References

Allen, Henry. 1999. *What It Felt Like, Living in the American Century*. Pantheon Books, a division of Random House, Inc. New York.

Angle, Paul M. 1967. *A Pictorial History of The Civil War Years*. Doubleday and Company, Inc. Garden City, New York.

Axelrod, Alan, Ph.D. 2009. *The Complete Idiot's Guide to American History, Fifth Edition*. Alpha Books, The Penguin Group.

Axelrod, Alan, Ph.D. 2009. *The Complete Idiot's Guide to The American Presidency*. Alpha Books, The Penguin Group.

Brady, Patricia. 2005. *Martha Washington*. Penguin Books.

Bunting III, Josiah. 2004. Edited by Arthur M. Schlesinger, Jr. *Ulysses S. Grant, President 1869-1877*. Times Books, Henry Holt and Company New York

Caroli, Betty Boyd. 2010. *First Ladies from Martha Washington to Michelle Obama*. Oxford University Press, New York.

Cappon, Lester J. 1988. *The Adams-Jefferson Letters: The Complete Correspondence Between Thomas Jefferson and Abigail and John Adams*. The University of North Carolina Press, Chapel Hill and London.

Cary, John H. and Weinberg, Julius. *The Social Fabric: American Life from 1607 to 1877*. Little, Brown and Company, Boston. Toronto.

Channing, Edward. 1901. *A Student's History of the United States*. The Macmillan Company, New York.

Christman, Margaret C. S. 1996. The *1846 Portrait of a Nation*, Smithsonian Institution Press for the National Portrait Gallery, Washington DC, and London.

Cox, Clinton. 1997. *Fiery Vision: The Life and Death of John Brown*. Scholastic Press of New York

Croom, Emily Anne. 2003. *The Genealogist's Companion and Sourcebook*, 2nd Edition. Betterway Books, Cincinnati, Ohio.

Davis Kenneth C. 2009. *Don't Know Much About the Presidents.* HarperCollins Children's Books, New York.

Durant, Will and Ariel. 1968. *The Lessons of History.* Simon and Schuster, New York.

Fawcett, Bill. 2008. *Oval Office Oddities, An Irreverent Collection of Presidential Facts, Follies, and Foibles.* Harper Collins Publishers, New York.

Goebel, Julius Jr and Smith, Joseph H. 1964. *The Law Practice of Alexander Hamilton.* Columbia University Press.

Goodwin, Doris Kearns. 2018. *Leadership in Turbulent Times.* Simon & Schuster, Inc. New York.

Hardorff, Richard G. 2008. *Washita Memories: Eyewitness views of Custer's Attack on Black Kettle's Village.* University of Oklahoma Press

Hargrove, Jim. 1986. *The Story of the Black Hawk War.* Children's Press, Chicago.

Hazelgrove, William. 2016. *Madam President, The Secret Presidency of Edith Wilson.* Regnery History, Salem Media Group. Washington, DC.

Harper's Weekly; Scribner's Magazine. 1895. *The Pony Express, a Thrilling and Truthful History.*

Hart, Albert Bushnell. 1914. *Essentials of American History (from the Discovery to the Present Day).* American Book Company, New York – Cincinnati-Chicago.

Hilton, Suzanne. 1975. *The Way it Was – 1876.* The Westminster Press, Philadelphia.

Holt, Stephen. 1956. *We Were There with the California Forty-Niners.* Grosset & Dunlap, New York.

King, C. Richard. 1976. *Susanna Dickinson, Messenger of the Alamo.* Shoal Creek Publishers, Inc. Austin, TX.

Lederer, Richard. 2009. *Presidential Trivia.* Gibbs Smith, Layton, Utah.

Leiby, Adrian C. 1992. *The Revolutionary War in the Hackensack Valley.* Rutgers University Press, New Brunswick, New Jersey.

Mattes, Merrill J. 1960. *Indians Infants and Infantry: Andrew and Elizabeth Burt on the Frontier.* Fred A. Rosenstock, The Old West Publishing company. Denver, Colorado.

Middlekauff, Robert. 1982. *The Glorious Cause: The American Revolution 1763-1789*. Oxford University Press, New York. Oxford.

Millichap, Nancy. 1994. *The Stock Market Crash of 1929*. New Discovery Books, New York.

Morris, Seymour Jr. 2010. *American History Revised, 200 Startling Facts that never made it into the Textbooks*. Broadway Books, imprint of Crown Publishing Group, division of Random House, Inc, New York.

Muzzey, David Saville. 1922. *American History*. Barnard College, Columbia University, New York.

Rhodes, Richard. 1990. *A Hole in the World: An American Boyhood*. Simon and Schuster.

Robson, Lucia St Clair. 2012. *Shadow Patriots: A Novel of the Revolution*. St Martin's Press.

Sherman, Josepha. 2004. *The Cold War: Chronicle of America's Wars*. Lerner Publications Company, Minneapolis.

Skolnik, Richard (editor). *Our Great Heritage from the beginning 1784—1800*. Consolidated Book Publishers, New York-Chicago.

Sosin, Jack M. 1969. *The Opening of the West*. Harper & Row, Publishers. New York, Evanston, and London.

Stone, Irving. 1951. *The President's Lady: A Novel about Rachel and Andrew Jackson*. Rutledge Hill Press, Nashville, Tennessee.

Szucs, Loretto Dennis & Wright, Matthew. 2001. *Finding Answers in US Census Records*. Ancestry Publishing, Orem, Utah.

Taylor, Dale. 1997. *Everyday Life in Colonial America* from 1607-1783. Writers Digest Books, F&W Publications, Cincinnati.

Ural, Susannah J. 2013. *Don't Hurry me down to Hades, The Civil War in the Words of those who Lived it*. Osprey Publishing, Oxford, UK, New York.

Ward, Christopher. 2011. *War of the Revolution*, two volumes. Skyhorse Publishing.

Wecter, Dixon. 1941. *The Hero in America*. Charles Scribner's Sons, New York. 530 pp.

American History from Revolution to Reconstruction and Beyond. Department of Alfa-Informatica of the University of Groningen (The Netherlands).
https://www.let.rug.nl/usa/about.php

Williams, Glenn F. 2017. *Dunmore's War: The Last Conflict of America's Colonial Era*. Westholme Publishing, LLC, Yardley, Pennsylvania.

Woodward, W. E. 1944. *The Way Our People Lived*. E. F. Dutton & Company, Inc. New York

Worton, Stanley Ph.D. *American History to 1865*. College Notes & Texts, Inc. New York.

Zimmer, Louise. 1987, 2nd printing 1992. *True Stories of Pioneer Times, Northwest Territory 1787-1812*. Broughton Foods Company, Marietta, OH

Online References

Creative Commons: A Creative Commons (CC) license is one of several public copyright licenses enable the free distribution of an otherwise copyrighted work.

America's Best History; where we take a look at the timeline of American History and the historic sites and national parks that hold history within their lands. 2017. https://americasbesthistory.com/about.html

1820s American Farm Frontier Culture Museum of Virginia. http://www.frontiermuseum.org/exhibits/1820s-american-farm/

Abigail Adams Biography: National First Ladies' Library. http://www.firstladies.org/biographies/firstladies.aspx?biography=2

Seminole Wars. http://military.wikia.com/wiki/Seminole_Wars

Facts about the Presidents: https://www.newsweek.com/presidents-facts-50-strange-united-states-list-slideshow-954314 https://www.history.com/topics/us-presidents

Frances Folsom (Mrs. Grover Cleveland): http://www.firstladies.org/biographies/firstladies.aspx?biography=23

Woodrow Wilson and the League of Nations. 1974: http://www.digitalhistory.uh.edu/teachers/lesson_plans/pdfs/unit8_12.pdf

JSTOR is a digital library for scholars, researchers, and students. https://daily.jstor.org

Knight, Sarah Kemble. 1704. Pub 1865. *The Private Journal of a Journey from Boston to New York in the Year 1704*. F.H. Little. 92 pp. Google Play Books. https://play.google.com/store/books/details?id=295hAAAAcAAJ&source=ge-web-app&writeReview

Hemings, Madison (1805-1877) https://en.wikipedia.org/wiki/Madison_Hemings

Wikipedia references: Various information about different presidents as well as photos were obtained from www.Wikipedia.org. For all practical purposes on Wikipedia, the public domain comprises copyright-free works: anyone can use them in any way and for any purpose. Permission to reproduce and modify text on Wikipedia has already been granted to anyone anywhere by the authors of individual articles as long as such reproduction and modification complies with licensing terms. The only Wikipedia content you should contact the Wikimedia Foundation about are the trademarked Wikipedia/Wikimedia logos, which are not freely usable without permission.

Index

About the Author

C arolyn B. Leonard loves America and its amazing history. She shares her passion for family history with her husband as they explore historic places, photograph interesting tombstones, and rummage through old courthouse records.

Gov. Ernie Fletcher named her an honorary KY Colonel for publicizing the 18th century Reformed Dutch migration from New York to New Jersey through Pennsylvania to Kentucky. The Sons of American Revolution (SAR) awarded her a medal of honor for locating graves of Revolutionary War veterans. Researching family history led her to Germany, England, the Netherlands, New England, the LDS Library in Salt Lake City, libraries, museums, and cemeteries across the US.

Leonard was named an honorary lifetime member of the OK Writers Federation, Inc of which she is a past president. She is also past president of the OKC Writers and Writers of the Purple Sage. A former newspaper editor, she's won many writing awards. She is an active member of Daughters of American Revolution (DAR), Daughters of 1812, the prestigious Mayflower Society, genealogical and historical societies in several states; and a graduate of OKC University.

She enjoys presenting programs or teaching classes to help people find and write about their family's place in history.

She can be reached through her website at

www.CarolynBLeonard.com

Email at: CarolynLeonard@me.com

Testimonials

"Carolyn Leonard's First Hundred Years weaves a tapestry of presidential and American history that provides a glimpse in a concise way to engage the reader with a bit of whimsey and satire. She also presents important details of how the annual decennial census has evolved as the national population grew. Leonard aids family historians as to the how and why aspects of census data is added and utilized making the material more enriching for researchers."

—William D. Welge,
Certified Archivist, Director Emeritus, American Indian Culture
and Preservation Office, Oklahoma Historical Society

"The First Hundred Years by Carolyn B. Leonard covers the US presidents and Federal Census procedures from 1790-1890. This book is a rich source of factual material and is especially effective in providing the reader with a keen sense of the times, something so often missing in reference materials. If you are climbing the family tree or are simply a curious reader interested in your ancestors' daily lives and experiences, this is the book for you. Not only is it well researched, it is also an enjoyable and fast paced read, filled with rare and fascinating details of our past. When you reach the top of that tree, you will not only know who your ancestors are but what they lived."

—Dr. Sheldon Russell,
author of the Oklahoma Book Award winner *Dreams to Dust*, *The Hook Runyon Mystery Series*, and his latest historical novel, *A Forgotten Evil*

"Leonard's book, The First Hundred Years, is so interesting no one will put it down. Meticulous research and detailed creativity went into the writing of Leonard's book. Tidbits of the lives of past US Presidents makes parts of this history read like a testy novel."

—Gwen Hewitt, writer, reader, owner-operator Hewitt Farms

"I finished your advance copy of the First Hundred Years and I thought it was excellent! I look forward to your follow-up book. It was very informative and had a lot of info about many of the presidents that I was not aware of. Once again, it was a very interesting book."

—Larry Rhodes, reader

"The First Hundred Years is an essential guidebook for genealogists, family historians, and anyone who wants to learn more about our country's early years. Award-winning author Carolyn Leonard offers meticulously researched information about each US census and an overview of events during each decade, including a wealth of intriguing historical facts you never learned in school. Keep this book close by your side as you research your family tree."

—Maria Polson Veres,
author of Oklahoma Book Award Finalist *Church People,*
Adjunct Instructor, Francis Tuttle Technology Center

"The First Hundred Years by Carolyn B. Leonard provides a unique perspective on American History. The author uses the census as an outline to develop an entertaining and unusual approach to life in the United States. Whether the reader is simply studying history or wanting to learn about the life his or her ancestors lived, she presents the reader with well-researched facts about each decade. Leonard unites her passion for history with her talent as an excellent writer who uses the threads of the census to weave an entertaining tapestry of the American experience. History teachers will find this book a useful supplement to dry textbooks. History aficionados will find it a delightful read that is as hard to put down as a gripping, suspenseful novel."

—Leon Beall,
author, BA, MSA, 25-year career teaching Social Studies

www.ingramcontent.com/pod-product-compliance
Lightning Source LLC
Chambersburg PA
CBHW030238030426
42336CB00009B/157